Popularity Explained
The Social Psychology of Grade School

Popularity Explained

The Social Psychology of Grade School

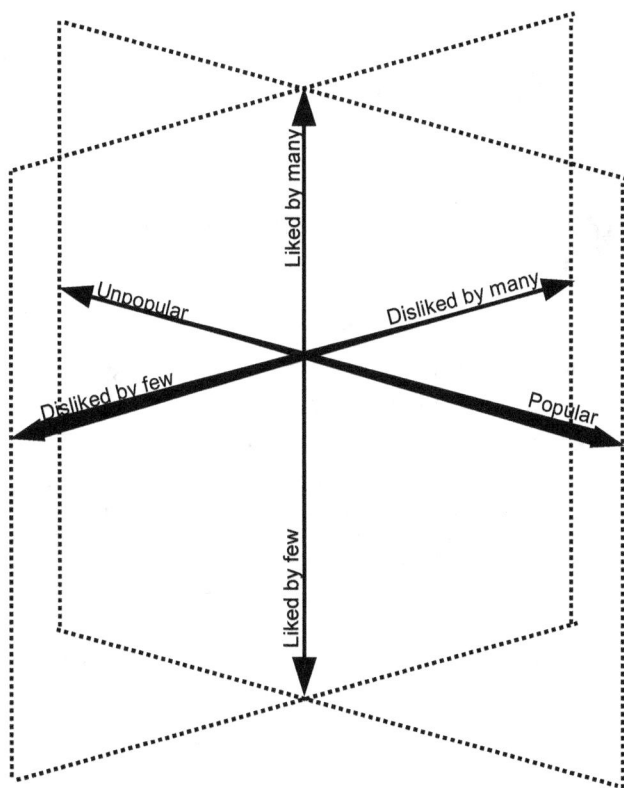

Liked by many

Unpopular

Disliked by many

Disliked by few

Popular

Liked by few

A. L. Freedman

Published by: Ravi Seyed Mahmoud, Edmonton, Canada

ISBN 978-1-927588-63-5

Student readers should not try to recreate the suggestions of this book without consulting a responsible adult such as a parent, teacher, or counsellor. The content of this book is only suggestion. Author claims no responsibility for any deleterious outcomes incurred by readers as a result of reading or attempting to recreate said suggestions.

Although all personal anecdotes in this book are based on true stories, key details have been changed to preserve anonymity.

Publication assistance and
digital printing in Canada by

PageMaster
PUBLICATION SERVICES INC.
www.pagemaster.ca

Dedicated to the original
Hollywood Protagonist:
my unsuspecting mentor,
grades 9, 10, 11, 12.

PREFACE

I love people. People fascinate me and for as long as I can remember, I have reflexively analyzed the behaviour of myself and others. On entering university, there was no question in my mind that I would major in psychology. Even today, I am always thinking about *thinking* and asking the question, "why do people do what they do?"

I was obviously this book's original audience. Like most adolescents, I was mesmerized by popularity during grade school. I was never bullied or without friends but this wasn't good enough for me. I wanted to be "popular" and so I analyzed the phenomenon intently. If I could understand it, I reasoned, I could achieve it.

Popularity Explained has been over a decade in the making. Its origins are roughly scribbled journal entries that I started making in grade 9 and would continue making throughout grade school. It took several years of observation before concepts such as the "Hierarchy of Attraction" began to appear in my notebooks and it wouldn't be until graduation that I wrote the essay on which this book is partially based (See Appendix I).

For a long time post high-school, I didn't think much about popularity. It wasn't until my final year of undergraduate study that I returned to the subject. I was curious to know if professional psychologists formally studied the same things I had. After some preliminary research, I was delighted to discover that yes they did. Encouraged, I devoted an Independent Study to the subject and spent an entire semester combing through published, scientific, psychological literature.

The impulse to write a book came soon after completing my research. By combining my first hand experiences with the formal research of professional psychologists, I realized that I could formulate a unified and comprehensive explanation of popularity. I skimmed the Internet to see if anyone else had ever produced something similar. On discovering that "no," the next step was obvious.

The evolution of this book did not end with the first draft. Serendipitously, in the same month I finished writing it, I entered medical school which proved instrumental in shaping its final form. For reasons discussed in Chapter 8, medical school resembles grade school in terms of its social dynamics. For two years I had the unprecedented opportunity to watch all the things I had written about unfold, quite literally, all around me. Emboldened by what I saw, I continued taking steps towards publication.

I truly believe that the *experience* of popularity is available to anyone; albeit, not in the clichéd form of the prom queen or quarterback. Popularity, it turns out, isn't exclusive to the "popular" students. Grade school social dynamics are a system that can be studied and manipulated like any other. With some creativity and understanding of what to look for, anyone can achieve popularity.

That being said, *Popularity Explained* is not a self-help book which promises a quick fix. It is an unapologetic attempt to describe reality regardless of how unjust it is at times.

Although I originally intended this book to be for adolescents, it is now written for for parents and educators. Armed with superior maturity and wisdom, they are uniquely positioned to help guide dissatisfied students through the requisite processes of planning, action, and reflection required to make substantive changes. Without guidance, the content of this book is too blunt to be appropriate for all students. The experience of popularity may be available to anyone but a major theme throughout is that not *everyone* can be *everything*.

The second reason why *Popularity Explained* is written for adults is because the phenomenon isn't unique to grade school. The human behaviours which underlie it are present throughout the life span meaning anyone can benefit from understanding the "phenomenon that is." Look for it: glimmers of grade school social dynamics can be found anywhere there are people. Even the adult reader, I hope, will find this book interesting and applicable.

CONTENTS

CHAPTER 1

INTRODUCTION

When I was fourteen, I made a stunningly obvious discovery: some people are popular and others are not. On September 4, 2001, I hastily scribbled down some preliminary observations in a journal. The popular students had everything an adolescent could want—everything I could want. It was the outset of grade 9 and I was determined to understand this fascinating social phenomenon.

Even if I was capable of understanding the concept of "popular" much earlier, it isn't surprising that I suddenly felt the impulse to write about it at the age of fourteen. Social scientists have found that concern with popularity follows an inverted U shape across grade school.[1] Starting in the first years of elementary, the desire for popularity slowly increases until reaching a fever pitch in high school before quickly dropping off in the years after graduation. Perhaps you're reading this book because you know someone whose current situation is similar to mine on that September night: an average student, stuck in the tumultuous throes of adolescence, facing several more years of grade school and painfully aware that some people are popular and others are not.

---

1 LaFontana & Cillessen, 2009

Popularity is a global phenomenon that exists generation after generation. It happened to me, it happened to you, and it will happen to your children. If you don't believe me, ask your peers, your children, or even your parents if they can relate to the phenomenon of popularity in school. Regardless of culture or ethnicity, everyone will invariably answer, "yes." Popularity is a contemporary fact of life.

The oldest formal studies concerning children and their friendships date back as far as the early 1900s[2] and the concept is evident in a number of hit Hollywood movies: *Rebel Without a Cause (1955), Splendor in the Grass (1961), Bye, Bye Birdie (1963), The Last Picture Show (1971), American Graffiti (1973), Carrie (1976), Grease (1978), Fast Times at Ridgemont High (1982), Sixteen Candles (1984), The Breakfast Club (1985), Heathers (1988), Dazed and Confused (1993), Clueless (1995), Not Another Teen Movie (2001), Mean Girls (2004),* and *Mean Girls 2 (2011).* If popularity concerns you, you're not alone! Hollywood wouldn't produce so many high school movies unless there were interested audiences.

It's easy to understand why so many students are concerned with popularity. Popular students, along with their clique, seem to have everything an adolescent could want: money, good looks, and access to epic social events. They command respect and admiration from their same-sexed peers and consistently attract the most desirable boyfriends/ girlfriends. In the 1995 movie *Clueless*, the main character, Cher Horowitz, summarizes this point. As she narrates the movie's introduction, the film shows her speeding along in a brand new jeep en route to pick up a friend. "Here's where Dionne lives!" she happily narrates as she pulls up in front of a beautiful mansion. "She's my friend because we both know what it's like to have people be jealous of us!"

---

2   Wellman, 1926

Such, it would seem, is the life of popular students. They have countless friends and acquaintances flock around them wherever they go. Even though I graduated in 2005, a decade after *Clueless* was released, the words of Cher Horowitz are equally applicable to my generation. The lives of popular students at my school seemed somehow easier, better, and more interesting.

With so much to be envied, it's not surprising that countless stories document students jumping at the first opportunity to be popular. In the book *Cliques*, author Demi Chang tells the story of how she was lured into betraying her best friend: a week before winter break, Rachel—the most popular girl in school—pulls Demi aside and offers her the chance of a lifetime: Demi could join the popular clique so long as she was willing to do one thing... betray her best friend Jenny. Demi agrees because, in her words, she "wanted to taste" what it was like to be popular.[3]

Stories like Demi's are so common that Hollywood has taken note. In the 1988 movie Heathers, the main character, Veronica, confesses to the audience that "Betty Finn was a true friend and I sold her out for a bunch of swash dogs and Diet Coke heads." As Demi and Veronica exemplify, more than one student has been mesmerized by popularity and done whatever it takes to attain it.

Betrayal seems to go hand in hand with popularity. In their seminal work, *Peer Power: Preadolescent Culture and Identity*, Patricia and Peter Adler document how popular students commonly manipulate their less prominent peers[4] by dangling favours and friendship in front of them like a lure. Clearly, popularity is not just laughter and smiles—it has a dark side.

---

3   Chang, 2010
4   Adler & Adler, 1995

The dictionary definition of popularity is "to be liked by many." Based on this definition, you might predict that popular students are the cheeriest and most agreeable people in a school: kind to everyone and always willing to lend a helping hand. Such a conclusion couldn't be further from the truth! In the novel *How to Be Popular* by Meg Cabot, the protagonist's mother naively asks, "Aren't the most popular kids the nicest at your school?"

"No Mom!" the protagonist retorts in a sarcastic tone.

It's not just fictional characters who make the outlandish conclusion that popular students are nice to everyone. In fact, when social scientists first began studying the social dynamics of grade school, they too assumed that popularity was dependent on what they called "prosocial behaviour"[5]— a term referring to the combination of kindness, helpfulness, sociability, and respect.

Too often, it seems, popular students are the exact opposite of prosocial: often depicted in the popular media as a ruthless band of social marauders bent on spreading rumours and excluding anyone they deem unworthy. In all fairness, the popular students at my school were not as bad as those shown on television and in the movies, but they shared many of the same characteristics.

What causes such an inexplicable mix of contradictory social behaviour? Popularity is a hierarchical and hegemonic social phenomenon that depends on the acquiescence of the student body. "Why are popular students worshipped when they rule over us like evil dictators?" asks Janice Ian, the anti-hero of the 2004 movie *Mean Girls*.

A central goal of this book is to explain how popular students do "it" and why the student body submits to them. How do they make friends so easily? How are they always in

---

5   Dunnington, 1957

the right place at the right time? How is it that embarrassing moments never stick to them? How is it that their jokes are always funny? How do they keep their peers coming back no matter how terribly they treat them? For some students, being popular comes naturally. For others, popularity is an intangible state of being that is somehow tantalizingly out of reach.

Just as the student body's collective desire for popularity reaches a maximum in high school, graduation arrives and the social phenomenon that dominated for so long vanishes. The hierarchical social rigidity fades as each student spirals out into the adult world. By the time most students have completed some form of post-secondary education, popularity is a thing of the past. The intangible social structure that was once so captivating becomes trivial in hindsight, a silly distraction in the overall scheme of life after high school.

Graduation is a symbolic event. Every high school graduate can attest to the fact that, biologically, it isn't developmentally relevant. The day after, your mind and body aren't materially different from the day before. Nothing has changed except that society now recognizes you as having completed a high school diploma. So why then is popularity so closely associated with grade school? Where does it go? What happens to the popular and unpopular students after graduation? Do the same attributes that lead to popularity in grade school also lead to success later in life? Or, does the glamour and prestige of popularity end with graduation?

***

This book is the culmination of countless observations from grade school, an undergraduate degree in psychology, and two years of documenting the social forces that shaped my medical class. At its root is the September 4 journal entry

I made in the beginning of grade 9. "This year," I wrote in my journal all those years ago, "I have set out to crack the code of popularity." In hindsight, the yearlong timeline I gave myself was laughably ambitious. It took me until the end of grade 12 before I was able to produce my first attempt at a theory; an undergraduate degree in psychology before I was able to write the paper that became the precursor to this book; and two years of watching the phenomenon re-emerge in medical school before I was able to produce a version of the book I was happy with.

These days it all seems so obvious. Looking back, I can hardly believe that it took me so long to understand something that is ultimately so simple. After I finished writing the original manuscript, I asked close friends and family to read it. When I asked them what they thought, they all responded by saying something to effect of, "Well, yeah, I agree. It's kind of obvious, isn't it?" After you finish reading this book, my goal is to have you saying the same thing.

That being said, the secrets of popularity are not obvious. In the 2011 book, *Popularity in the Peer System*, social scientists Lara Mayeux, John Houser, and Karmon Dyche write:

> *Does a little boy become popular because of his attributes, such as the combination of being wealthy, funny, and athletic, which then kick-starts a self-perpetuating dynamic of behavioural change and status reinforcement? Or, does a child make a conscious decision to be popular and seek the proper social accoutrements (the right friends, the right clothes, skillful aggressive acts) to become that way? Researchers have yet to propose a true developmental model of popularity.*[6]

The explanations you can find on the Internet aren't any more satisfying than the quotation above. If you glance through half a dozen articles concerning popularity, you're likely to come across the same tired clichés again and again. An example pulled from a *Wikihow* article reads: "Remember, the only thing you need in order to be popular is a good set of people skills!" This is frustratingly simplistic. If the key to popularity was as simple as people skills, why is the stereotypical popular girl always depicted in the media as an "anorexic, superficial bitch. A whore who lacks any long term goals?"[7] In the movie *Sixteen Candles*, "Ted the Geek" asks this same question. To the most popular girl in his school, he says, "I can't believe you're so popular acting like this!"

The secrets of popularity are mysteriously elusive for a variety of reasons and there are excellent explanations for why it has been a generational constant since the inception of grade school: why the lunchroom always divides up along clique lines; why popular students always seem to be arrogant jerks; and a host of other questions.

***

I was the original audience for the content of this book. My first attempt at understanding the social world in which I lived was an essay which I have included as an appendix. At the time, I had an obvious goal in mind: I wanted to take control of my social destiny. "If I can start by understanding popularity," I reasoned, "then I can set out to achieve it."

Popularity Explained relies heavily on published psychological literature and has been written for the parents and educators of dissatisfied students. It has never been intended as a *How-To Guide*—the social dynamics that shape the emergence of popularity are too complex for "a one size fits all" approach. Rather, my intention is to offer a theoretical framework on which clever parents and educators can engineer

---

7 Columbia Pictures, 2001. Janey Briggs from the movie *Not Another Teen Movie (2011)*

more equitable and forgiving social circumstances for those under their care. I hope what I have written will help readers as they guide dissatisfied students through the process of uncovering personal strengths/weakness and the social opportunities/threats they face.

There are two opposing paradigms from which to approach social destiny:

1. The belief that anyone can be anything and that all social roles are open to everyone.

2. The belief that nothing can be changed and that social roles are predetermined.

After writing this book, I can confidently say that I don't subscribe to either extreme. My position between the two can be succinctly stated as follows: If, after reading this book, the reader is able to help a student confront the social realities they *can* change, accept those they *cannot*, and learn to differentiate between the two, I've been successful.

A primary theme of this book is the fact that life is unfair; not everyone can be everything. Nearly a decade ago, I was volunteering as a camp counsellor. One night, while supervising a game of nighttime capture the flag, I stumbled across a camper known for his bilateral hip brace. He was sitting alone in a dark room overlooking the field and quietly crying while he watched his peers play through the window. After noticing his tears, I asked the obvious question, "What's the matter?"

"Isn't it obvious?" he retorted, "All I want is to run and to play, but I can't and no matter how many times I tell people, 'it's not my fault,' the boys don't respect me, the girls don't like me, and there's nothing I can do about that."

If I could write a book to solve the root cause of this boy's problems, I would. Unfortunately I can't and I won't pretend that I can. Nothing can reverse the vicissitudes of fortune but that doesn't mean this boy is helplessly tethered to the social plight described.

If I was given the choice, I would choose (for myself and the aforementioned camper) a life of social dominance and prowess in perpetuity. Perhaps, however, it has been a blessing for me to have lived at many levels on the social totem pole given my desire to understand the circumstances of others. I know that social roles aren't static. On the contrary, the social landscape is continually changing and where a student falls is not, by any stretch, irreversibly predetermined. Near the end of this book, I share the story of a hockey player who found himself in different social roles depending on the context he was in. The same phenomenon can happen to anyone, including the camper with the bilateral hip brace.

The social world is complex, but this does not mean it cannot be understood and manipulated to great effect. Like any other system, it can be studied and broken down into component parts. Once these parts are understood, predictions and purposeful modifications can be made. Although not everyone can live as the clichéd image of *popular*, the experience of *popularity* is available to anyone.

Originally, this book was intended for students but has ultimately been published for parents and educators. Students, although astutely aware of popularity, don't necessarily have the wisdom and insight to appreciate what constitutes reasonable social aspirations. Furthermore, I don't believe that it is always appropriate for the average student reader to be confronted with painful—though self-evident—facts about them self. I approach the subject of grade school social dynamics through a paradigm of logic and reason that, at times, is brutally unsympathetic.

Armed with wisdom and legitimate authority, parents and educators are well positioned to guide dissatisfied students through the planning, action, and reflection required to initiate social change in their lives. In fact, the struggling student need not be aware of the manipulations occurring on their behalf. For the bullied or rejected student, invisible help may be the most appropriate form of intervention. After reading this book, I hope that parents and educators will be able to creatively help engineer positive social change in the lives of those who need it.

CHAPTER 2

STUDENTS WE
ALL KNOW

When I was in grade 11, I participated in a two-day drama festival organized by my high school. The purpose of the festival was to bring drama students from around the city together and let them share and celebrate each other's work. In addition to presenting our respective plays, we had the opportunity to join various breakout sessions.

The two-day festival was a whirlwind of activity with students hustled from one venue to the next, first to watch a play and then to participate in their chosen session. The first night was crowned with a dance party, complete with a live D.J. The atmosphere was electric with hundreds of jittery teenagers all itching to share their work and brimming with energy.

One memory from those two days remains prominent in my mind. Among the participants was a girl named Daisy who was embedded in the popular clique of my high school. She was, as would be expected, outgoing, socially adept, and pretty. Although I was not part of her immediate circle I had enjoyed some interaction with her before the festival, occasionally sharing the same AP (advanced placement) classroom. In addition, chance encounters with her clique prior to grade 11 gave me some knowledge of her and her friends. Coming into the drama festival, we were simple acquaintances. At the festival, like school, our groups overlapped slightly. But we never made a point of finding each other.

What strikes me about my memory of Daisy is not our interactions at the festival but rather the effect she had on me every time I noticed that we had chosen the same session. Each time, I was overcome with positive emotion that wasn't just excitement—I felt that almost every time I was in proximity to someone from the popular clique. Happiness is a better way to describe it. I was genuinely happy to know that we would be in the same session, and the feeling was so uncanny and unexpected that my immediate response was to analyze it vigorously. "What," I wondered, "was driving these distinct feelings of happiness?" The emotional response was perplexing. Daisy was popular but not the most popular, pretty but not the prettiest, an acquaintance but not a friend.

For the remainder of the festival, and ultimately the school year, I paid special attention to how other students interacted with Daisy and how they behaved in her presence. I also made a point of listening to their opinions of her when she wasn't around. Eventually, it became clear to me that it wasn't only in my mind that she stood out. The student body's collective perception of her was unique. Daisy was distinct from every other student, including those more popular than her. Why? What differentiated her from all of the other students?

***

More than just adolescents are interested in popularity. It is such an influential phenomenon that social scientists have been formally studying it for decades now. In fact, books on the subject began to appear as early as 1959.[8]

If you were a social scientist studying popularity, how would you define it? Take a moment and think about it. If, by chance, your definition of popularity involved the word "liked," you're not alone. In her novel *How to Be Popular*, Meg Cabot defines it as "widely liked or appreciated; liked by acquaintances; sought after for company." The dictionary definition isn't much different. According to the Canadian Oxford Dictionary, to be popular is to be "liked or admired by many people or by a specified group." Dictionary.com is similar. "Popularity: adjective, regarded with favour, approval, or affection by people in general."

Based on these definitions, you might imagine that liking and disliking represent opposite ends of a single continuum, similar to the image in Figure 2.1.

Figure 2.1 *A single continuum representing how much a student is liked or disliked.*

In 1982, social scientists John Coie, Kennetis Dodge, and Helde Coppotelli discovered something different while working with 311 students from grades 3, 5, and 8.[9] The number of times a student was "liked most" varied independently from the number of times they were "liked least." In other words, being liked by many students was not the opposite of being disliked by many. Some students were liked by many while being simultaneously disliked by others. Others were almost

---

8   See Grolund, 1959
9   Coie, Dodge & Coppotelli, 1982

entirely forgotten! These neglected students were almost never nominated as "liked most" or "liked least." Based on the data collected, Coie, Dodge, and Coppotelli concluded that Figure 2.1 was inadequate.

The problem with Figure 2.1 can be understood using a simple example. Imagine the following four hypothetical students:

- Student #1 receives 5 "liked most" nominations and 0 "liked least"
- Student #2 receives 5 "liked most" nominations and 5 "liked least"
- Student #3 receives 0 "liked most" nominations and 0 "liked least"
- Student #4 receives 0 "liked most" nominations and 5 "liked least"

If you tried to use the formula accompanying Figure 2.1, student #1 would receive a score of 5; students #2 and #3 would receive equivalent scores of 0, and student #4 would receive a score of -5. If you plotted all four students on Figure 2.1, it would look like Figure 2.2.

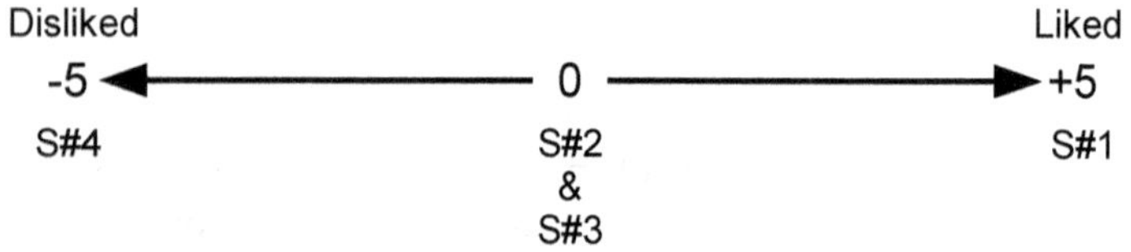

Figure 2.2 A plot showing where students #1, #2, #3 & #4 would fall on Figure 2.1

Looking at Figure 2.2, you can see that information is missing. When we add and subtract "liked most" and "liked least" scores, students #2 and #3 appear to be equivalent—something that is clearly not true. Student #2 received a total of ten nominations and student #3 received none at all. Obviously there are some big differences in how each is perceived by their peers.

Coie, Dodge, and Coppotelli were the first to outline a solution. Instead of using a single continuum to describe popularity, they used two. Their classification system is depicted in Figure 2.3. When the four hypothetical students are plotted, it is obvious that each is unique in how they are perceived by their peers. The difference between students two and three is how visible they are. Student #2 is simultaneously liked and disliked while student #3 is effectively forgotten.

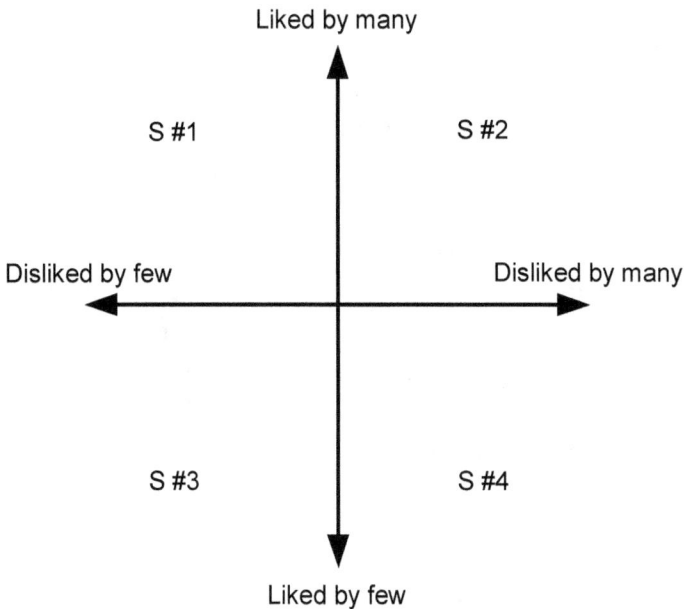

Figure 2.3 The classification system developed by Coie, Dodge and Coppotelli. Students #1, #2, #3 and #4 are plotted with their respective labels.

THE PERCEPTION
OF POPULARITY

The Coie, Dodge, and Coppotelli classification system provides a much more comprehensive representation of the social landscape when compared to Figure 2.1. For this reason
it was the standard used by researchers studying popularity
for many years. In the early 1990s, however, a major flaw
was discovered. Think about the most popular person you
can remember: were they also the most liked? For elementary school children the answer might be yes. For junior high
and high school students, however, the answer is more likely no. The definition of "popular" changes around grade 6.
Throughout middle school and high school, the most popular students are rarely most liked. During late adolescence
there is almost no relationship between being well liked and
being popular. After the transition to middle school, some
of the most popular students are actually disliked by their
peers.

Because the standard definition of popularity is based
on being well liked, social scientists thought that being liked
and being popular were synonymous. It wasn't until the early 1990s that researchers discovered that their definition of
popularity was wrong.

Clever researchers began asking students directly, "who
is the most popular in your class?" instead of "who do you
like the most?" As soon as they did, they made an interesting discovery. Members of the popular clique are not necessarily the most liked. Some are, but some are so *disliked* that
Coie, Dodge, and Coppotelli would have classified them as
"rejected!"[10]

---

10 Kosir & Pecjak, 2005

As more researchers began to ask students "Who is the most popular?" it became clear that the popular clique is a mixed bag. Some popular students are aggressive jerks. Others are quiet observers or extroverted socialites. Somehow the Canadian Oxford, Dictionary.com, and author Meg Cabot have gotten the definition of popularity wrong. Popularity does not equal being well liked by many. Being "popular" can mean being well liked, disliked, both, or neither.

Researchers concluded that popularity, as understood by students, was simply a perception. As soon as the student body recognized someone as being "popular," that was enough. Any student could be perceived as popular—even those that everyone hated. Let me explain.

Popularity, as perceived by students, is one dimensional. In other words "popular" and "unpopular" are opposites along a single continuum. In contrast to liking, a single dimension is enough to map perceived popularity because there is a large consensus among the student body with respect to who is and is not popular. Unlike choosing who is "liked most" and "liked least," all students seem to agree when it comes to labelling popular or unpopular. As a result, all students can be classified somewhere along the graph shown in Figure 2.4.

Figure 2.4 *Popular and unpopular students can be classified along a single continuum representing popularity.*

Although useful, the Coie, Dodge, and Coppotelli classification system isn't enough because liking and disliking are not the same as popular and unpopular. Since 1982, when Figure 2.3 was proposed, many researchers have found that the "popular" students can belong to any of its four quadrants. To get the fullest picture of the social landscape, it is necessary to combine Figures 2.3 and 2.4. The end result is Figure 2.5. Notice that there are now eight quadrants, each representing a different prototype of student:

- Queen Bees[11] and Kingpins
- Sidekicks

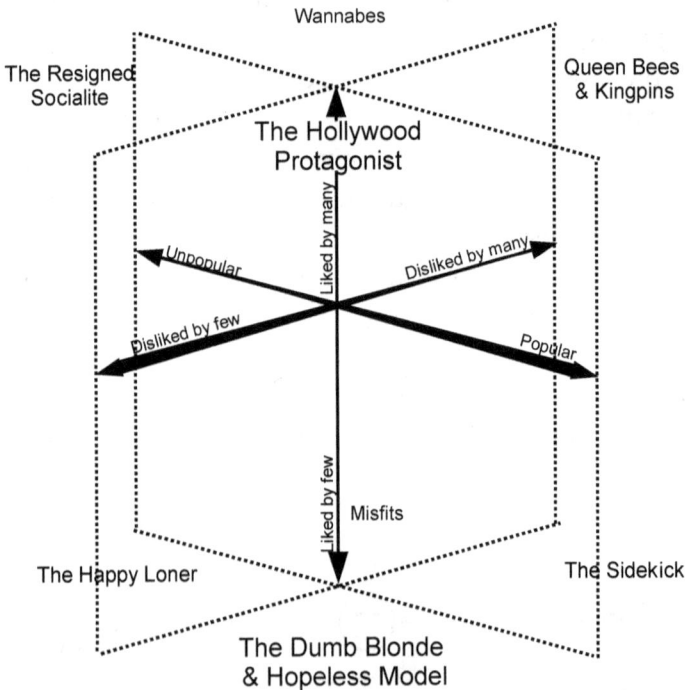

Figure 2.5 A combined classification system depicting all three concepts of liking, disliking, and perceived popularity.

---

11 The term 'Queen Bee' was first coined by Rosalind Wiseman in her excellent book, *Queen Bees & Wannabes*.

- Dumb Blondes and Hopeless Models
- Hollywood Protagonists
- Wannabes
- Resigned Socialites
- Happy Loners
- Misfits

THE STUDENTS AMONG US

I have labelled each of the eight quadrants in Figure 2.5 with a prototypical student description for the purposes of explanation only. Don't think that all students fit one of these titles perfectly. In reality, a student can fit anywhere on the diagram. If, hypothetically, each axis were given a scale ranging from 0 to 10 (where 5 is the midpoint on each axis), there would be 1,000 potential places a student could be plotted. The eight labels represent only the most recognizable student types and are extremes. Rarely will anyone fit one of the eight prototypes perfectly.

QUEEN BEES & KINGPINS:
PERCEIVED AS POPULAR / LIKED
BY MANY / DISLIKED BY MANY

Of the eight types, Queen Bees and Kingpins are the most recognizable. Every school has them. You can probably still remember the names of the Queen Bees and Kingpins of your own graduating class. They are depicted in movies and books as snobbish and stuck up. They think they own the school because they wear designer clothes and own the latest gadgets. They won't hesitate to stab another student in the back if it means preserving their position on the social totem pole. Somehow, these manipulative jerks get away with their bad behaviour and seem to rule the hallways.

In her influential book, *Queen Bees and Wannabes*, Rosalind Wiseman offers an excellent description of Queen Bees. "Through a combination of charisma, force, money, looks, will, and manipulation, this girl reigns supreme over the other girls and weakens their friendships with others, thereby strengthening her own power and influence".[12] For boys, the Queen Bee is an irresistible vixen. Even if she treats them like dirt, they still let her borrow their pencil if she asks. For girls, the Queen Bee can be a good friend, a mortal enemy, or both. On a whim she can convince other girls to turn on them or she can elevate their status by choosing them as a new best friend. If they hate her because she's cruel to them, it can be difficult to understand why everyone else seems to love her so much.

The Kingpin is the male version of the Queen Bee. He is physically intimidating relative to the majority of his peers and often good at sports. If you are familiar with the television show Glee, Noah Puckerman is a good example of what it is to be a Kingpin—a rebellious football-playing tough guy that all the girls love. Despite being jerks to almost everyone but their clique, Kingpins manage to retain their popularity. Joey Donner from the movie *Ten Things I Hate About You* is another good example. He's a male model who drives around in a red sports car making bets about which girls he can bed. In one scene he draws a penis on another student's face as punishment for stepping out of line and talking to him without permission.

One pattern of Queen Bee behaviour well documented by social scientists is a rapid flip flop between friendly behaviour and cruelty.[13] Jane, a Queen Bee from my school, used to dangle popularity in front of my friend Tanner. In

---

12 Wiseman, 2002, p. 25
13 See Aikins, 2011

English, the seating arrangement forced her to sit beside him and far from her clique. During the period, he played to her whim and she rewarded him with smiles and conversation. In Science, the story was much different. Jane sat surrounded by her friends; she no longer had use for Tanner. Every class, she made a point of reminding him that he was a Wannabe: a wanderer on the periphery of the cool group. Books about bullying are filled with similar anecdotes detailing the type of everyday cruelty Queen Bees and Kingpins regularly dole out.

SIDEKICKS: PERCEIVED AS POPULAR / LIKED BY FEW / DISLIKED BY MANY

Poking her head out from behind the shadow of the Queen Bee is the Sidekick. Sometimes everyone but the Queen Bee has something to dislike about this person. She's the evil enforcer. As Rosalind Wiseman states, "Together they appear to other girls as an impenetrable force. They commonly bully and silence other girls to forward their own agenda".[14] Without the Queen Bee, the sidekick is nothing. With the Queen Bee she is a force to be feared. Even though many girls might dislike her, her connection with the Queen Bee keeps her in the popular clique.

In the novel *How to Be Popular*, Alyssa Kruger is the perfect example of a Sidekick. Her Queen Bee is Lauren Moffat. Wherever Lauren goes, Alyssa lurks close behind. When the novel's protagonist, Stephanie Landry, becomes a threat to the popular clique, Lauren instructs Alyssa to write her a note reading: "U STUPID HO. WHY DON'T U GET A LIFE".[15] Alyssa dutifully obeys and drops the note on Stephanie's binder one day. Throughout the novel, Alyssa supports Lauren in various

14 Wiseman, 2002, p. 28
15 Cabot, 2006, p. 167

ways, including laughing at her jokes, writing hurtful e-mails on her behalf, and giving dirty glances to anyone who dares cross her.

Kingpins can have one or more Sidekicks as well but for whatever reason they are less apparent in the scientific literature and less frequently the focus of the popular media. Often, a male doesn't need the title "Sidekick" to earn a place in the lower left hand corner of Figure 2.5 (perceived as popular, liked by few, and disliked by many). He need only be a member of the popular clique and a jerk to everyone.

DUMB BLONDES & HOPELESS MODELS: PERCEIVED AS POPULAR / LIKED BY FEW / DISLIKED BY FEW

I named this category of students after the character Karen Smith from the movie *Mean Girls*. According to the movie's antihero, Janice Ian, Karen is "one of the dumbest girls you will ever meet." She can't catch a ball or spell the word "orange," and she thinks that her breasts predict rainfall.

Often students don't dislike Dumb Blondes the same way they dislike Queen Bees and Sidekicks because Dumb Blondes don't initiate cruelty in the same way. Even if she goes along with bullying, the Dumb Blonde likely has the feeling that what she's doing is wrong. The problem is that the prestige associated with being popular tends to outweigh any moral objections she might have. The Dumb Blonde is likely to toe the line because she is easily influenced.

The character Darlene Staggs, from the novel *How to Be Popular*, is an excellent example of what it is to be a Dumb Blonde. She's described as follows:

> *Darlene Staggs is possibly the dimmest person I have ever met who was not actually in Special Ed. Once in eighth grade biology, she finally figured out that honey comes from bees, and she*

was so grossed out that her favourite condiment came, as she put it, "out of a bug's butt" that she actually had to be sent to the nurse's office to have a cool compress applied to her forehead.

But while God was short-changing Darlene in the brains department, He went overboard on the beauty [...] she's the prettiest girl in our whole school and so is constantly surrounded by boys, who flock to her in hopes of someday being able to sink into her soft good-smellingness.

The other thing about Darlene is, when she, Lauren, Alyssa Krueger, and Bebe Johnson were in the line to get meanness from God, Darlene must have seen a butterfly and gone running after it, or something, since she doesn't have a mean bone in her body. But Lauren still lets Darlene hang out with her and the other Dark Ladies of the Sith, because Darlene's too pretty not to keep her around, in case one of them needs to catch her dregs.[16]

As exemplified by this quotation, Dumb Blondes aren't particularly liked or disliked. Boys are attracted to them for obvious reasons and so are the girls because they make an attractive addition to their clique. Although Dumb Blondes receive a lot of attention, this doesn't necessarily mean that they are well respected.

Examples of Hopeless Models—the male equivalent of Dumb Blondes—are less common in the popular media. The best example might be someone like Derek Zoolander, title character from the movie *Zoolander*, a man who thinks that being bulimic gives you the power to read minds. Hopeless Models confound their male peers because no matter how stupid they are, the girls still love them. In my school, there was a Hopeless Model named Josh. He wasn't influential and most of the time he just sat in class without participating.

Behind his back, the boys made him the butt of jokes because he was caught covering a blemish with makeup. Nonetheless, the girls kept courting him, one after the other. At parties, they would pull him into closets, cover him in hickeys, and drop him just days later.

HOLLYWOOD PROTAGONISTS: PERCEIVED POPULAR / LIKED BY MANY / DISLIKED BY FEW

Chris Hargensen from *Carrie*, Carolyn Mulford from *Sixteen Candles*, Kurt Kelly from *Heathers*, Joey Donner from *Ten Things I Hate About You*, and Regina George from *Mean Girls* all have what Rosalind Wiseman likes to call, "evil popularity".[17] Not all popular students, however, are cruel and/or clueless. Some are genuinely kind and engaging people. In addition to being "in" with the popular clique, they are also friendly with everyone else. Somehow, they separate themselves from the nastiness of the Queen Bee but stay on her good side. Students in this category are not as common as Queen Bees or Kingpins, but they certainly exist.

I call this group of students "Hollywood Protagonists" for two reasons: first, they are almost too good to be true; and second, students in this group embody the characteristics and personality of all high school movie protagonists. In addition to being beautiful, intelligent, and talented, they're also genuinely kind and compassionate people. Unlike Queen Bees and Kingpins, Hollywood Protagonists act with confidence without belittling their fellow students or acting snobbish. They are the ideal peer and the type of son/daughter every parent wishes for.

Because every high school movie has one, examples of the Hollywood Protagonists are easy to find. Cady Heron, from *Mean Girls*, is the perfect example of what a Hollywood

17 Wiseman, 2002, p. 23

Protagonist should be. The speech she gives after being elected "Spring Fling Queen" is an excellent demonstration of just how genuine of a person she is: "You know, I've never really been to one of these things before and when I think about how many people wanted this [crown], and how many people cried over it and stuff... I mean, I think everybody looks like royalty tonight. Look at Jessica Lopez [a paraplegic], that dress is amazing. And Emma Gruber [an overweight girl] that hair must have taken hours and you look really pretty. So why is everybody stressing over this [crown], it's just plastic." Cady then proceeds to break her crown into pieces and shares it with the student body.

Another classic example is Veronica Sawyer from the 1980's movie *Heathers*. After heroically saving her school from the sadistic bomber Jason Dean, Veronica walks pensively back into school. Having spent the entire movie in remorse for selling out her best friend to join the popular clique, Veronica decides to make a change in her life. Instead of returning to the Queen Bee, she walks straight up to Martha Dunnington, a Misfit, and invites her to watch movies on prom night.

In real life, Hollywood Protagonists can be hard to find for two reasons. First, they are statistically rare (see Chapter 3) and second, even if they want to be genuinely nice people, Hollywood Protagonists can often come across as arrogant (see Chapter 11, question 3). Students in this category do, however, exist.

I have a friend named Justin. When he's not helping under privileged children in Brazil, he studies medicine. At just over 6 feet tall and approximately 175 pounds weight, he is a well-proportioned man. His chiseled jaw line, prominent cheekbones, and dark complexion once got him noticed by a modelling scout. The amazing thing about Justin is that he is surprisingly modest and genuine. In the words of one of my female friends, "He isn't arrogant although he has every reason to be." Justin treats all girls equally—even those he could easily think are "below" him. He is the perfect example of a Hollywood Protagonist and the girl who finally captures his heart should count herself lucky.

WANNABES: PERCEIVED AS UNPOPULAR / SOMETIMES LIKED / SOMETIMES DISLIKED

Hovering around the periphery of the popular clique are the Wannabes. Along with Queen Bees and Kingpins, they are some of the most recognizable students. Wannabes desperately want to be popular and they are constantly vying for membership in the popular clique. More than other students, they are prone to mimicry and influence. When popular students adopt a new style or trend, Wannabes are the first to copy them. They are the "yes men;" when a popular student voices an opinion, Wannabes immediately agree. Despite their best efforts, however, Wannabes never attain the allusive adjective "cool." The following quotation from Stacey, a popular fourth grade girl, summarizes the point:

> *The wannabes try to hang around, and try to be in, and try to do stuff that is cool, but they aren't really cool. But they think they are, and if we play with them, they think they'll get cooler, so they're always ready if we want them.*[18]

Another common tactic used by Wannabes is luring students with material possessions, lucrative invitations, privileged information, or other benefits. One guy I used to know regularly bought cans of soft drinks for people he thought were his "friends." Because Wannabes are always looking to please those above them on the social totem pole, they can

---

18 Adler & Adler, 1996.

easily get themselves into trouble by doing the dirty work. Although such strategies might work temporarily to elevate the Wannabe's status, any gains are short lived.

Wannabes' constant attempts at inclusion don't go unnoticed. Constant ingratiation ultimately serves to weaken their social position. A self-perpetuating, detrimental cycle is often the result: Wannabes want to be cool, so they try to be cool, which makes them even less cool.

What comes to my mind when I think of Wannabes is a guy from my high school named Allan. Although he had a respectable number of friends among the student body, he desperately wanted to be part of the popular clique. Whenever I was with him and a group of less popular students, Allan wasn't a bad guy. As soon as someone from the popular clique was around, however, his allegiance could turn on a dime. Sometimes I liked him, sometimes I didn't.

FOOD FOR THOUGHT:
BEING

Spencer was the exact opposite of a Wannabe. He rarely spoke unnecessarily and never tried to attract attention to himself. He was a talented soccer player but would always pass the ball to give someone else a chance while playing. His girlfriends came and went but his status was always a little bit of a mystery because he never advertised it. He would come to school with an arm cast and say only that he had gotten into a little bit of fight—shrugging it off as nothing. Not once did he make an effort to project a particular image and yet, among his peers, he was "badass" and always "such a beauty."

RESIGNED SOCIALITES: PERCEIVED AS UNPOPULAR / WELL LIKED BY MANY / DISLIKED BY FEW

Resigned Socialites have little flare or social visibility. If they want to be popular, they hide it well. Unlike Wannabes, Resigned Socialites don't bother making desperate attempts to be included in the popular clique; neither do they act superior to those around them. Instead, they happily congregate with other students of the same status and get to know whoever they meet without discrimination. Resigned Socialites are genuinely pleasant people with many friends from various social circles. They are not a threat or nuisance to the popular clique and, as a result, they rarely become the targets of aggression. With so many high quality friendships, it's tempting to assume that Resigned Socialites would be considered popular by their peers but this is not the case. Somehow this title eludes them.

My good friend from high school, Darren, was the perfect example of a Resigned Socialite. Everybody loved him because he was pleasant and always interested in fostering meaningful relationships with anyone he met. Because he was an active member of the school band, rugby team, and drama productions, he maintained friendships across an array of different cliques. Now that he has graduated and become an avid traveller, his network of friendships literally spans all of Canada. When his birthday reminder is sent out via Facebook, he receives hundreds of posts. He was never, however, perceived as popular.

HAPPY LONERS: PERCEIVED AS UNPOPULAR / LIKED BY FEW / DISLIKED BY FEW

Not everyone wants to be popular or socially central. Some students value academics, sports, or music more than their social status. These students can be found wandering the hallways, content to ponder the secrets of the universe. The introverted math genius is the stereotypical example of what it is to be a Happy Loner. Generally, they will have one or two close friends but remain mostly disengaged from the social world. Happy Loners aren't necessarily socially inept—just uninterested. Other students rarely target Happy Loners for bullying because they react with muted responses or general indifference. As a result, they are often left to their own devices. When researchers such as Coie, Dodge, and Coppotelli ask students to nominate who they like most and who they like least, Happy Loners are entirely forgotten: they are neither liked nor disliked.

MISFITS: PERCEIVED AS UNPOPULAR / LIKED BY FEW / DISLIKED BY MANY

For every Queen Bee or Kingpin, there is a social Misfit stranded at the bottom of the social totem pole. Unlike the Happy Loner, Misfits are preferred targets for all sorts of aggression. Even at young ages they eat lunch by themselves or socialize with the adult supervisors at recess. Their friendships are often the result of necessity and with other Misfits. A teacher can always spot these students by observing who is chosen last for group projects. As they age and move to larger schools, Misfits find each other and form their own cliques. In this way, they find a reprieve from the constant mockery doled out everywhere else in the school.

It's well known that Misfits suffer systemic discrimination from the student body. Teen books are full of stories detailing the type of horror that social exclusion can create. Steve, author of the short story "I was Bullied Because I was Different," paints a chilling description of what rejection can feel like:

My hell is a bit different from how mythologies or religions depict it. My hell is Hadfield Elementary School. Elementary school is perhaps the most vicious, ruthless, unaccepting atmosphere that exists on this planet. The groups, the cliques, the gangs are unstoppable and unbearable. [...] If you are different you are wrong, and therefore are punished verbally, physically, and mentally.[19]

WHAT MADE DAISY SO SPECIAL?

Looking back at the drama festival mentioned at the outset of this chapter, I know in hindsight what made Daisy so special. Compared to all of her friends, who were best described as Queen Bees, she was a Hollywood Protagonist. In addition to being popular, she was genuinely liked by students of all social strata because she didn't snub her nose at anyone or demean others. If she knew you she would acknowledge you in the hallways, and if you happened to be standing beside her she would ask how your day was. If you needed a favour, Daisy would make the offer regardless of which clique you were in. Whenever I learned that we had chosen the same breakout session, I felt happy because I, like the rest of the student body, genuinely *liked* her.

Often, authors and screenwriters rush to demonize the entire popular clique as superficial and cruel. Implied in their works is the message that all popular students are phonies and have no real friends.[20] When I read books or watch movies that depict popular students solely as stereotypical jerks, I think of people like Daisy and Justin. They prove that life is never so simple. It is possible to be popular and genuinely well liked.

---

19 Steve, M., 2010
20 See Chang, 2010

"GREAT, NOW HOW DO I HELP SOMEONE BECOME A HOLLYWOOD PROTAGONIST?"

By itself this chapter isn't very useful because it doesn't explain how a student comes to occupy their social position. Most students (except perhaps the Happy Loners) want to be popular at some point and so the remainder of this book is dedicated to answering the question: "how?"

FOOD FOR THOUGHT:
CARING AND NOT CARING

A student who decides to "not care" has chosen a safe option. By not caring, nothing can hurt or disappoint them. Unfortunately, it can also prevent them from confronting what might be legitimate character flaws. In other words, "not caring" can turn into a crutch which keeps students from making positive changes in their life. Unfortunately, some students are likely to care a little too much and this too can be a bad thing. The goal, I suggest, is to help students find a happy medium between caring and not caring.

CHAPTER 3

THE HIERARCHY
OF ATTRACTION

Every year, my high school held a "Battle of the Bands" style concert. In senior year, the concert was held in the drama room and, like any professional black box theatre, the room was complete with spotlights and a sound system. A two-foot stage was erected in the centre of the room with seating arranged around it and a small standing space at the front. When the show started, the glow of acoustic guitars under spotlights and the bustling crowd gave the concert an authentic feel.

One of the performers that night was a multi-talented musician named Patrick. He and two friends had prepared a three guitar acoustic set complete with vocal harmony. I was excited to see Patrick play because he and I were good friends throughout junior high and high school. One of the reasons Patrick and I clicked was because neither of us outshone the other with respect to friends, status, or girls.

In addition to seeing Patrick perform, I had another motivation for attending the concert that evening. One of the girls in my class, Shirley, was hosting a newly arrived Swedish exchange student and wanted her to meet our group—specifically me. That day at school, Shirley had given me a heads up that she would be introducing Emily to me in particular. As you can imagine, I was delighted to hear this.

The concert did not disappoint. The professional ambiance and high quality performances made for an exhilarating evening; Patrick and his band were no exception. Their set was beautiful, well performed, and just long enough. He himself did an excellent job singing and playing. I would have congratulated him immediately after the show if it hadn't been for my meeting with the Swede. As planned, Shirley found me after the concert and introduced me by saying "Emily, this is my friend Alex..."

I'll never forget her response. She shook my hand, introduced herself quickly, then turned to Shirley and said, "That's nice, now where is that boy who played guitar?"

***

Popular media enforces the stereotype that mathematically inclined students make for unpopular nerds. "Ted the Geek," from the movie *Sixteen Candles*, is an excellent example. Short, skinny, and pale, his appearance screams computer nerd. Given this stereotype, it is ironic that the secret of popularity begins with statistics. Underlying the social drama that permeates every grade school in the world is the well-known statistical phenomenon known as the "normal distribution." It, together with the natural human experience of attraction, combine to form what I call the "Hierarchy of Attraction:" a diamond shaped concept that can be used to classify how attractive students are relative to each other. Before I discuss statistics, however, it is necessary to define the word "attractive."

When I discuss popularity with people, almost invariably they eventually say, "Yeah but different people find different things attractive" or, "Yeah, but being beautiful isn't the only thing that matters." My response to these people is always that I agree. Hundreds—if not thousands—of different details make people attractive. Furthermore, no two people are attracted to exactly the same things. When I use the word "attractive" in this book, I am not referring synonymously to "beautiful." Being beautiful is important, but it's not the only thing that makes someone attractive. Any quality that exerts a magnetic pull on another person can be referred to as attractive.

ALL THE THINGS THAT MAKE US ATTRACTIVE

At the university where I completed my undergraduate degree, there is a hallway lined with small 6 by 10 feet practice rooms, each housing a piano. At the very end of the hallway was my favourite room. Unlike the others, it was brightly decorated with posters and artificial plants. Among the decorations was a small photo sized picture of Johnny Depp playing the piano and smoking a cigar. It was obviously such an attractive picture that one day, one of the female vocal students stole it and took it home. Many posters of Johnny Depp exist but this picture in particular is well known. What makes it so special?

In the picture, Johnny Depp is sitting in profile at an old, upright, piano. His tanned skin and loose muscle shirt give the impression of a muggy ambient temperature. (If you have convenient access to the Internet, I highly suggest that you Google "Johnny Depp playing piano" and see for yourself.) In addition to accentuating his physical features, the photographer also included the following details to portray a particular persona:

1. Johnny Depp is smoking, communicating a rebellious, macho, and carefree attitude. This persona is reinforced by his long unkempt hair, tattoos, and ragged muscle shirt.

2. His surroundings, including the piano he is playing, are old and worn. This suggests that Johnny Depp appreciates the rustic side of life. It also places him far from the mundane context of suburbia.

3. Finally, he happens to be playing with limp wrists and lax fluidity: only talented musicians can make a piano sing with such ease and comfort. Perhaps the point here is to communicate that underneath his rebellious and rustic nature is a softer, more artistic, side. If Rosalind Wiseman was to see this photograph, she would likely characterize Johnny Depp as, what she calls, "the misunderstood guy." A male that is "intoxicating to girls because he combines the dangerous bad boy elements with sweetness. He acts hard and dangerous in public and then sweet in private with a girl".[21]

Your interpretation of the picture may differ from mine. The point, quite simply, is that more than physical appearance can make someone attractive—the photographer who took the picture knew this.

If I asked you to describe all of the things that make someone attractive, you could probably write a book; in fact, it's been done.[22] For the purpose of crafting a theory, however, what's needed is not a long list of attractive qualities but rather a rule of thumb for predicting what makes someone attractive. Luckily, psychologists have already done this. It

21 Wiseman, 2002, p. 180
22 See Berscheid & Walster, 1969

turns out that if you want to predict attractiveness, it's not enough to know about the target (i.e. Johnny Depp in the above example), you also need to know something about the observer (i.e. the person viewing Johnny Depp). The reason both are relevant is because what makes someone attractive changes according to the wants and desires of the observer. In other words, you need to know what someone wants in order to predict what they are going to find *attractive*.

Imagine a large group of business men gathering for an investment luncheon. The vast majority are middle aged and married with kids. At this point in their lives, their number one desire is to maximize success which, for them, means making as much money as possible. Among the crowd is Mark Zuckerberg (the billionaire founder of Facebook) and he is looking to invest his money in an interesting business venture. Also among the crowd is a failed salesman who wears cheap suits and is known for barely being able to make his minimum loan repayments. Under these circumstances, who do you think will be more attractive to the business men in the room: the billionaire or the failed salesman? The answer is obvious. Having billions of dollars is going to make someone very attractive to a group of business men looking for investment capital and networking opportunities. In this situation, wealth equals attractive.

Now, let's change the scenario and context. Instead of middle aged married business men at a luncheon, let's imagine a group of young male medical students. Unlike the business men, they're rowdy, single, and not motivated primarily by money. Instead of a business luncheon, let's imagine they're at the bar after a final exam. In this particular situation, who do you think is going to be the most attractive person in the bar? The answer is of course the girl with the most sex appeal. What do young, single, and rowdy male medical students generally want when they go to a bar? Sex, of course. Mark Zuckerberg, Bill Gates, and Donald Trump could be sitting in the back of the room having a beer and none of the students would likely pay much attention to them. In this situation, sexual appeal equals attractive.

Let's change the scenario one more time. Imagine a singles "get-together" organized by a traditional Christian community. The group in attendance is composed of males and females in their early twenties, all of whom want to get married. Unlike the first two examples, it is much more difficult in this scenario to equate one or even two qualities with being attractive. If I had to guess, I would say that the average person in the room is looking for a combination of qualities including physical appearance, future ambition, a compatible personality, and so forth. In this scenario, it is multiple qualities that combine to equal attractive.

The rule of thumb given earlier (the desire for various rewards causes attraction) is useful because it reminds us that "attractive" is not synonymous with beautiful. Many different things can make us attractive, depending on the wants and desires of the observer. Attraction is not one thing.

Even if the feeling of attraction is subjective, this does not mean that useful generalizations cannot be made. Across a wide range of scenarios, there are four things that make people attractive to the average person: physical appearance, socioeconomic status, similarity, and efficacy (being good at what you do). Why physical appearance and socioeconomic status are important isn't hard to understand. How someone looks is always the first thing people notice. As for higher socioeconomic status, it is generally attractive because being wealthy implies access to resources that can be used for any number of things. No matter what a person's interests are—photography, raising children, travelling, etc.—money is a requirement. Being in a relationship with someone who is wealthy therefore facilitates access to the things that people want.

The fact that similarity is an important predictor of attraction is less intuitive. Have you heard the sayings "opposites attract" or "birds of a feather flock together?" Of these contradictory sayings, all evidence points to "birds of a feather" as correct. Because it is difficult to quantify, similarity is often overlooked as a predictor of attraction. Although less obvious than physical appearance and socioeconomic status, its importance should not be underestimated. It applies to a large range of tangible characteristics, such as ethnicity, as well as a large range of intangible characteristics, such as similarity of attitudes, interests, and beliefs. Perhaps the reason why similarity is so important is because it ensures compatibility. If you are a devout Baha'i (an independent world religion that teaches abstinence from alcohol) living with an alcoholic would be difficult no matter how attractive he or she might otherwise be. On the other hand, if both partners abstain, the consumption of alcohol becomes a non-issue in their relationship. For a detailed discussion of similarity leading to attraction, see Chapter 9.

A friend once told me that there is nothing more attractive than a man in his element—this is efficacy. In general, people are attracted to those who are competent and good at what they do and this applies to all domains and occupations. Think of a sports team. When a player demonstrates skill with ease and confidence, the media is immediately focused. This is why Johnny Depp's posture and disposition in the photograph is so important: the lax fluidity in his hands communicates efficacy at playing the piano.

One reason why being good at something is attractive is because demonstrations of skill and ability are rewarded with positive praise and attention. Esteem is a basic human need and, as a result, members of the same and opposite sex feel a natural tendency to bask in the reflected glory of their efficacious peers.[23]

Between myself and Patrick, neither was significantly better looking or more popular. With respect to similarity and socioeconomic status, I can only speculate that relative to Emily, he and I were roughly equivalent. In hindsight, however, Patrick easily outshone me that evening of the concert—his musical talent was what Emily had responded to. Just like Johnny Depp playing the piano, Patrick communicated musical efficacy and Emily was attracted to him because of it. Over the next few months Patrick and Emily became a couple and enjoyed each other's company until she left Canada. Although it would be unfair to judge Patrick's other personal qualities, sometimes I wonder how things would have turned out if Emily had met the two of us in a situation where I was more dominant.

Disclaimer

Before I explain the details of the Hierarchy of Attraction, it's important to emphasize an unfortunate part of life. In order to understand popularity, it must be accepted that life is unfair. Everyone has strengths and weaknesses—it's just that some people have more strengths than others. My brother has Down's syndrome and a handful of other problems. As much as I love him, I have to accept that with respect to success in the physical world, he does not have the same potential as I do. And as hard as it is to accept, some people are simultaneously smarter, kinder, better looking, and more genuine than I will ever be. As will be explored later in this chapter, rigid equality is impossible. That's just the way it is.

---

23 Cialdini & Richardson, 1980

FOOD FOR THOUGHT:
GROUPS ARE INHERENTLY ATTRACTIVE

Even if the members of a group aren't particularly attractive in and of themselves, when they come together a synergy develops that makes them more attractive than any member individually. Everyone wants to have friends and be accepted and so as soon as people see the camaraderie between two or more individuals, they commonly want in. Every time I organize get-togethers (bike rides, cards, etc.) with a small group of friends, I'm amazed at how many people "want in" the next time around—people who otherwise would never seek my attention.

A strategy for students who always feel on the periphery is to take a look around and see who else is "on the outside looking in." If they can find common ground and group with each other, they will discover that unlikely people are suddenly attracted to them and their new friends.

THE HIERARCHY
OF ATTRACTION

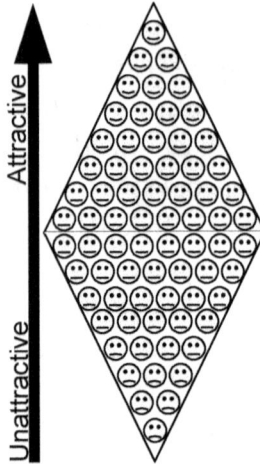

Figure 3.1 The Hierarchy of Attraction

In short, the Hierarchy of Attraction is a depiction of how attractive people are relative to each other. Everyone finds some people attractive and some people unattractive. Johnny Depp, for example, is attractive to millions around the world. Likewise, the hockey player Sydney Crosby. In fact, one of his fans showed up to a game wearing a wedding dress and holding a sign proposing marriage. A fan of pop singer Britney Spears took his attraction too far and ended up with a restraining order issued against him. Without ever having met any of them, a large percentage of the population finds people like Johnny Depp, Sydney Crosby, and Britney Spears attractive. People like these three are at the top of the Hierarchy of Attraction.

For every superstar who is attractive to a large percentage of the population, there exist people who are attractive to only a small percentage.

On YouTube, there is a video of a man trying to get inside of a giant inflated weather balloon (search, "Balloon Fail"). The star of the show is a middle-aged man wearing sweatpants and a loose, plain white t-shirt. He is bald on the top of his head with curly black hair on the sides. The video begins with him orienting a massive weather balloon that fills the camera frame. He then pokes his head inside and eventually gets his arms and torso in as well. As he tries to pull the balloon over his hips, the nozzle becomes caught on his pants and begins deflating rapidly. "Oh great," he says, "I'm becoming trapped in the balloon."

As the balloon nears full deflation, the man becomes disoriented and falls to the ground—a giant balloon wrapped around the upper half of his body. "I can still breath," he says hopefully before making a first and then second attempt at standing. Eventually, he manages to escape the balloon but not before accidentally flashing his white boxer briefs. I don't know what percentage of the population finds this man attractive. You be the judge.

The Hierarchy of Attraction is just a depiction of the fact that some people are attractive to many and others are attractive to few. Therefore, a person's position in the Hierarchy is determined by the percentage of people in any group that finds them attractive. As depicted in Figure 3.2, percentage is represented by the shaded area: the larger the area, the larger the percentage.

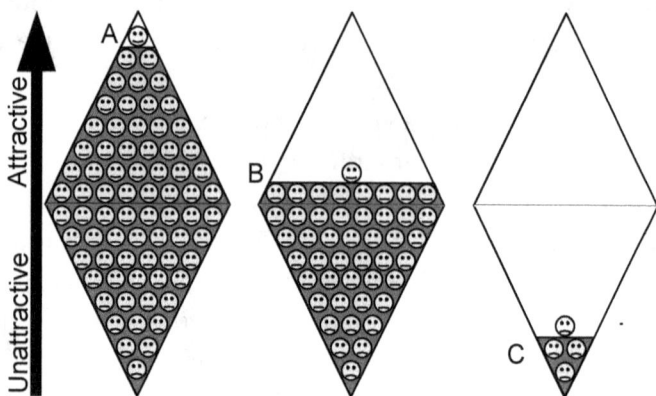

Figure 3.2 A person's position in the Hierarchy is determined by the percentage of people that finds them attractive. People like Johnny Depp are at position A while people who are attractive to few are at position C. The majority of people are somewhere around position B.

Imagine a classroom with 30 students, 15 male and 15 female. A student who is attractive to all of the girls and all of the boys will be at the top of the Hierarchy because 100% of his/her peers find him/her attractive (remember: "attractive" is not synonymous with "physically attractive"). Such a student would occupy position A because 100% of the Hierarchy falls underneath them. A student who is attractive to approximately 60% of the students would occupy position B. Finally, a student attractive to approximately 5% of his peers would occupy position C.

The Hierarchy of Attraction is not something I invented to impose on the social world. It's a statistical phenomenon that can be deduced from five facts of life.

FIVE FACTS OF LIFE

Fact #1: An Infinite Number of Characteristics Define Each Individual

If you take a moment and think about all of the characteristics—physical, emotional, intellectual, and spiritual—that define a particular student, it doesn't take long to appreciate that the list can be very, very long. If you actually tried to include all characteristics, it would become apparent that even straight forward traits like beauty can be broken down into component parts. It, for example, depends partly on proportion, symmetry, and the shape of features such as jawline, eyes, and alignment of teeth. If you wanted to go further, you could even consider just the eyes in terms of colour, shape, and size. In short, an almost infinite number of characteristics define each individual because each can be continuously broken down.

Fact #2: Every Individual is a Unique Combination of Possible Characteristics

How would you respond if someone told you that all people with red hair were abnormally smart and that all people with black hair were abnormally dumb? If you're thinking that hair colour has nothing to do with intelligence, you're correct of course. What if someone told you that anyone who is athletic cannot be good at music? If you're thinking that's ridiculous, you're correct again. People who are good at sports can also be good at music just like people with black hair can be intelligent. The reason why things like physical appearance/intelligence and athleticism/musicality are not related is because different genetic and environmental factors influence each. As a result, any combination of these traits is possible. Some people are going to be physically attractive, intelligent, musical, and athletic. Others are going to be physically unattractive, unintelligent, unmusical, and nonathletic.

Even related characteristics like height and weight can vary more or less independently. People can be tall and big like Arnold Schwarzenegger or they can be tall and skinny like the basketball player Steve Nash. People can also be short and stocky like the hockey enforcer, Tie Domi, or short and skinny like a horse jockey. The important point is that even though height and weight generally go together, a wide range of combinations is still possible.

Think of the all the characteristics that define an individual and appreciate that all of these characteristics can vary semi, or entirely, independently. Just imagine the huge number of possibilities if you started changing this or that aspect of a person! Together, facts #1 and fact #2 prove the well-known adage that no two people are exactly the same.

Fact #3: The Existence of "Positive" Qualities Necessitates the Existence of "Negative" Qualities

Personal characteristics are all examples of relative concepts that do not exist as absolutes. Consider the following rhetorical question: how tall is tall? Look at the picture in Figure 3.3. Who is tall and who is short in frame A? Now, look at frame B. Who is tall and who is short? This silly example demonstrates an important point. The definition of the adjective "tall" depends on what is available for comparison. Whether Tom is considered tall or short depends entirely on who he is standing beside. If Thomas didn't exist, Tom would be the tallest.

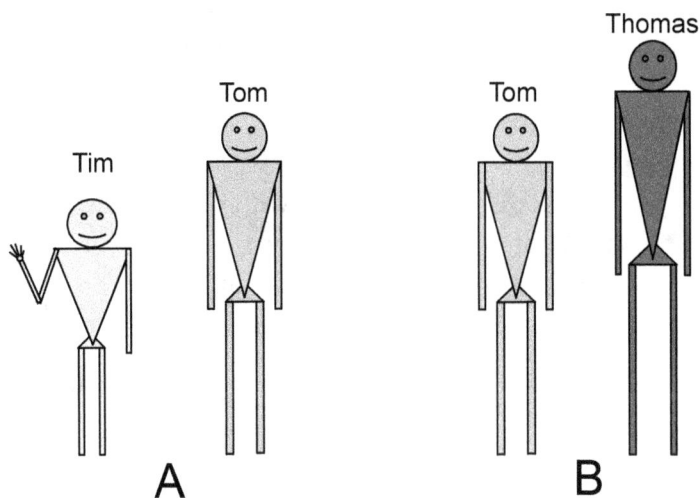

Figure 3.3 The adjective tall depends on context. Tom is only tall when compared to Tim.

Just like the concept of "tall" depends on the opposite concept of "short" to have meaning, so too do all other relative concepts. Without a corresponding opposite, many common adjectives would have no meaning. Rich/poor, talented/untalented, intelligent/unintelligent, and athletic/nonathletic are all good examples of relative concepts. As soon as you label one individual as talented, rich, or intelligent, you necessarily imply that another individual is untalented, poor, or unintelligent by comparison.

Fact #4: Attraction is a Universal Human Experience and is Itself a Relative Concept

Everyone has experienced the pull of attraction and knows what it feels like. Attraction can be romantic and/or sexual in nature, but it is also a fundamental part of many non-sexual types of relationship including those with friends or family.

In addition to the big four mentioned earlier (physical appearance, socioeconomic status, similarity, and efficacy), there are other characteristics that can make people attractive, especially during adolescence:

- acting tough or rebellious,
- emotional displays consistent with gender roles[24]
- having a lot of friends and being socially connected,
- owning or having access to a car, and
- access to mature and/or exciting opportunities (e.g., parties).

Of course, the five characteristics listed above are not universally attractive. Not everyone is going to be attracted to gender consistent emotional displays because attraction is a uniquely individual experience. The point, quite simply, is that everything that makes someone attractive is a relative concept and, as a result, the experience of attraction is itself relative. Think back to your time as a student. Who were you most attracted to? The fact that you are able to mentally identify one or two individuals preferentially implies that you find everyone else less attractive by comparison. Try to imagine what the world would be like if everyone found everyone else equally attractive. If this were the case, you wouldn't even know what the word "attraction" meant! Unless you are attracted to some and *not attracted* to others, the concept of attraction has no meaning.

Fact #5: A Normal Distribution of Positive and Negative Trait Combinations can be found in Any Population

The normal distribution, also known as "the bell curve" is a statistical concept that depicts the probability of an event when graphed. It's found again and again in nature hence its name sake, the normal distribution. How it relates to

24 Tracy & Beall (in press). DOI 10.1037/a0022902

popularity and the Hierarchy of Attraction can be demonstrated using a series of simple examples.

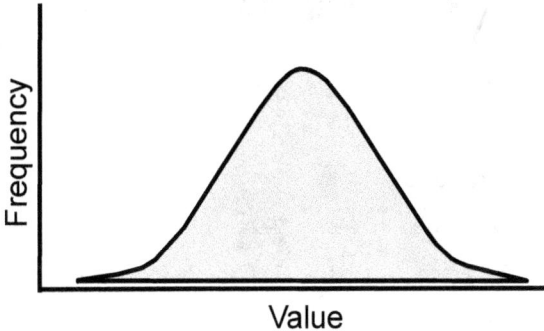

Figure 3.4 A normal distribution. The y-axis represents the number
of times an event occurs. The x-axis represents the numerical value
of an event.

Example 1: First, let's consider two characteristics that
are applicable to all people: physical appearance and intelligence. For simplicity, assume that with respect to each characteristic, people can be: (1) lowest, (2) low, (3) average, (4)
high or, (5) highest. In other words, a person can be: (1) very
ugly, (2) ugly, (3) average, (4) beautiful, or (5) very beautiful,
and with respect to intelligence: (1) very dumb, (2) dumb,
(3) average, (4) smart, or (5) very smart. Because physical
appearance and intelligence vary independently from one
another, a total of 25 trait combinations are possible:

5 different ways to look
* 5 different ways to be smart
= 25 different trait combinations

If it helps a student to understand, they can think of rolling two funny shaped dice each with five sides. On their first
roll, they can score a 1, 2, 3, 4 or 5 and on their second roll

they can score 1, 2, 3, 4 or 5. All of the possible combinations are written in the table below.

Table 3.1		DICE 1 *(Physical Appearance)*				
		1	2	3	4	5
		Very ugly	Ugly	Average	Beauti-ful	Very Beautiful
DICE 2	1 Very Dumb	1+1	2+1	3+1	4+1	5+1
(Intelli-gence)	2 Dumb	1+2	2+2	3+2	4+2	5+2
	3 Average	1+3	2+3	3+3	4+3	5+3
	4 Smart	1+4	2+4	3+4	4+4	5+4
	5 Very Smart	1+5	2+5	3+5	4+5	5+5

What Table 3.1 shows is that in the lottery of life, some people roll a double 5 and score a total of 10: these people are both very beautiful and very smart. Other people roll a double 1 and score a total of 2: these people are very ugly and very dumb. If you compute the sum of all possible combinations, what you will find is that some people have the same total score even though they roll different numbers. For example, 4+3=7 and so does 5+2. Each combination's total is listed in Table 3.2.

Table 3.2		Dice 1 (Physical Appearance)				
		1	2	3	4	5
		Very Ugly	Ugly	Average	Beauti-ful	Very Beautiful
Dice 2	1 Dumb	1+1=2	2+1=3	3+1=4	4+1=5	5+1=6
(Intelli-gence)	2 Very Dumb	1+2=3	2+2=4	3+2=5	4+2=6	5+2=7
	3 Average	1+3=4	2+3=5	3+3=6	4+3=7	5+3=8
	4 Smart	1+4=5	2+4=6	3+4=7	4+4=8	5+4=9
	5 Very Smart	1+5=6	2+5=7	3+5=8	4+5=9	5+5=10

Looking at the totals, what you will notice is that the same totals (e.g., 5 & 6) occur often and others occur only a few times (e.g., 2 & 10). Figure 3.5 is a graph depicting which totals are most common and which totals are least common. As you can see, only one combination (5+5) sums to the maximum of 10 and only one combination (1+1) sums to the minimum score of 2. The most common total is the average score of 6.

Example 2: To make the above example more interesting, a third characteristic could be added such as athleticism. Like the other two characteristics, someone can be (1) very nonathletic; (2) nonathletic; (3) average; (4) athletic; or (5) very athletic. If a student followed the same procedure as in example 1, what they will discover is that there are now 125 different combinations:

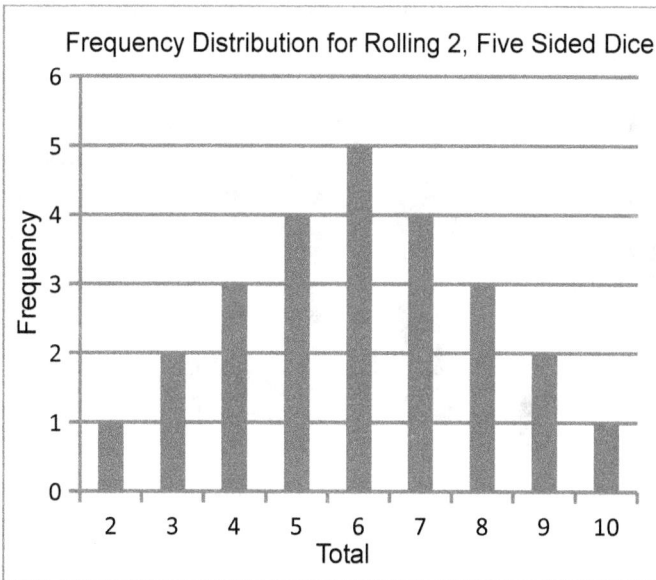

Figure 3.5 *Frequency distribution showing how many times each total occurs after rolling 2, five sided dice.*

5 different ways to look
* 5 different ways to be smart
* 5 different ways to be athletic

= 125 different trait combinations

Tabulated, the following three things would be obvious: first, there is only one way to get the minimum score of 3 (1+1+1); second, there is only one way to get the maximum score of 15 (5+5+5); and third, the average score of 9 is the most common total. The corresponding graph is shown in Figure 3.6.

What will happen if a fourth characteristic, such as socio economic status, was added should be obvious. The equation would look like this:

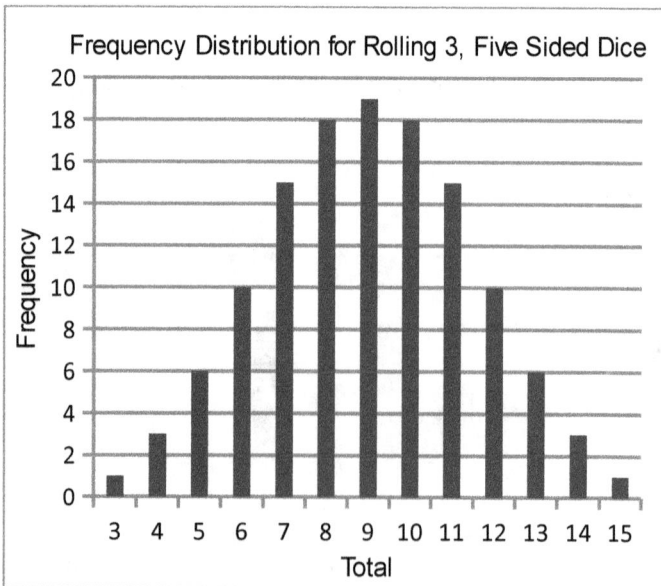

Figure 3.6 *Frequency distribution showing how many times each total occurs after rolling 3, five sided dice.*

5 different ways to look

* 5 different ways to be smart

* 5 different ways to be athletic

* 5 different ways to have money

= 625 different trait combinations

Tabulated, the following three peculiarities would be obvious:

1. There is only one way to get the minimum score of 4 (1+1+1+1).

2. There is only one way to get the maximum score of 20 (5+5+5+5).

3. The average score of 12 is the most common total.

Graphed, it would look like Figure 3.7.

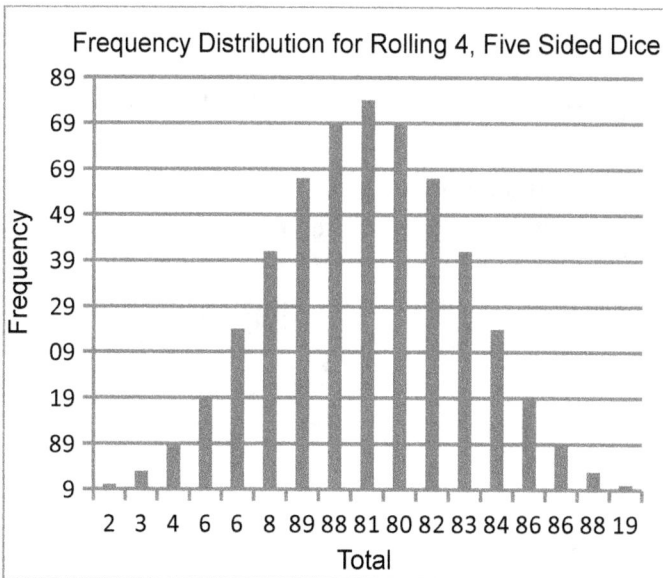

Frequency Distribution for Rolling 4, Five Sided Dice

Figure 3.7 Frequency distribution showing how many times each total occurs after rolling 4, five sided dice.

A student can appreciate the link between the graphs created and the normal distribution by looking at Figure 3.8. If characteristics kept being added, eventually the associated graph would look exactly like the bell curve on the right. Even if an infinite number of human characteristics were considered, the basic shape would always remain the same.

In everyday language, all that the complicated graphs and statistics are saying is that it is rare that any student will have only "positive" qualities and equally rare that they will have only "negative" qualities. The vast majority have some combination of both.

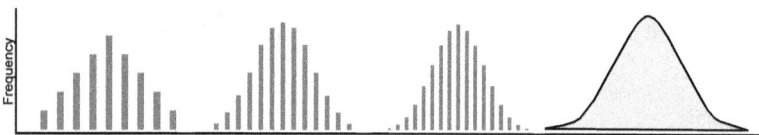

Figure 3.8 The frequency distributions of Figures 3.5, 3.6, 3.7, and 3.4 shown side by side. Notice the consistent shape of a bell.

"What," a student might ask, "does this have to do with the Hierarchy of Attraction?" The answer is that individual variation comes from Facts of Life #1 and #2; the top and bottom labels of "attractive" and "unattractive" come from Facts #3 and #4; and, the shape comes from Fact #5. As can be seen, the Hierarchy of Attraction isn't just an arbitrary invention I came up with. It's the combined result of Five Facts of Life!

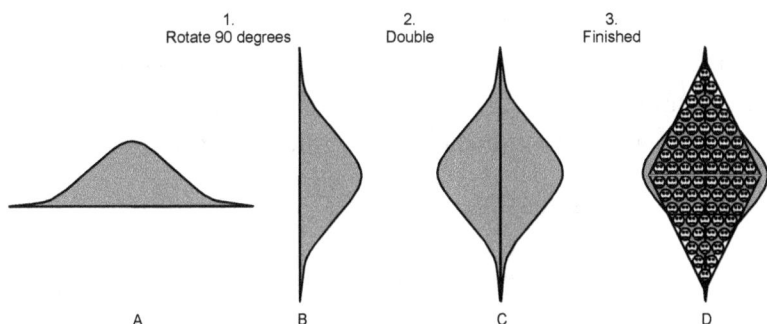

Figure 3.9 The diamond shape of the Hierarchy of Attraction is not arbitrary. It's a stylized version of the normal distribution as illustrated above.

No matter what group a student finds them self in, a Hierarchy of Attraction will exist. In fact, none of us can escape it because we all participate in the lottery of life at the moment of conception. Some people get very lucky and roll all 5s. These are the Alicia Keys of the world. Not only is she a beautiful, wealthy, and talented pop superstar, she is also intelligent. She was valedictorian of her high school graduating class and I'm willing to bet that, in addition to everything else, she was also good at sports as an adolescent.

Unfortunately, for every Alicia Keys there is someone else who has much less going for them. I feel sympathy for a girl I knew throughout grade school who is a good example of someone who seemed to have rolled nearly all 1s in the lottery of life. In addition to being academically average, she was physically unattractive, didn't play sports, wasn't particularly talented, and had odd social mannerisms. No one at my school found this girl attractive. Whenever she was brave enough to face the barrage of mockery and come to a school dance, she inevitably danced alone.

The vast majority of us are not as lucky as Alicia Keys or as unlucky as the girl just described. Most of us can safely say that we are good at some things and not so good at others. We are just average: stuck somewhere in the middle of the Hierarchy.

FOOD FOR THOUGHT:

WHY?

At the university where I study, there is a medical resident who, in addition to being a future doctor with "modelesque" features, is a song-writing, piano playing, weightlifting, genuine, person. I once had the opportunity to watch him audition for a concert and I remember thinking, to myself, "why do people like this exist?" When he apologized for not being totally prepared, his four female judges responded in unison by saying, "Just play and we'll think that anything you do was amazing."

THREE IMPORTANT POINTS TO REMEMBER

Above all, there are three important points to remember about the Hierarchy of Attraction. First, a student's position is not a constant and changes depending on the group that they are in. Imagine a small town business man known to be worth between $4 and $5 million dollars. Because there are not many millionaires in his small town, he is going to be very attractive to the majority of participants at any business luncheon he attends. Under such circumstances, this small town millionaire will occupy a high place in the Hierarchy. If he moves to upscale New York, however, his few millions will pale in comparison to the fortunes of his new neighbours. In this new social context, he will occupy a much lower position in the Hierarchy.

The same is true for all of us. Where we sit in the Hierarchy is always changing depending on the circumstances. Imagine a charming and charismatic old man living amongst a cohort of retirees. Within the social context of his retirement home, he may find himself at the top of the Hierarchy. However, imagine what would happen if the same man decided to return to university and live in residence. Do you think he would ascend or descend the Hierarchy? Except under exceptional circumstances, it is difficult to imagine that other students would find him more attractive than the young and virile roommates that surround him.

The second important point to remember about the Hierarchy of Attraction is that personal effort can affect someone's position. The Hierarchy is not a static or rigid structure. People cannot be permanently classified into rungs or percentiles because it is fluid and changing over time. Should a person lose a noticeable amount of excess weight, for example, the number of people who find them physically attractive is likely to increase given current standards of beauty. Likewise, when an employee transitions from entry level job to a senior position, their place in the Hierarchy increases because socioeconomic status is generally attractive.

A student who knows deep down that they scored a couple of 1s in the lottery of life need not feel too bad. Perhaps they are not Hollywood beautiful but they can take consolation in the fact that a majority of people are in the same boat thanks to statistics. Furthermore, if the same student is not satisfied with their position, they need not feel that it is dependent solely on characteristics that cannot be changed. People cannot choose to look like Marilyn Monroe, for example, but they can attend to personal hygiene and style. People cannot choose to be built like Arnold Schwarzenegger but they can exercise regularly. People cannot choose to be brilliant like Einstein but they can choose to study diligently. In short, even if a student rolls a low score in the lottery of life, they retain significant control over their final position in the Hierarchy of Attraction.

The third and most important point to remember about the Hierarchy is that it is not prescriptive. In other words, someone who is in the 75% percentile is not necessarily going to find someone in the 80% attractive nor are they necessarily going to find someone below them in the 70% unattractive. Said differently, a person at position A in Figure 3.2 might find a person at position B incredibly attractive. Such a situation is not impossible because the Hierarchy only depicts what is true *in general*. It does not in any way determine who will be attracted to whom as a guarantee. If someone at the top of the Hierarchy is attracted to someone at the bottom, it doesn't matter what the rest of the world thinks. In fact, anytime you hear someone say, "he/she could have done so much better," it is a reflection of the fact that there is a perceived discrepancy between the hierarchical positions of the two individuals in question.

FOOD FOR THOUGHT:

THE OVER COMPENSATOR'S SYNDROME

Everyone has insecurity and it can be tempting to try and overshadow a personal weakness with a personal strength. Because there are many things that make someone attractive, this can be a very practical strategy up to a certain point. It becomes detrimental, possibly pathological, when an individual becomes consumed with the need to overcompensate for a particular, self-perceived, flaw.

CHAPTER 4

INPUT OF ENERGY

Any grade school student knows that classroom seating arrangements are not a trivial detail. Getting a spot near friends is essential. If they are unlucky enough to get a seat far away, the outcome is a semester of gazing longingly from across the room at a cluster of their friends laughing and enjoying each other's company.

My grade 11 biology teacher didn't care where we sat so long as we picked a seat and stuck to it. In the first week of the semester, the seating arrangement in his class was fluid because no one really knew who was going to be there permanently. New students joined and others dropped out within a couple of days so everyone had about a week to settle into their permanent spot.

On day one of grade 11 Biology, I scanned the classroom after everyone had taken their seats. With me in the class was a prominent member of the popular clique. Like her peers, Kate was physically attractive and gregarious—the type of girl most boys cross their fingers to sit beside. On that first day, I got unlucky and ended up sitting several seats back from both her and my two long-time friends. On day two, however, someone sitting in front of me was interested in swapping seats and I made the trade willingly. On day three, I caught another lucky break. A student sitting directly ahead of me dropped the class so I claimed his desk immediately. I loved my new spot not only because the desk itself was nicer, but because the location was excellent. I was near two of my friends and right beside Kate.

Several months later, I noticed (for the first time) something strange and amusing in the seating arrangement. While scanning the room, I realized that the entire class was divided down the middle with boys on one side and girls on the other. The only exception was Kate—she was surrounded by boys. At first, I figured it was because she didn't know any of the girls on the other side of the class but she soon proved this hypothesis wrong by joining them every time the class broke up for group projects. "What," I wondered, "could be responsible for this odd seating arrangement? Was it just chance?"

THE BRAIN ON ATTRACTION

As mentioned in Chapter 3, feelings of attraction are a universal human experience. Deep inside every human brain are circuits designed to trigger feelings of attraction in response to specific stimuli. As intuitive as it might seem, sex and sexual reproduction are actually a complicated affair. If you are a male, sexually receptive females aren't always available (e.g. being a boy in an all-boys boarding school). If you're a female, sexually receptive males aren't always available either (e.g. being a girl in an all-girls boarding school). Even when mates are available, they are not always acceptable. Think back to the person you found most unattractive in your school—would you?

Assuming that all of the males and females in a room are mutually acceptable to each other, the outcome is still not a free-for-all. Competition for sexual opportunities is the inevitable outcome if there is a discrepancy between supply and demand. When a receptive female rat is let loose amongst a group of males, they will literally pile on top of her, tumbling and wrestling with each other in a desperate attempt to mate.

More direct and violent male/male competition is observable in a number of species. Hippopotamus, deer, walrus, and a large number of other animals regularly fight vicious battles in order to win access to females. For their part, females are generally less violent when it comes to mating because they are the more discriminating sex: carefully choosing from amongst those available only the most attractive partners.

To ensure that males brave serious injury and females hold off until the right suitor comes along, evolution has produced the psychological process of sexual attraction.[25] Along with our animal instincts, humans have inherited the neurological systems that underlie feelings of attraction. The brain circuitry underlying these feelings is so thoroughly embedded that just looking at physically attractive people is rewarding. A "reward," in the lingo of neuroscience, is the "activation of neural circuits in the brain that function to maintain an animal's contact with certain environmental stimuli, either in the present or in the future."[26] In everyday language, a reward can be anything that feels good: when you score a goal playing sports it feels good; when you eat chocolate, it feels

25 Fisher, 2000
26 Kolb & Wishaw, 2005, p.433

good; when you have sex, it feels good; and so on. Everyone
has an intuitive understanding of what it feels like to experience a reward.

Attraction is not exclusive to heterosexuals nor is it always sexual in nature (a fact emphasized in Chapter 3). All
forms of it, however, rely on shared elements of the same
brain circuitry. The most studied of these circuits is the
mesolimbic system and it in particular is important when it
comes to motivating everyday behaviours. In brief, anytime
you experience a reward by doing something like scoring a
goal, eating chocolate, or having sex, this circuit releases the
neurochemical dopamine which is well known for being associated with the feelings of wanting and pleasure.

In 2008, the neuroscientist Jasmin Cloutier and his team
used functional magnetic resonance imaging (fMRI) to look
inside the brains of people while they viewed pictures of
strangers.[27] What he and his team discovered was that viewing
pictures of physically attractive people is enough to activate
the brain's reward circuitry. In essence, looking at beautiful
people is in some ways similar to scoring a goal, eating chocolate, or having sex.

Once feelings of attraction—sexual or otherwise—stimu-
late our brains, an amazing thing happens: our behaviour
changes in ways that are predictable. Sometimes these changes are obvious and consciously motivated. At other times,
they occur without any conscious awareness. Deep inside the
human brain are pre-programmed behavioural responses to
feelings of attraction; in other words, instincts. After reading
the rest of this chapter, you should start to notice subtle (and
sometimes funny) changes in the way people interact with
one another when under the influence of attraction.

---

27 Cloutier et al., 2008

INPUT OF ENERGY

Think back to your adolescence and imagine you are walking through a school hallway. You're busy laughing and joking with your friends when all of a sudden you see a new—and beautiful—student coming towards you. You've never seen this student before but you're impressed by his/her confident stride as they come close. Rays of light seem to emanate from their perfect form as time seems to slow down. Like Romeo when he first sees Juliet, you immediately feel the pangs of Cupid's arrows sinking deep into your adolescent heart. Its love at first sight and you know it. But how, you wonder, will you ever be able to attain this stranger's good pleasure? How will you get them to notice you?

Before you even have the chance to recover from your initial enchantment, let alone come up with a plan of action, your brain has already kicked into overdrive and begun priming an array of motivated behaviours designed to help you win your new love's heart. Thanks to millions of years of evolution, your brain comes pre-programmed with behavioural responses designed to facilitate the process of matchmaking. I call this repertoire of innate behaviours, "input of energy."

In its simplest and most obvious forms, input of energy compels people to do things like seek physical proximity. In its subtlest and most inconspicuous forms, it changes how intelligent, funny, and cool you think someone is. Despite its many forms, input of energy always has one common purpose: to help you meet and bond with people you find attractive romantically or otherwise.

INPUT OF ENERGY IS:
ATTEMPTS AT PHYSICAL PROXIMITY

Sometimes the most interesting insights are right in front of us. Input of energy, a major piece of the popularity puzzle, can be inferred from the English language itself. Consider the words "alluring" and "physically attractive," two common synonyms of the adjective beautiful. If you think about it, both imply getting close to the targeted individual. The word "alluring" is derived from the word allure which means to attract something. The term "physically attractive" obviously has a similar meaning. Both imply that beautiful people have a special magnetic pull that draws others toward them.

It's easy to understand why the words "alluring" and "physically attractive" became synonymous with beautiful during the evolution of the English language. Think about the beautiful strangers you see on a daily basis: do you not feel a subtle desire to interact with them? Popular culture is full of examples of beautiful people demonstrating their magnetic power over others. When Romeo first sees Juliet from across the hall of the Capulet's house, his first instinct is to approach her and then, after only a brief first meeting, risk his life to famously find his way to her balcony.

Attempting to get close to people who are attractive is one of the most common forms that input of energy takes. To create a relationship with someone, you must find opportunities to get to know them. This involves getting within communicating distance.

One day while riding the school bus, my younger brother noticed a beautiful girl sitting several rows ahead of him who was surrounded by empty seats. At the next bus stop, three boys (none of whom knew each other or the girl) got onto the bus. The first boy chose to sit in front of the girl, the second boy chose to sit beside her, and the third chose to sit behind.

Unless every other spot on the bus was taken, their choice of seats was no accident. Because the girl was beautiful, each of the three boys was motivated to choose a seat close to her. By doing so, they increased their chances of interacting and starting a relationship.

Often, there are situational constraints that prevent people from acting outright on their desire for proximity. If the dream girl/boy of a student happens to be in a different homeroom, it's going to be difficult for them to choose a desk close by, because they're stuck in a different classroom. No matter how much they might like to do otherwise, the situation prevents them from seeking proximity.

If not a physical barrier, it is often social constraints that prevent people from acting on their desire for proximity outright. Imagine that the same student sees his/her dream girl/boy sitting in the school cafeteria. Although they might want to choose the closest possible seat, social norms can prevent them from doing so even if the seat beside the object of desire is empty. It is a well-known fact that high school cafeterias are usually divided up into cliques. If the girl/boy is part of a clique different from the student's, they cannot just sit down beside them without good reason. Not only would they risk immediate rejection, they risk becoming the subject of embarrassing rumours. Ignoring social norms can be tantamount to committing social suicide.

Because situational and social constraints so often prevent people from making overly obvious attempts at proximity, more subtle variations are much more common. Have you ever noticed that when teachers number students from 1 to 5 and then ask them to form groups, it never works out exactly as would be expected? One year at summer camp, I remember being frustrated by the fact that I was always unlucky when it came to making groups using this method.

Even on those occasions when I was sure that the girl I liked got the same number as me, she would mysteriously end up in the same group as the most popular boy. At first, I couldn't understand what was going on. In time, however, I discovered that she was actively trading her numbers with someone else so that she could be in the same group as him—that's input of energy. The girl I liked was attracted to the popular boy and, as a result, she made a subtle but targeted effort to get close to him.

Another example involving the same girl and boy is also worth sharing. During group activities, campers regularly got up and left the main hall to go for water at the fountain. I could get up, go for water and come back... Go for water again and come back... Leave and return once more and nothing worth mentioning would happen. The popular boy could go for water once and the girl would always get thirsty at exactly the same time—how convenient. The next time you witness students being numbered and asked to form groups, watch how the numbers change. The students will actively swap numbers and switch groups in order to be with their friends or those they are attracted too.

Attempts at proximity occur around us all of the time. When you're in a school or near students, look for the different ways in which they try to get close to one another. Pay special attention during times of unrestricted movement such gym class, drama class, school dances, lunch, and recess. Even if they won't admit it, where people chose to stand and/or sit is often motivated by attraction.

At times, what people think are subtle attempts at physical proximity can be humorously obvious. In grade 10 cooking class, my teacher brought her teenaged (and beautiful) daughter to school as part of "Bring Your Kid to Work Day." The classroom had six small kitchens around the perimeter of the room and, for whatever reason, the teacher directed her daughter to work in the same kitchen as me and my friends. Amazingly, for the rest of the class period, my kitchen and the two kitchens adjacent to it became the most popular in the classroom. Boys from every other group were finding any reason imaginable to visit my kitchen or those adjacent.

When I asked why they were suddenly so interested in being around my kitchen, they gave answers that never failed to make me smile. Some were there to borrow salt or a can opener. Others would come to visit with friends while others would give no reason at all. Not surprisingly, none of them said, "I am attracted to the teacher's daughter therefore I'm making a not-so-subtle attempt at physical proximity in hopes of improving my chances of meeting her." In all the days prior to "Bring Your Kid to Work Day," my kitchen had never been so popular. In the days that followed, it would never be so popular again.

FOOD FOR THOUGHT:
STUDENT'S WILL BE STUDENTS ALL AROUND THE WORLD

For seven months I taught English at a small school in Tanzania, Africa. Every time I tried to group the kids using numbers, it always took two or three tries before they got it right. This failure was not because my Swahili wasn't good enough to explain the process. It was because Tanzanian students are just like North American students— always inputting energy behind the scenes in a subtle attempt to influence who's in what group.

INPUT OF ENERGY IS:
SUBTLE CHANGES IN BODY LANGUAGE

Bored at university one day, I zoned out and directed my attention toward two strangers, a boy and girl, who had just begun a conversation two rows ahead of me. I couldn't hear what they were saying yet I could tell that the boy was fighting a losing battle. Even though I had never met either individual, it was obvious that the girl was not interested in talking. Just as I had suspected, their conversation was short lived and it wasn't long before she went back to her work and he went reluctantly back to his music.

Learning the ins and outs of nonverbal communication is something that all social animals must do. Humans are no exception. From the time of infancy, the human brain is primed to learn nonverbal cues. Even if you cannot list the nonverbal cues that you respond to during conversation, you and everyone else has a sophisticated understanding of what to look for.

Along with attempts at proximity, nonverbal communication is one of the most obvious forms that input of energy takes. When someone is or is not attracted to another, an array of nonverbal cues conveys this message. Imagine a boy who wants to borrow a textbook from a girl sitting at a desk in front of him. Standing behind her, he taps her on the shoulder and asks if she has the book. Recognizing his voice, she flips her hair over her shoulder to expose one side of her neck, rotates her torso towards him, looks up, cocks her head to the side, smiles, and says, "Of course, it's under my desk." In this situation, what would you think if you were the boy?

Now, imagine that instead of flipping her hair, turning toward him and looking up, the girl continues to do her work. Speaking into her desk she says, "Of course, it's under my desk." If you were the boy, what would you think now?

In the two scenarios, the verbal communication is exactly the same but the message conveyed is clearly different. In the first scenario the boy is going to conclude that the girl is happy to lend him the book and excited to have his attention. In the second scenario, his conclusion will be that her interest is minimal and strictly business.

Since the 1960s, researchers have been cataloguing different behaviours that communicate attraction and rejection. In 2010, the psychologist Monica Moore compiled a review of nonverbal courtship behaviour.[28] What she found was that if a girl is interested in a boy, she is likely to do one or more of the following: hair flipping, a scanning glance, short darting glances, smiles, repeated eye contact and acceptance of mutual gaze, mild physical contact such as a delicate touching, head nodding, and close attention to the conversation. Men communicate attraction through short glances, acceptance of mutual eye contact, leaning forward, and tilting their heads. Most men will increase the frequency of touch between them and their male buddies when in the presence of an attractive female (e.g. putting their hand on a friend's shoulder or mock punching). They also attempt to maximize the space they occupy by doing things like spreading their arms across adjacent chairs.

The nonverbal communication of rejection often involves behaviours that are opposite to those that communicate attraction. Both men and women generally adopt closed body postures when interacting with people they find unattractive: crossing the arms, putting hands in pockets, keeping the legs tightly closed, and turning the torso away. Also important are yawning, frowning, avoiding the other's gaze, staring upward, sneering, grooming fingernails, picking at one's teeth,

---

28 Moore, 2010

avoiding eye contact for more than 10 seconds, or staring coldly.

There is no secret to nonverbal communication. Most socially adept people are able to decode the nonverbal messages implied by other people's behaviour. If you are interested in learning more, several books have been written on the subject.[29] The important point is that nonverbal communication changes depending on how attractive two people are to one another.

INPUT OF ENERGY IS:
INDIRECT CHANGES TO VERBAL
COMMUNICATION AND THE QUALITY/
CONTENT OF CONVERSATION

Just like nonverbal communication, verbal communication also changes depending on how attractive two people find one another. One of the best ways to kill a romantic moment is to bring up a third person and begin talking about them. In fact, this is a common way for women to communicate rejection. If a woman is interested in a man, she sets an exclusive tone by focusing her attention on him and will not mention other people. For their part, men communicate attraction during conversation by making a special effort to understand the woman's perspective and appreciate her point of view.[30]

There are other ways attraction can be communicated indirectly during conversation. Think of the person you are closest with romantically. Take a moment and imagine yourself talking with them. What are you discussing? What information are you sharing? Regardless of gender, people are motivated to share personal information with those they find attractive because personal disclosure facilitates the process

29 See Quilliam, 2004
30 Garcia et al., 1991

of interpersonal bonding.[31] The next time a student finds that one of their peers is telling them all sorts of secrets about their personal life, they can take it as a sign that they are attractive.

Think back to the boy asking the girl for a textbook and her response, "Of course, it's under my desk." One of the differences you probably imagined between the two scenarios was a change in the girl's tone of voice. Sometimes, *how* you say something is more important than what you say. In 1981, psychologists Susan Andersen and Sandra Bem tested this by asking participants to get to know a stranger over the phone.[32] The critical manipulation in their study was that some of the participants were led to believe that the stranger they were talking to was beautiful. After collecting all of the data, judges who didn't know what the experimental condition was were asked to rate how responsive each participant was to the conversation. To do this, they filled out standardized forms with questions such as: How animated or enthusiastic [was] the participant?; How interested [was] the participant in his or her partner?; and, How intimate or personal [was] the participant's conversation? What Andersen and Bem found was that participants were more responsive and enthusiastic when they believed the stranger to be beautiful.

INPUT OF ENERGY IS:
ATTITUDINAL CHANGES AND
SOCIAL INFLUENCE

Switch on the television and watch some commercials. What types of people are chosen to represent brand names? For the most part, all spokespersons are beautiful. Naomi Wolf, author of *The Beauty Myth*, and others like her argue

31 Brundage, Derlega & Cash, 1977
32 Andersen & Bem, 1981

that corporations are responsible for Western society's obsession with beauty. The truth is that advertisers are not subservient pawns seeking to further an evil corporate agenda. Rather, they have a single and simple goal in mind: to sell their product. After decades of practice, the advertising industry has come to appreciate how shallow human nature often is. People are more likely to accept endorsement from someone who is beautiful. Advertisers have known this for decades. Using properly controlled experiments, social scientists have demonstrated time and again that the public is more likely to accept a message, buy a product, or purchase a service if it is endorsed by someone beautiful.[33]

One of the reasons why beautiful people have more social influence is because they are consistently judged more favourably with respect to a range of personal characteristics. For whatever reason, beautiful people are judged more intelligent, moral, emotionally adjusted, and so on. This tendency forms the basis of the bias "beautiful-is-good" and books have been written on the subject.[34]

Perhaps you can remember someone from your time in school who was physically attractive but not smart. If you concluded as a result that what a person looks like is not a good indicator of how smart they are, you would be right. Dumb people can be good looking and smart people can be ugly. Unfortunately, the truth is that if you give someone two pictures and ask them to judge "who's smarter?" they generally choose the more physically attractive person—that's just the way it is.

The fact that beautiful people have more social influence has important implications in the grade school setting. When it comes to setting trends at school, beautiful students

33 Ahearne, Gruen & Jarvis, 1999
34 Ray & Rumsey, 1988

are much more successful because other students are willing to accept their opinions and actions as inherently "cool."

Try the following thought experiment: bring a physically *unattractive* girl to mind. Imagine that one day she comes to gym class wearing a white sleeveless shirt pulled over a purple bra. Furthermore, she has cut two strategically placed holes so that her bra shows through at the nipples. How do you think the student body would react? Now, change the scenario by imagining that, instead, a beautiful girl pulled this stunt. Do you think the student body's reaction would be any different?

It seems ridiculous but this is exactly what happens in the movie *Mean Girls*. As a prank, Janis Ian (a Misfit) cuts two holes in the beautiful Regina George's white tank top causing her bra to show through at the nipples. Instead of having the humiliating effect that the prankster intended, all of the girls are in awe of Regina's new style. The next day, every girl has a shirt cut in the same way. Reflected in the *Mean Girls'* script is the fact that beautiful students have significant social influence.

If the world was fair, an idea or action would be judged solely on its intrinsic merit. In reality, the merit of an idea or action is also dependent on who said and/or did it. If you're gagging at the notion that society could be so superficial, I'm not sure what to tell you. The following quote from the book, *Queen Bees and Wannabes*, concisely demonstrates the point that *what someone is* biases interpersonal judgments about them:

> *A few footnotes from the girls: Being athletic is acceptable only if the girl has a thin, "feminine" body—a large, "masculine" build is unacceptable, which is why many excellent female athletes worry about getting bulky if they lift weights. Sexual promiscuity is more acceptable (meaning she won't be called a*

*slut) if a girl is popular. A girl with few friends who is low in
the social hierarchy will get a reputation as a slut for the same
behaviour that doesn't cost a popular girl anything, and very few
girls will associate with her.*[35]

If you still don't believe me, search the following titles in
Google Scholar:

- Shared Brain Activity for Aesthetic and Moral
  Judgements: Implications for the Beauty-is-Good
  Stereotype. Tsukiura, T. & Cabeza, R. (2011) in *Social
  and Cognitive Neuroscience*, volume 6.
- What is Beautiful is Good Because What is Beautiful
  is Desired: Physical Attractiveness Stereotyping as
  Projection of Interpersonal Goals. Lemay, E. P., Clark
  M. S., Greenberg A. (2010) in *Personality and Social
  Psychology Bulletin* volume 36.
- Positive Illusions about a Partner's Physical
  Attractiveness and Relationship Quality. Dick B. &
  Dijkstra, P. (2009) in *Personal Relationships*, volume
  16.
- Is Beautiful Always Good? Implicit Benefits of Facial
  Attractiveness. van Leeuwen, M. L. & Macrae, C. N.
  (2004) in *Social Cognition*, volume 22.
- Origins of a Stereotype: Categorization of Facial
  Attractiveness by 6-Month-Old Infants. Ramsey, J. L.,
  Langlois, J. H., Hoss, R. A., Rubenstein, A. J. & Griffin,
  A. M. (2004) in *Developmental Science*, volume 7.

Undeniably, it matters what a student looks like.

---

35 Wiseman, 2002, p.39

FOOD FOR THOUGHT:

WILLINGNESS TO CHANGE

Because attitudinal changes and social influence are two of the forms that input of energy takes, you can gauge someone's attraction to you by their willingness to conform to your idiosyncrasies. For example, let's say you love watching the nightly news and you're seeing someone who normally doesn't. Under these circumstances, it's a good sign if they willingly take up the habit.

Never assume that you're immune to social influence. I consider myself a "non-texter" because my text messages are short and to the point. I cannot understand why people have text conversations that last hours about nothing. Nonetheless, under certain circumstances, and with the right person, I've caught myself willingly texting for hours on end. Obviously, social influence due to input of energy can be inevitable even if you are aware of it.

INPUT OF ENERGY IS:
COGNITIVE INTRUSION

In the summer after high school, I became friends with a girl two years my senior who had studied psychology in university. She claimed that psychology allowed her to "read between the lines" of what people said. I was sceptical at first and so I tested her by asking: "Who's the girl that I have a crush on?" Although my psychology friend didn't know it, mine was a trick question because she had never seen this girl and myself interact. As such, I was expecting her to answer something to the effect of, "No one." When she guessed the name correctly on her first try, I was surprised and suitably impressed! I hadn't shared my secret with anyone and so it wasn't possible she had heard the answer from someone else. How did she do it?

The human brain is designed to notice attractive people; they grab our attention and hold onto it. Whenever I'm driving, I am always amazed at how much effort it takes to keep my eyes on the road when I notice a girl on the sidewalk. The same thing happens to me at the gym. I can't help it. My attention is automatically drawn to look so it takes considerable effort on my part to thwart this natural instinct. I freely admit this fact because I know that I am not alone.[36] Anyone who tells you that they feel no such impulse is lying. Think back to a crush you had in school: how much did you know about their daily routine? If you knew a creepy amount of information back then, don't feel too bad. As illustrated by the following quote, it's a common phenomenon:

> I was obsessed with this guy named Scott. I have no idea why. I look back and laugh at this now, but at the time I was totally serious. I would write in my journal the different things he had done that brought me closer to the conclusion that he liked me. I would show off, try to be near him. Every day during recess, my friend and I would play tag near where he played soccer with his friends and count the number of times he smiled at me. It was pathetic — Julia[37]

Attractive people have a tendency to invade our minds and hijack our thoughts. The love-possessed may even focus their attention on specific events or objects that involve the target of their affection, as Julia did.

---

36 Fisher, 2000
37 Wiseman, 2002, p. 205

Having studied psychology, my friend knew about cognitive intrusion and was able to exploit it to her advantage. At various times she had inconspicuously asked me open-ended questions that required a list of names to answer. Because the image and name of my crush was primed in my mind at all times, her name was perpetually on the tip of my tongue. Even if she wasn't the first person I listed, she was invariably included somewhere in my answer. In the end, even though I hadn't told anyone, it was a pattern in my behaviour that betrayed my secret and tipped off my friend.

FOOD FOR THOUGHT:
STARING

For the unmarried reader: Wait until you're in a group with a person of interest and a third party. During the conversation, notice what happens when you and the third party try to talk at the same time: where does the person of interest direct their attention first? If the three of you are sitting in a line and the person of interest is in the middle, this test can be particularly effective. Thanks to cognitive intrusion, attraction will keep them focused on you even if they are talking with the third party. If you make even a small comment, they'll re-orient their head and pick up on your conversation as if they had been looking at you the whole time. In way, they have been!

INPUT OF ENERGY IS: HELPING BEHAVIOUR

The following is an excerpt from Meg Cabot's book, *How to Be Popular*. It features the busty bombshell, Darlene Staggs:

> *Darlene picked up her Diet Coke can and shook it, indicating it was empty. "Oh no. All gone! Can you be a sweetie and go get me another?" Todd practically tripped over his own feet in his haste to get her another soda. Darlene glanced at Becca and me with a smile. It was hard not to crack up.* [38]

Even though it's fiction, this excerpt accurately reflects an important truth: when it comes to helpful behaviour, attractive people get more than their unattractive peers. This was demonstrated by psychologist David Wilson in 1978.[39] His simple experiment involved physically attractive and unattractive actors asking strangers for help mailing a letter. The results were shocking: 95% of the strangers agreed to help mail the letter when the actor was physically attractive whereas only 45% agreed when she was unattractive.

As always, *attraction is not synonymous with beautiful* and preferential helping behaviour doesn't just occur in potentially romantic relationships. In the television show *90210: The Next Generation*, the main character, Annie Wilson, demonstrates this in the pilot episode. Annie is struggling to find friends and fit into her new school, and not long into the episode, the popular girl, Naomi Clark, emerges as her social saviour. Not only is Naomi popular, she's also fun and exciting. To Annie, who is timid and overwhelmed, Naomi is attractive as a potential friend.

---

38 Cabot, 2006, p. 164
39 Wilson, 1978

When things start to go poorly for Naomi with respect to school, it's not surprising that Annie comes to the rescue of her new friend on account of the attraction she feels.

"Are you kidding me?" Naomi gasps as she reads a text message, "My mom just texted me. I have to write that paper for Mathew by tomorrow."

"How much have you written?" Annie responds.

"I haven't even started yet! Oh my God, I can't do this right now... this is so not what I need. I mean I know if I just sat down and started writing it that I could get it done, but just thinking about staring at a blank piece of paper... What am I going to do?"

"Well, I can help. I told you I got an A on that paper last year so I could give it to you and you could take some ideas from it."

"Really? That would be so awesome."

"Sure, that way you can see what it should look like. I'll just e-mail it to you when I get home!"

In this excerpt, Annie wasn't forced to help Naomi. She could have shrugged her shoulders and simply said, "Too bad. You're on your own." Of course, Annie doesn't do this because Naomi is attractive as a potential friend. By offering to help, she is reinforcing their budding relationship.

INPUT OF ENERGY IS: NOT ONLY THE RESULT OF BEAUTY!

It bears repeating once again that "attractive" IS NOT synonymous with "beautiful." Although many researchers have studied input of energy in the context of beauty, this does not mean that their results are not relevant when attraction is based on something else.

Many things make one person attractive to another and input of energy is always the result regardless of what the attraction is based on. When someone is trying to sell you something, for example, you are attractive because you are the key to them getting paid. As such, you can expect to notice input of energy in its various forms being directed towards you throughout the interaction.

INPUT OF ENERGY IS: OFTEN UNCONSCIOUS

Although you are probably not aware of it, a large part of your behaviour is the result of unconscious processes that occur automatically in your subconscious. Timothy Wilson, a prominent social psychologist and author of *Strangers to Ourselves: Discovering the Adaptive Unconscious*, uses the metaphor of a plane to describe just how influential the unconscious mind is.

> *The mind operates most efficiently by relegating a good deal of high-level, sophisticated thinking to the unconscious, just as a modern jumbo jetliner is able to fly on automatic pilot with little or no input from the human, "conscious" pilot. The adaptive unconscious does an excellent job of sizing up the world, warning people of danger, setting goals, and initiating action in a sophisticated and efficient manner.*[40]

No matter how hard you try, unconscious processes influence your behaviour, emotions, and decisions. Malcolm Gladwell, author of the bestseller *The Tipping Point*, has written an entire book on the power of the unconscious mind entitled *Blink*. In it, he argues that some of the best decisions you make actually originate from the unconscious in the blink of an eye—hence the title of the book.

Your unconscious does a number of things but two are particularly relevant to grade school social dynamics and will be discussed here: interpreting social cues and goal

---

setting. First, let's consider the unconscious's role as interpreter. In order to appreciate just how much interpretation goes on behind the scenes of your conscious thought, try the following:

1. Read this sentence out loud: "I like to eat 1ate at n1ght."
2. Now, read out loud this series of numbers: "1O, 11, I2"

Did you have any trouble reading either the sentence or the numbers? Of course not. The sentence clearly states, "I like to eat late at night" despite the fact that the letter L in "late" and the letter I in "night" have both been replaced with the numeral 1. In fact, you interpreted the number 1 as two different letters depending on the context. Likewise, did you having any trouble counting from ten to twelve in the second example? Of course not. Even though the number zero in 10 was replaced with the letter O and the one of 12 was replaced with a capital I.

You are constantly being bombarded with ambiguous stimuli and it is the responsibility of your unconscious to interpret these stimuli so that your consciousness does not become overloaded. The circle that represents the zero or the letter O is ambiguous until placed in context—otherwise it's just a circle! Depending on what's around it, the circle can be interpreted as either a letter or a number.

Just like your interpretation of the circle was dependent on context, so are many interpersonal judgements. The act of cutting two holes in a shirt so that the bra shows through at the nipples, for example, is ambiguous with respect to how "cool" it is. It can be interpreted differently depending on the context (was it the popular girl who did it or the unpopular girl?). Without conscious awareness, people can judge the same action as cool or *un*cool in the same way that they can interpret a circle to be either a number or a letter. The same principle applies when you judge the humour of a joke or the quality of someone's fashion sense— your final judgement depends on *who* you are judging as much as *what* you are judging.

Unconscious processes are a large part of the reason why the stereotype known as "beautiful-is-good" perpetuates. In his book *Blink*, Gladwell devotes an entire chapter to what he calls the "Warren Harding Error: Why We Fall for Tall, Dark and Handsome Men."[41] Warren Harding was the 29th President of the United States and although he is widely regarded as one of the worst presidents of all time, his physical appearance was everything that a President's should be. "People only had to see Harding," Gladwell writes, "and hear that magnificent rumbling voice to be convinced of his worthiness for higher office". Because the "beautiful-is-good" stereotype works on an unconscious level, it is incredibly hard to stop. As soon as people see someone who is physically attractive, their behaviour is affected without them even knowing it. In the case of Warren Harding, the relevant behaviour was voting. In the case of grade school popularity, the relevant behaviour is input of energy.

Another important function of the unconscious mind is to set goals and prioritize opportunities. As Wilson writes, "people's adaptive unconscious might acquire goals of which they are completely unaware".[42] In the book *How to Be Popular*, the protagonist Stephanie Landry provides a great example of how this is relevant to popularity. As part of a fundraising effort, the boy she likes—Mark—agrees to endorse any store that "purchases" him for an advertising

---

41 Gladwell, 2005, p. 74
42 Wilson, 2002, p. 34

campaign. During the fundraiser, Stephanie gets herself into a bidding war and ultimately ends up spending $1,000 to buy Mark's services. "Your endorsement is really going to help bring business to [my family's store]", Stephanie says to Mark, in an effort to make it clear that she bought his services for the store and *not* for herself.[43]

The word "confabulate" means "to bullshit" and it is a favourite word among psychologists who study unconscious processes because everyone, it turns out, is an excellent confabulator when explaining their own behaviour. If Stephanie actually believes her own excuse about buying Mark on behalf of the store, she's delusional. Mark is the boy she's had a crush on since the beginning of the book and she clearly "bought" him for herself.

The moral of the story is that input of energy is like breathing: some conscious control can be exerted over it but ultimately it finds expression in our behaviour. When you speak to an attractive or unattractive person, it isn't necessary for you to consciously change your nonverbal behaviour. Without effort on your part, it changes regardless of whether you want it to or not. Likewise, when someone asks you to do them a favour, you don't consciously make your decision based on how attractive they are—the bias just happens. Unconscious influence is one reason why input of energy is such a powerful indicator of attraction. Even people like me, who study and write books about it, cannot fully stop it from influencing our behaviour.

43 Cabot, 2006, p. 200

FOOD FOR THOUGHT:
CONVERSATIONAL DIP

I was at a Martini party socializing with peers around a table of nicely prepared appetizers when an attractive girl commented that the dip was delicious. Moments later, I thought to myself, "that dip does look good" and tried some.

On reflection, I began wondering if my behaviour had been motivated by a desire for the dip or for the girl. Maybe I tried the dip because it looked good and it wouldn't have mattered who made the comment. Or maybe my primordial instinct was to try the dip so that I could begin a conversation. Both are plausible explanations and it is not difficult to appreciate that even if the latter was true, I could still convince myself of the first. Either way, the dip was terrible.

CONCLUSION AND IMPLICATIONS

Returning to the story that began this chapter, you probably have an idea now about what caused the seating arrangement in my grade eleven biology class. Unconsciously, every boy (including me) was automatically and instinctively directing input of energy towards Kate. Each of us had slowly but surely moved closer to her until she was completely surrounded.

For my part, I hadn't acted consciously. I truly believed my final position was the result of good luck. Today I know that my unconscious had an active role in influencing fate. During the first days of semester, when the seating arrangement was fluid, desks were opening up all over the classroom. However, whenever a desk far from Kate became available, I declined it under false pretences. I would tell myself that, "the far desk was a bad choice because it was dirty on top" or because, "it put me at a bad angle to the chalkboard." In reality each was just an excuse. My justification for choosing the desk right beside Kate was also a lie. I told myself that the reason I liked it was because it was newer and closer to the chalkboard, when I really liked it because it was closer to her. The same, I suspect, was true of the other boys as well. Input of energy was compelling us to seek proximity to Kate whether we knew it or not.

Input of energy, in all its forms, is constantly occurring. Now that you have an idea of what to look for, pay attention and you will notice it in all social situations. Consider the following:

- I once overheard a girl saying to her friend, "Do you remember when we used to ride our bikes back and forth in front of his house hoping that he would notice us?" — that's input of energy.
- I saw a girl offer the boy she liked a ride home after a chemistry class — that's input of energy.
- A Queen Bee asked me to steal my friend's lunch for her in grade ten and I did it — that's input of energy.
- When my friend Justin posted a Facebook request for help moving to a new house, four girls responded almost immediately — that's input of energy.

Look for it. It's happening all around you.

CHAPTER 5

ATTRACTION, LIKING, AND ATTACHMENT

Hedonism, the pursuit of pleasure for its own sake, is not really the answer to the riddle of drug addiction. The pursuit of pleasure does not explain why so many addicts insist that they abuse drugs in a never-ending attempt to feel normal. With compulsive use and overuse, much of the pleasure eventually leaches out of the primary dysphoria-relieving drug experience. This does not, however, put an end to the drug-seeking behaviour. Far from it. This is the point at which non-addicts tend to believe that there is no longer an excuse—the pleasure has dribbled away, the thrill is gone—but even when addicts aren't getting the full feel-good benefits of the habit, they continue to use.

The above quotation is from a blog entitled the *Addiction Inbox*.[44] It describes the irrational and paradoxical feelings experienced by many drug addicts. Even though they learn to hate their drug of choice they can't stop themselves from wanting it. Recovering addicts who have successfully struggled through all of the primary withdrawal symptoms often describe a persistent desire to use whenever they're

44 Hanson, 2010

around old friends or hang outs. Even though they know the terrible consequence of relapse, the cravings never fully subside. Desiring something so strongly disliked is completely illogical to everyone, including the addict, yet the paradoxical sensation is common.

"What," you might be thinking, "does drug addiction have to do with popularity?"

***

After the Hierarchy of Attraction and input of energy, there is one more piece of the popularity puzzle that must be explored before the phenomenon can be fully explained. Think for a moment about the words "attraction," "liking," and "attachment." How would you define each concept in terms of interpersonal relations? How similar or different is each concept in your mind? During everyday conversation, it is easy to get the three mixed up and use them interchangeably. When one student asks another "Who do you have a crush on?" the question is more ambiguous than they probably realize. Perhaps they want to know who the other student finds attractive. Perhaps they want to know who the other student likes. Or, maybe they want to know who the other student is emotionally attached to? Maybe having a "crush" on someone is a combination of all three. What do you think?

Because feelings of attraction, liking, and attachment commonly go together in situations of friendship, love, and affection, it is easy to consider them as varying levels of the same basic feeling. In other words, *attraction* eventually turns into *liking* which ultimately becomes *attachment*. Like most things in life, the truth is not so simple. It turns out that each of these three concepts is distinct and dissociable. What I mean is that feelings of attraction are different from the feelings of liking which are different again from feelings of attachment. Therefore it's possible to feel any one without feeling either of the other two. For example, it is possible to be attracted to someone while simultaneously disliking them. It is also possible to be *un*attracted to someone and yet still like them or even be attached to them, despite disliking them! When it comes to popularity and grade school social dynamics, the distinction between attraction, liking, and attachment is important since each is responsible for a unique set of behaviours.

ATTRACTION

Attraction is the experience of *wanting*. It is the *desire* for a hedonistic reward. It is the *magnetic pull* that you feel towards objects, people, or places that are pleasurable and gratifying. The important point to remember is that attraction is motivated by the thought of future benefit. Being attracted to something is not a pleasurable experience in and of itself. For example, during strenuous exercise you sweat profusely and this loss of water triggers a switch in your brain that causes you to want a drink. This *wanting* causes the experience of attraction and results in automatic gravitation toward water fountains and vending machines.

People aren't always consciously aware of why they are attracted to something; many researchers have designed clever experiments to demonstrate this. In 2000, Piotr Winkielman, Kent Berridge, and Julia Wilbarger inconspicuously tampered with people's wanting a simple fruit drink. Before offering participants in their experiment a pitcher of the drink, the three scientists asked them to guess the gender of emotionally neutral faces flashed on a screen. What the participants didn't know was that before each emotionally neutral face, a happy, neutral, or angry face was flashed so fast that they saw it but had no conscious awareness of this fact.

You wouldn't expect that happy or angry faces flashed subliminally for 1/60 of a second could have any real effect on a participant's consumption of fruit drink. The amazing thing is that it did! The subliminal faces were significant enough to change the amount of fruit drink that participants poured for themselves and how much they would be willing to pay for a can of the same. Those who saw the happy faces poured more of the drink and were willing to pay more. In contrast, those who saw angry faces poured less and were not willing to pay as much. Afterwards, participants were asked questions about what they had seen during the experiment. No one was aware of anything other than the emotionally neutral faces whose gender they had guessed! The happy and angry faces were truly subliminal.

With respect to subliminal messaging and other experiments that deal with it, a word of caution is necessary. As interesting and exciting as Winkielman, Berridge, and Wilbarger's results are, they should not be over interpreted. Subliminal messaging is not equivalent to mind control. Often, the actual difference in behaviour between participants in these experiments is very small. In the real world, outside of the controlled environment of a laboratory, the subtle effects of subliminal messaging often disappear entirely. The take-home message is that attraction is not always conscious or deliberate. Sometimes, we can be attracted to things for reasons we aren't fully aware of.[45]

The brain circuit largely responsible for feelings of attraction is the mesolimbic pathway and it was briefly described in the previous chapter (see Chapter 4, "The Brain on Attraction"). The exact details concerning the neuroscience

---

45 See Berridge, 2002

of this circuit are beyond the scope of this book. The important point is that it is activated during all sorts of motivated behaviours, from seeking out a song you heard on the radio to craving an illicit drug. Anyone who has been addicted to drugs knows that attraction can be a powerful force. Animals and humans often expend a surprising amount of effort in order to obtain the object of their desire. For example, a specialized cage known as the "Columbia University Obstruction Device" has been used by scientists to measure the sexual motivation of rodents. This diabolical chamber is diagrammed in Figure 5.1.

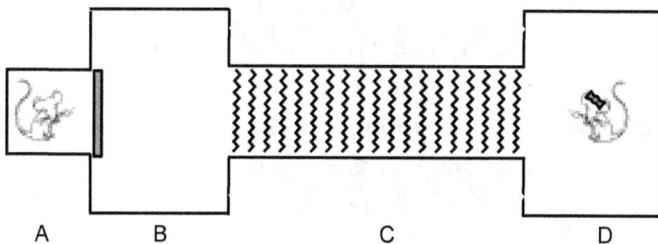

A   B   C   D

Figure 5.1 A diagram of the Columbia University Obstruction Device. The electrified floor along hallway C is no obstacle for the motivated male in room A.

The test subject (often an innocent and unsuspecting male rodent) is first put into room A where a divider blocks his view into room B and beyond. Next, some sort of incentive—often a sexually receptive female—is placed beyond the hallway in room D. The diabolical twist is that the hallway can be booby-trapped with any number of painful or noxious stimuli: electric floors, heated water, poisonous odours, and so forth. The purpose of these experiments is to see how motivated the male is to mate. Once the divider between rooms A and B is lifted, the experimenter times how long it takes the male to cross the obstruction.

It's not just rodents who'll risk their wellbeing and suffer pain in order to achieve the object of their desire. After all, what is Romeo and Juliet's first meeting other than a dramatized version of the Columbia University Obstruction Device? Drug addiction is perhaps the best example of how far humans will go to acquire the object of their desire. Junkies, desperate to get high, risk almost anything to get their next fix.

LIKING

Where attraction is the desire for future reward, liking is the pleasurable experience of reward. Once you find a water fountain after strenuous exercise and push the button, the feeling of water in your mouth is bliss. As soon as it touches your lips and swishes around in your mouth, it is as if your brain is rejoicing. In the words of neuroscientist Kent Berridge:

> Sweetness or other natural pleasures are mere sensations as they enter the brain, and brain systems must actively paint the pleasure onto sensation to generate a "liking" reaction—a sort of pleasure gloss or varnish.[46]

In other words, after we experience something our brains must decide whether or not the experience was pleasurable. If it was, we *like* whatever the stimulus was. If it wasn't, we *dislike* the stimulus. In contrast to attraction, which is largely mediated by the brain chemical dopamine, feelings of liking are mediated by natural opioids manufactured in the brain. Natural opioids have a chemical structure similar to that of heroin and morphine, which is why the use of these drugs

46 Berridge, n.d.

is so enjoyable: they flood the brain with the same type of chemical that signals pleasure.

As I write this paragraph, it is a hot, sunny day and I am sitting at my kitchen table sipping a ginger ale. Every time I lift the bottle to my lips I smell the delicate aroma of ginger and, as the drink floods my mouth, I taste sweet carbonated deliciousness. The drink is refreshing, so my brain actively paints a "pleasure gloss" onto the experience, mentally re-affirming that ginger ale is a stimulus that I like. The people we meet day-to-day are environmental stimuli, just like my ginger ale. When it comes to interacting with them, we must decide whether or not we like them.

How one student can make another *like* them is no mystery. The golden rule—do unto others as you would have them do unto you—is probably the best and most concise advice that can be given on this matter. If a student wants something more specific, they should check out the time-less classic *How to Win Friends and Influence People*, written by Dale Carnegie in 1936. In the section entitled "Six Ways to Get People to Like You," he gives the following advice:

1. Be genuinely interested in other people,
2. Smile,
3. Remember that a person's name is to them the sweet-est and most important sound in any language,
4. Be a good listener and encourage others to talk about themselves,
5. Talk in terms of the other person's interests, and
6. Make the other person feel important and do so sincerely.

Just like attraction, people are not always consciously aware of why they like something. A phenomenon known as "the mere exposure effect" is a good example. In the 1960's, Robert Zajonc was the first psychologist to formally recognize the fact that repeated exposure to a particular stimulus could increase how much people liked it.[47] Have you ever run into a stranger day after day in the same public place? A coffee shop for example? The added familiarity of seeing them on a regular basis is enough to increase how much you like them. The effect is small but real.

ATTACHMENT

Attachment is an intense emotional bond between two people characterized by separation anxiety. Attachments are not necessarily romantic. The relationship between a child and caregiver is also characterized by a profound attachment between individuals. So too is that between two close friends.

Humans are not the only species to experience intense attachment relationships. A species of monogamous prairie voles is actually the specimen of choice when it comes to studying the neuroscience of attachment. Thanks in large part to research on this species, scientists have identified oxytocin as a major hormonal modulator of attachment. During the attachment process, this hormone is released, triggering a cascade of physiological events. Areas of the brain normally used for critical social assessment are deactivated to allow individuals to overcome social distance. Furthermore, reward circuitry is activated, making the object of attachment a source of attraction.[48] Nipple stimulation during breastfeeding, for example, is a potent stimulator of oxytocin release in females. No doubt this serves to foster an attachment relationship between the mother and her infant.[49]

Just like attraction and liking, attachment has its own unique brain signature of electrical activity. When people

47 Zajonc, 2001
48 Zeki, 2007
49 Young & Wang, 2004

look at pictures of their romantic partners, a pattern of brain activation occurs that is different from that of face recognition, visual attention, sexual arousal, or other emotional states.[50]

FOOD FOR THOUGHT:
THE LANGUAGE OF ATTACHMENT

A friend of mine once described his girlfriend in the following terms, "I get anxious when we aren't together. I genuinely like her. I miss her when she's not around and I can't stop thinking about her." This is the language of attachment. The key words and gold standard are the anxiousness associated with separation. As soon as you hear someone describe their significant other in these terms, drama is guaranteed if the relationship collapses.

ATTRACTION, LIKING, AND ATTACHMENT ARE DISSOCIABLE

Drug addiction has been a topic of research for many years. Currently the most comprehensive theory is known as the "Incentive Salience Model" proposed by two neuroscientists working at the University of Michigan, Kent Berridge and Terry Robinson. What makes the Incentive Salience Model so powerful is that it can explain why addicts continue to use (and seek) their drug after the pleasurable effects have faded. Central to this model is the fact that the subjective experience of attraction (i.e. wanting) is distinct and dissociable from the subjective experience of liking.

50 Insel & Young, 2001

According to the Incentive Salience Model, drugs hijack the brain circuits responsible for wanting. After repeated drug use, these circuits become hyper-sensitive to all drug related cues in the environment, such as pipes and other paraphernalia. When an addict sees these cues, a large surge of dopamine in the brain causes an uncontrollable craving to use. Unfortunately for addicts, drugs have the exact opposite effect on the brain circuits responsible for the experience of liking. Instead of becoming hyper-sensitized, liking circuits become tolerant to the euphoric effects of a drug. The addict needs to continually increase the dosage in order to achieve the same "feel-good" effect. In short, drugs cause the experience of *wanting* to increase and the experience of *liking* to decrease with repeated use.

The Incentive Salience Model proposed by Berridge and Robinson is relevant to popularity because it makes clear the fact that feelings of attraction are dissociable from feelings of liking. When it comes to relationships, *it is possible to be attracted to someone without liking them and vice versa*. Most people can easily think of someone they are *attracted* to but don't actually *like* and others whom they *like* but aren't actually *attracted* to. Can you?

In hindsight, it might seem obvious that attraction and liking are different but people often get them confused for a good reason. In general, people are attracted to the things they like because attraction is the desire for future reward. People like things that reward them and therefore become attracted to the same. For example, most people find eating chocolate to be a pleasurable experience. As a result, most people are attracted to chocolate because they anticipate the pleasure associated with eating it. Likewise with our friends: interacting with them is pleasurable, therefore an attraction to them develops.

The development of an attachment relationship is more complex than that of attraction or liking. Generally, it always involves three steps: initial approach, repeated interaction, and reciprocal emotional investment. If you think about what these steps entail, it's obvious why attraction and liking facilitate the process of attachment. Attraction, as discussed in Chapter 3, promotes approach behaviour through input of energy while liking promotes repeated exposure so that, ultimately, an intense emotional bond can form. Despite being intimately linked, attachment remains a distinct feeling because it is associated with its own unique physiological changes and pattern of brain activation.[51]

ODD AND INTERESTING BEHAVIOUR

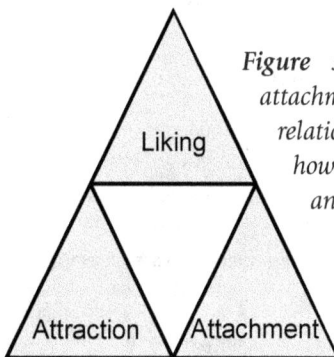

Figure 5.2 When attraction, liking and attachment come together, an ideal relationship is achieved. Not all three, however, are necessary in all relationships and any combination is possible.

Because attraction, liking, and attachment are distinct and dissociable, it is possible to feel any combination of the three. If you think about it in terms of Figure 5.2, you can cover up one or even two of the three triangles and still maintain a relationship. In other words, it is possible to:

51 Fisher, 2000

1. Be attracted without liking the person or being attached.
2. Like the person without being attracted or attached.
3. Be attached without being attracted or liking the person.
4. Be attracted and like the person without being attached.
5. Be attracted and attached without liking the person.
6. Like and be attached to a person without being attracted
7. Be attracted and attached to a person who is liked.

Try thinking about each category in terms of people in your life. I can think of someone who fits each category except for 5. This situation usually occurs in abusive relationships—something I've luckily never had to deal with.

Table 5.1		
Category	Description	Possible Examples
1	Attraction without liking or attachment	The Queen Bees of high school
2	Liking without attraction or attachment	Chance acquaintances who are pleasant but not attractive
3	Attachment without attraction or liking	Old friends who have grown apart
4	Attraction and liking without attachment	Strangers who are pleasant and attractive
5	Attraction and attachment without liking	Abusive partners
6	Liking and attachment without attraction	Past mentors or role models
7	Attraction, liking and attachment	Significant others

In general, most relationships progress from initial feelings of attraction to liking and eventually attachment. When dissociation does occur and all three feelings are not present, some odd and interesting behaviour can result.

QUEEN BEE WORSHIPPING (ATTRACTION WITHOUT LIKING OR ATTACHMENT)

You can probably guess what Queen Bee worshipping is. Most males and females have been guilty of it at some point during grade school. Somehow, even though we tell ourselves again and again how much we dislike them, all it takes is one smile from the Queen and all of our stern determination dissolves. Soon, we find ourselves bending over backwards to please her. All because of a smile!

Books about grade school are full of similar examples. Recall the example of Demi Chang who writes about how she betrayed her best friend for Queen Bee Rachel. Her opening words are, "I wished it had never happened. I wished I had never done what I did". In the story, Demi describes how she and her best friend would fantasize about what it was like to be popular and have everyone "love" them. A week before their winter holidays, Rachel pulled her aside and offered her the opportunity to be just that. All Demi had to do was betray her best friend. Mesmerized by the Queen Bee, she agreed.

Why would she do such a thing? Why on earth would students like Demi betray their best friend? In the words of Demi herself: "I agreed because I wanted the taste of popularity".[52] If you remember the rule of thumb for understanding what makes someone attractive—the desire for various rewards—it's easy to understand why Demi would be attracted to Rachel. In her case, the reward was popularity and Rachel was her ticket to becoming popular. This attraction is enough to hijack the wanting circuitry in Demi's brain even if Rachel is not her true friend. Demi knew that what she was doing was wrong but because she desperately wanted to be popular, nothing else mattered. She couldn't help herself—feelings of

---

52 Chang, 2010, p. 67 & 69

attraction overcame her better judgement and caused her to make what was ultimately the wrong decision.

Think back to the chapter's opening excerpt on hedonism and recall the description of what it is like to be addicted to drugs: "[E]ven when addicts aren't getting the full feel-good benefits of the habit, they continue to use." When it comes to Queen Bee worshipping, the underlying cause is similar to that of drug addiction. Demi knows what she did was wrong, but it didn't stop her. Just like drug addicts desperately seek to satisfy their wants, she risked hurt feelings to attain the object of her desire. Even though she might not like the Queen Bee, her attraction to the glamour of popularity was enough. The following is an excerpt from the book, *Odd Girl Out*. In it, Michelle describes a Queen Bee to author Rachel Simmons:

> *Erin's the kind of person so that when you're first friends with her, it's like a drug almost. She just seems like such a good friend. She's so nice and fun, not to mention the fact that she's really popular, and you're like, why is she friends with me? She says everything that you want her to say and she acts like she's such a good friend and acts like you're the best thing ever to happen to her, and you're kind of excited because you're like insecure and you're her everything.*[53]

Even Hollywood screenwriters have picked up on the intoxicating effect of popular students. The protagonist from the movie *Heathers* puts it best: "Betty Finn was a true friend and I let her hang for a bunch of swash dogs and diet coke heads. Killing Heather [the Queen Bee] would be like offing the Wicked Witch of the West. [...] Tomorrow I'll be kissing her aerobicized ass but tonight, let me dream of a world without Heather; a world where I am free."

---

53 Simmons, 2002, p.89

GOOD TIMES NOT TO BE HAD AGAIN (LIKING WITHOUT ATTRACTION OR ATTACHMENT)

Generally, attraction precedes liking because input of energy is designed to pull people together so individuals can decide if they like each other or not. Attraction is not always necessary, however, because chance occurrences can also bring two people together without input of energy. When this happens, it is possible to find yourself in relationships where you like the other person but feel no sustained attraction.

Intuitively, you would think that if you met someone you really liked, you would seek their company on a regular basis. This is not always the case. Think about all the pleasant people you meet by chance at parties, in line ups, or on the way to school. Do you always make an effort to keep in touch with them?

Perhaps because I'm a little antisocial, I can think of many instances where liking has not motivated me to seek repeated interaction with someone else. In my final year of undergraduate studies, I sang with my university choir. In this capacity, I met a girl who could take any awkward moment and turn it into a pleasant memory. She was funny, bubbly, and an absolute joy to be around. Although I genuinely liked this girl, I never made a special effort to seek her out and our interactions remained limited to choir practice.

ABUSIVE RELATIONSHIP (ATTRACTION AND ATTACHMENT WITHOUT LIKING)

For some unfortunate people, attraction and liking can fade from a relationship while the attachment remains. Consider the following question submitted to the pop culture website TrèsSugar:

Dear Sugar,

Is it possible to love someone and no longer like them? I have been with my boyfriend for almost four years; we used to talk about marriage and children but for the past couple of months, I have been thinking that he may not be the one I want to spend the rest of my life with. I no longer have butterflies in my stomach when we talk and I don't even look forward to seeing him sometimes. He is the perfect guy in every way—he's loyal, honest, generous, and family oriented; however, there are a lot of things that I never noticed about him which are beginning to make me not even like him as a person anymore. He is very antisocial; he's moody, controlling and incredibly jealous.[54]

If the author of this quote had addressed her question to me, my answer would be an emphatic "yes." Attraction and liking can be momentary relative to attachment, which takes time to develop and time to fade. After an attachment has formed, it can easily outlast feelings of attraction and/or liking. Most long time couples no longer feel "butterflies in their stomach," but this doesn't stop them from loving each other intensely.

Although feelings of attachment are generally a positive force between individuals, persistent attachments can some-times have negative consequences. One reason why abused women don't leave their abusers is because of an intense at-tachment which has developed over time.[55] A similar situa-tion can occur between students and their friends. It sounds counter-intuitive, but it is possible for a student to find them-selves clinging to a friendship long after the joy of the rela-tionship has gone.

In the book, Rachel Simmons shares the sad story of Janet and Cheryl. Having grown up in the same neighbourhood,

54 Anonymous, 2008
55 Barnett, 2001

the two girls became best friends—bonding over long phone conversations and sleepovers. Outside of school they were the picture of friendship. At school, however, things were different. "Around the cool kids," Simmons writes, "Cheryl called Janet names and told her to get away. She nicknamed her 'bottle-eyes' and ordered the other girls to steal her glasses". As the two girls progressed through elementary and junior high, Cheryl's cruelty eventually expanded beyond school. At their houses, Cheryl dominated Janet, insulting her and pushing her to do things like trying on her first bra or pantyhose. Describing Janet, Simmons writes that she was, "broken and quiet, attached and abused by her only friend".[56]

A COMPLICATED INTERACTION

Feelings of attraction, liking, and attachment are dissociable but not entirely independent. Each affects the other. As a relationship develops over time, judgements of attraction, liking, and attachment become biased by each other in many ways. For example, even if you don't find someone attractive at first, just getting to know their personality can actually bias your initial assessment. In 2007, Garry Lewandowski, Arthur Aron, and Julie Gee did an experiment to demonstrate this.[57] They asked 78 undergraduate students to participate in a three part experiment. First, they asked them to rate the physical attractiveness of 36 strangers on a scale of 1 to 10. Second, they were instructed to complete an unrelated but challenging mathematical task for four minutes. Then, each was again asked to rate the same 36 people they had seen previously except for that this time, the pictures were accompanied by either positive or negative personality information.

56 Simmons, 2002, p. 165 & 166
57 Lewandowski, Aron & Gee, 2007

What the investigators discovered is that positive personality traits positively biased judgements of physical attractiveness and negative personality traits negatively biased judgements of physical attractiveness. In other words, having a positive personality actually made the photographed people more physically attractive!

FOOD FOR THOUGHT:
NONE OF MY FRIENDS ARE UGLY

Think about this: how many of your friends do you think are ugly? Probably none or few, if any. We see plenty of ugly people walking around but none of them are our friends. The reason no one has ugly friends because friends like each other and are mutually attached. Because we know their personality and all of their good qualities, our judgment of their physical attractiveness has become biased.

CHAPTER 6

THE EMERGENCE
OF POPULARITY

Imagine a co-ed high school where the incoming group of students comes from several different schools in the city. Almost no one knows each other. After returning from summer vacation, 25 freshmen are sitting nervously in their homeroom, looking at each other. Having survived junior high, they know that school can be a daunting place. While the teacher gives an introductory talk describing the mundane details of life at the school, the students muse privately about a more pressing issue. The social scramble for friends is about to begin and each is desperate to secure their place in the social hierarchy. As they look around the room at each other, they know that some students will be popular and others will not. Some will be Wannabes and still others Misfits. The stakes are high. Getting in with the wrong crowd could mean missing out on parties, girlfriends/boyfriends, weekend camping trips, and everything exciting for the next few years.

If this situation seems vaguely familiar, it's because something similar happens at the beginning of every year.

Although most returning students are familiar with each other from years past, the first day is always a new beginning. Students around the world know how important it is to get into the right crowd but, until now, no one has answered the question every student wants to know: "How do popular students become popular?"

THE THREE FACTOR MODEL

If you want to understand how a particular individual comes to occupy their social position, you always need to consider the following three factors. Factor #1 is how the individual in question relates to the group. Factor #2 is how the group relates to the individual and Factor #3 is the situation and its circumstances.

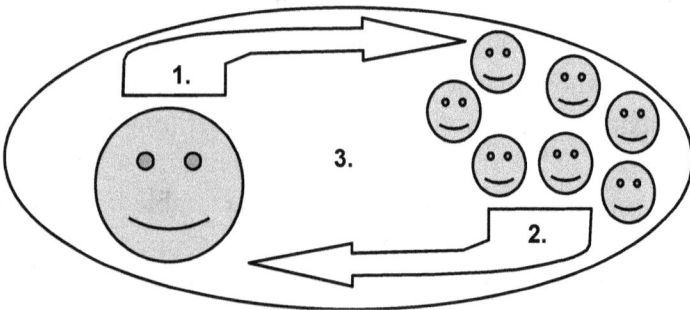

Figure 6.1 The Three Factor Model: (1) How the individual relates to the group; (2) How the group relates to the individual; and (3) The situation.

FACTOR #1: HOW THE INDIVIDUAL RELATES TO THE GROUP

If you ask yourself, "Who am I?" what would you say? Are you an introvert or an extrovert? An aggressive person or a non-aggressive person? An optimist or a pessimist? Factor #1, how the individual relates to the group, is a question of personality. In Chapter 3, the fact that innumerable physical characteristics define each individual was explored. The same is true of personality.

How many adjectives, do you think, exist in the English language to describe personality? One hundred, 1,000, or maybe 10,000? In 1936, Gordon Allport and Henry Odbert counted the number of adjectives used in the English language to describe personality and the total was an astounding 17,953 words![58] Just think about it: seventeen thousand, nine hundred, and fifty three different words can be used to define your personality. True, some of the adjectives they found are relatively obscure—decorous, debonair, and truculent for example—but they still exist.

In order to put Factor #1 into perspective, you don't need to consider all 17,953 adjectives and whether or not they apply. You just need to think about how the student in question treats other people on a day-to-day basis. Consider everything from the obvious (Do they bully others?) to the subtle (Do they smile when they pass someone in the hallway regardless of who it is?). Factor #1, how the individual relates to the group, includes everything from the smallest gestures to the most blatant of actions.

FACTOR #2: HOW THE GROUP RELATES TO THE INDIVIDUAL STUDENT

In addition to how the individual interacts with and treats other people, how people interact and treat them is equally important. A student's peers are constantly judging them and not always fairly. They consider what sports they play, their religion, the clothes they wear, how wealthy they are, and

---

58 Allport & Odbert, 1936

everything else. It all comes down to whether or not the individual appears to be a good candidate for friendship.

Sometimes, how people relate to an individual is dependent on Factor #1 (how the individual relates to them). If the student is aggressive and mean, for example, their peers generally learn to avoid them. If they are friendly and smile often, their peers will generally smile back. Unfortunately, who a student is as a person isn't the only thing that matters. In addition to who they are, what they are is also important. What I mean by "what they are" is everything that they represent and embody. For example: they are the school quarterback; they are a computer whiz; they are beautiful; they are ugly; they are the owner of a car; they are a talented musician; they are the smartest person in the class; and so on. When judging a particular student, what the student embodies is considered alongside who they are.

A simple example from the television show *The Simpsons* illustrates just how big of a difference what an individual is makes. In the episode, "Much Apu About Nothing," a group of students from Springfield Elementary circles a short, plump, exchange student named Üter and starts bullying him because he is an immigrant. Nelson, the class bully, grabs his suspenders and snaps them painfully against his back saying, "Hey, German boy, go back to Germania."

Üter protests, "Please, I don't deserve this! I've come here legally as an exchange student!"

"Young man," Principal Skinner chimes in, "the only thing we exchange for you is our national dignity."

Noticing the unfair treatment of the young immigrant boy, burly and muscular Groundskeeper Willie jumps into the circle of students and shouts, "So you want to pick on immigrants? Well then why don't you pick on Willie?!"

"Please, Willie," Principal Skinner says in response to this intrusion, "the children want to pick on someone their own size!"

Obviously, this scene is funny because the students wouldn't dare bully Willie unless they wanted to get badly beaten. Üter, on the other hand, is a plump little boy and thus an easy target. In this example, it isn't *who* Willie is that makes the difference but what he is that affects how the students relate to him. Üter is welcome to act as aggressively as Willie (a reflection of *who* he is) but the outcome (continued bullying) would be inevitable.

As silly as it is, all students in real life have an intuitive understanding of what makes this scene from *The Simpsons* funny. The following quote is from a short story entitled *Finding My Own Crowd*. The author is questioning a girl named Annie about why she acts and dresses the way she does.

> *"You pretend to be so tough at school. But you're really not like that at all. Why the act?"*
>
> *Annie responds: "Don't be fooled. I'm no angel. I like it that the 'popular' girls are afraid of me. I used to be made fun of, same as you. Then I got smart. I figured if I looked tough, I'd be left alone. I was right."*[59]

Just like in the example taken from *The Simpsons*, it's not *who* Annie is but *what* she is that affects how her peers relate to her, hence the importance of *looking* tough.

If you think back to Chapter 4 and the concept of input of energy, you will realize that it's entirely devoted to exploring how the group relates to the individual (i.e. Factor #2). In short, the more attractive a student is (in the broadest sense of the word), the more input of energy they will receive.

---

59 Blanco, 2010, p. 102

The less attractive they are the less input of energy they will receive.

FACTOR #3: THE SITUATION

Think back to Chapter 5 and the Columbia University Obstruction Device. Let's analyze a situation using the device and the Three Factor Model (see Figure 6.2).

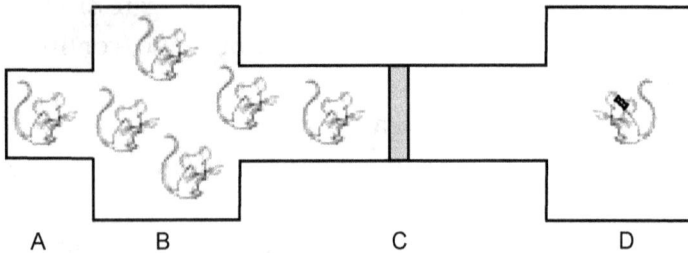

Figure 6.2 *The Plexiglas window in hallway C will prevent the male mice from reaching the female in room D.*

In this example, the female mouse in chamber D is the individual whose social situation is to be analyzed, the male mice in chamber A are the group, and the situation is the Columbia University Obstruction Device. Having been deprived of female company for weeks, what do you think the male mice are going to do in this situation? So long as they can get to her, the female mouse will be the most popular mouse in the cage. If the researcher puts a mild electric floor in the hallway, the male mice will dutifully input energy and accept the shocks in order to get to the female. If, however, the researcher puts a Plexiglas wall between the two rooms, the male mice will be stuck in room B no matter how hard they try. In this situation, what's blocking the female mouse from becoming popular is a situational constraint only. As the example illustrates, the situation (Factor #3) cannot be ignored when analyzing social outcomes.

Often a student cannot control the situation directly. Sometimes the stars line up and everything works in their favour and sometimes they do not. Fair or otherwise, changes to the situation can have serious implications for anyone trying to become popular. Imagine what would happen if a student were stuck in the wrong homeroom class and all of the popular kids were in another. No matter what they did, the situation would prevent them from sitting with the popular students during homeroom.

All sorts of situational variables have similar effects. Sports groups and extracurricular activities, for example, have a major impact on who becomes a friend to whom. Think about it: if every day the basketball team meets after school, the players are going to get to know each other. Friendships that otherwise wouldn't have existed often form simply because two people are in the same place at the same time.

When it works against students, an unlucky situation can be terribly frustrating. A couple of years ago I travelled to Nicaragua with a group of university students as part of a medical mission. While there, all of the students (except myself and one other) were housed next door to each other in the centre of town. In contrast, I had to walk a dangerous 10 to 15 minutes along the beach in order to get home at night. Every day when I arrived for morning roll call, I would find that everyone else had been up all night hanging out. Inevitably, their friendships with one another grew stronger every passing night. This wasn't because they didn't like me or because I didn't like them, it was because of the situation—such is life.

FACTORS #1, #2, AND #3 AFFECT EACH OTHER

When I first began studying popularity, a major source of confusion for me was the interplay between Factors #1, #2, and #3. Although each is separate, they all affect one another. The following three examples demonstrate what can be a confusing interplay between all three.

Example 1: If you are very sociable (Factor #1), you're likely to make friends easily. Having many friends is something most observers find attractive and therefore being sociable can affect how others relate to you (Factor #2). Most students know this intuitively and this is why occasionally you will see someone trying to exaggerate how many friends they have by greeting everyone they pass in the hallway. What they're trying to do is emphasize how well connected they are in an effort to manage the impression of others.

Example 2: During my research, I watched an old black and white educational film (Google: "1947 Coronet Film, *Are You Popular?*"). The point of the movie was to teach young men how to get dates with girls. The young male protagonist, Wally, calls up Caroline and invites her to a roller skating party. She accepts and the narrator congratulates Wally on his level-headed persistence.

In this example, Wally is attracted to Caroline and so he inputs energy. As a result, he successfully invites her on a date. Under these circumstances, the date (Factor #3) came about because of how Wally relates to Caroline (Factor #2). If Wally hadn't been attracted to Caroline, the date never would have occurred because he never would have called her.

Example 3: As discussed in Chapter 5, seeing someone on a regular basis can alter how attractive they are by virtue of the "mere exposure effect" (also referred to as the "familiarity principle"). In practice the effect is small, but people still have a slight tendency to prefer those they are familiar

with over complete strangers. In this example, seeing someone on a regular basis (Factor #3) changes how two students
relate to one another (Factors #1 and #2).

HOW POPULAR STUDENTS
BECOME POPULAR

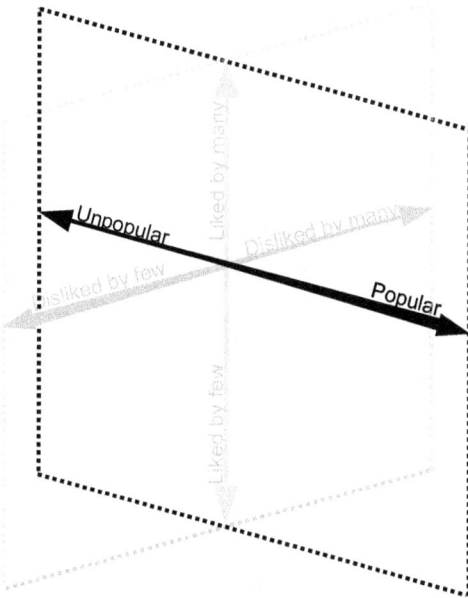

*Figure 6.3 A modi-
fied version of Figure
2.5 emphasizing axis
number 1: unpopular/
popular.*

In Chapter 2, eight prototypical students were mapped onto
Figure 2.5. These were Queen Bees/Kingpins, Sidekicks,
Dumb Blondes/Hopeless Models, Hollywood Protagonists,
Wannabes, Resigned Socialites, Happy Loners, and Misfits.
At the end of the chapter, the question I promised I would
answer was how any particular student came to occupy any
one of the eight positions. To begin answering this question,
let's first consider the axis labelled popular/unpopular from

Figure 2.5. The two other axes will be dealt with in the next chapter.

First, a quick review of what is meant by the word "popularity" in grade school: Popular students are socially dominant and influential. Their power is based on the recognition of their social superiority by their peers. Decisions they make and opinions they express are given more weight relative to others. They have more say in deciding what clothing is cool, what is funny, and—perhaps most importantly—which students are part of the popular clique. The lives of popular students are the object of intense interest. Not only do they engage in exclusive activities that pique the interest of the student body, they're also central players when it comes to the social dramas that characterize grade school.

The above description is often reflected in the popular media. Consider the main villain and her entourage from the movie *Mean Girls*: Regina George, Gretchen Wieners, and Karen Smith. All are beautiful, rich, and exciting. Like every stereotypical popular clique, they believe that they control the school. Although all movies exaggerate, they do mirror reality to some extent. Using the concepts discussed in this book, how can we explain the emergence of popular students like Regina George who are disliked and yet popular? The answer, in fact, is rather simple and you might have already guessed it. Popularity results when input of energy is preferentially directed towards a select group of students according to the Hierarchy of Attraction.

Look at the Hierarchy of Attraction and then look at the list of behaviours that constitute input of energy... Is it starting to make sense? People at the top of the Hierarchy are attractive to a large percentage of people and so you can imagine what the result is! Without doing anything other than existing, they attract a disproportionate amount of input of energy relative to their less attractive peers. When a group of students comes together, even for the first time, it's not long before the privileged position of those at the top of the Hierarchy of Attraction becomes obvious.

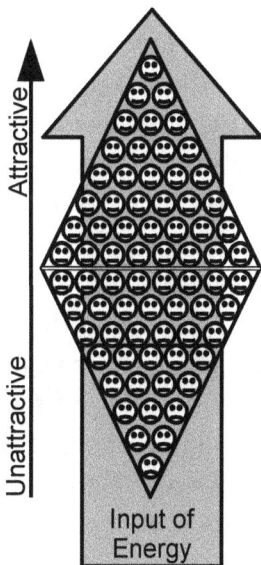

Figure 6.4 The Hierarchy of Attraction with an arrow representing how input of energy is directed preferentially upwards.

The students destined to be popular need not do anything special per se. Instead, their popularity is almost entirely mediated by Factor #2, how the group relates to the individual. Because input of energy takes on so many subtle forms, students cannot explicitly communicate what is so special about a select few of their peers. However, because input of energy is so pervasive, it's overwhelmingly apparent to everyone that some students are privileged. Ultimately the student body responds by labelling these special individuals as "popular." More concrete examples should put the emergence of popularity into perspective.

Let's consider the plight of protagonist Stephanie Landry from the novel *How to Be Popular*. Throughout the novel, Stephanie is infatuated with a boy named Mark Finley—a tall and handsome football player whose hazel eyes transfix every girl he cares to look at. Throughout the novel, Stephanie acts on her attraction by inputting energy into her relationship with Mark. Some notable examples are as follows:

- Page 25: Stephanie convinces herself that Mark is going to realize that they belong together. In her words, "He *has* to." This is a good demonstration of cognitive intrusion (i.e. infatuation).

- Page 26: Stephanie believes that Mark is a genuinely nice guy despite the fact they have never met. Also worth mentioning is the fact that she discovers otherwise by the end of the novel. This is a good demonstration of biased interpersonal judgements.

- Page 48: Stephanie states that she would build an observatory, complete with a high powered telescope, for Mark. This is a good demonstration of "helping" behaviour.

- Page 80: Stephanie notices Mark in the hallway and says "Hi Mark, hope you had a good summer." This is a good demonstration of the desire to seek proximity and natural changes to verbal communication.

- Page 96: Stephanie is consumed with joy when Mark smiles at her. Another demonstration of infatuation.

- Page 104: Stephanie makes a point of choosing a table close to Mark's at lunch, a good demonstration of seeking physical proximity.

- Page 197: Stephanie "buys" Mark at a talent auction under the pretence that she did it for her family's business. A good demonstration of confabulation (i.e. bullshit).

The irony throughout the novel is that Stephanie routinely criticizes the rigid social structure of her school and yet Mark Finley's popularity is a direct result of how girls like her relate to him.

Based on Stephanie's description of Mark, it is clear that he is everything a girl could want. What Stephanie fails to appreciate is that this places Mark at the top of the Hierarchy of Attraction. Over the course of the book, no mention is ever made of the fact that every girl in the school is likely thinking about Mark in exactly the same way. With input of energy coming from so many girls, it's no surprise that the student body has come to perceive Mark as the most popular boy. In contrast to Mark, how many girls in Stephanie's school do you think input energy into their relationship with the psychology nerd who writes books in his free time? NONE! Again, the irony of Stephanie's plight is that she is just as much a part of the problem as her "evil" antagonist Queen Bee Lauren Moffat.

Let's consider a female example. In the 1947 Coronet educational film *"Are You Popular?"* Wally calls Caroline on the phone and invites her on a date for Saturday night. About a minute later a second boy, Jerry, also calls Caroline and invites her out as well. Like a good 1940s female role model, Caroline politely turns Jerry down.

This is exactly the same situation encountered by Mark Finley. Caroline is at the top of the Hierarchy and, as a result, every boy in her school wants to call her and invite her out. Does the unattractive girl at the bottom of the Hierarchy get the same treatment? Of course not. Input of energy flows up the Hierarchy and not down. It is worth re-emphasizing that Caroline does very little to achieve her popularity. In the film, *it's the boys* that invite her to sit with them at lunch. *It's the boys* who invite her to help them in the school play.

And, *it's the boys* that call her up and ask for a date. All are examples of how the group relates to the individual. For her part, Caroline needs to do little other than smile in response to the positive attention to become popular.

In 2005, 58 years after the Coronet film was made, the mother of the girl to whom this book is dedicated told me, "When the boys call and invite her to a movie, they don't believe she is a busy girl." I would believe it. When everybody wants you, your nights must fill up quickly—I guess some things never change.

If the fictitious examples of Stephanie/Mark and Wally/Caroline don't convince you, perhaps an example from real life will. Here is a short story taken from Rosalind Wiseman's book, *Queen Bees and Wannabes*:

> *Emily and Kristi are seventh graders and both are in love with Brett. Each spends considerable quality time with Brett, including sending him notes, writing his name on their notebooks, calling him after school for tortuously long, awkward conversations, hanging out after school to see if she can bump into him, and "accidentally" walking by when his team practice is over. When the competition for his affections becomes unbearable, they make a pact that both will stop liking him. Neither girl has any intention of keeping her word, but each also believes that the other will. Each is also convinced that she has the right to be angry with the other if she goes back on her word. Which is, of course, what happens. Both girls quietly do everything they can behind each other's back to win Brett's affection.*

> *Things become much more complicated when they discover that no fewer than four other girls in their grade like Brett as well. Making matters worse, one of the girls, Liza, threatens to usurp Emily and Kristi's position as the front contender for Brett's affection. Emily and Kristi's response is to go after Liza, assured that they're in the right because (a) Liza knows they like him;*

(b) Liza is throwing herself at Brett; and (c) they staked their
claim first. Within a day the grade is abuzz watching the drama
unfold.[60]

In this example, it is not difficult to identify who's who.
Brett is clearly the Mark Finley of his classroom and Emily
and Kristi are like Stephanie and Lauren from the novel *How*
to Be Popular, battling it out for a boy's affection. The input of
energy is easy to spot:

- Spending considerable quality time with Brett.
- Sending him notes.
- Writing his name on their notebooks.
- Calling him after school.
- Hanging out after school so as to bump into him.
- "Accidentally" walking by when his team practice is
  over.
- Lying about agreeing not to like him.
- Working behind each other's backs to win his
  affection.
- Ganging up on Liza.

All of this energy is directed toward Brett by a total of at
least six girls (Emily and Kristi plus the four others) and can
only lead to one thing. In a very short time, the entire class
will come to perceive Brett as the most popular boy.

It is worth reiterating that attraction is not limited to
romantic relationships. Preferential attraction and input of
energy occurs in much the same way in platonic friendships.
How do you suppose the other boys relate to Brett? With so
many constantly showering him with attention, being one
of Brett's friends is like winning a golden ticket to all of the
most exciting activities and events. Not to mention it grants
access to his inner circle where opportunities to interact with
attractive girls abound. Just like a group of would-be business

60 Wiseman, 2002, p. 201

men will swarm around someone like Mark Zuckerberg (the billionaire founder of Facebook), less socially prominent boys will swarm around Brett. With both the boys and girls constantly inputting energy, Brett's ascent to top of the social totem pole will be swift.

FOOD FOR THOUGHT:
CONVERSATIONAL GRAVITY

I was out for lunch with friends and, as usual, silently analyzing the group. I was focused on the fact that the conversation continuously became centered on one guy in particular. Of no surprise, he was the "man amongst men" and his stories were full of sex, violence, and everything that adolescents idolize and respect. Thomas, without doubt, had what I call "conversational gravity" but he didn't draw attention because he was loud or boisterous. If he had done nothing but exist, the conversation would still have become centered on him.

When you consider the list of behaviours that constitute input of energy, the parallels between it and the advantages enjoyed by popular students are obvious. Compiled in Table 6.1 is a list of the behaviours discussed in Chapter 4 coupled with real life examples.

Input of Energy Type	Table 6.1
	Common Advantages Enjoyed by Popular Students
Attempts at proximity	• Popular students are always invited to the best parties.
	• Everyone tries to be around them.
	• Girls and boys "accidentally" walk by the target of their affection.
Subtle changes in body language	• Popular students always seem to have the undivided attention of anyone they talk to.
	• Everyone acts as if they like popular students.
Indirect changes in the quality/ content of conversation	• Everyone tells popular students secrets.
	• They are always juggling one or two conversations when in large groups.
	• The tone of voice a student uses is different when talking with popular students.
Helping behaviour	• Popular students never have trouble getting favours.
	• They never have a hard time finding help with homework.
	• Someone always lends them a pen or pencil in class.
Attitudinal changes and social influence	• Popular students decide what is and isn't cool.
	• They set trends and other students copy them.
Cognitive intrusion	• Everyone knows the popular students' names.
	• More than one student becomes obsessed with them.

A NEW DEFINITION OF POPULARITY

In Chapter 2, common definitions of popularity were reviewed. If you recall, each definition invariably focused on being well liked. By now it should be clear to you that popularity actually has little to do with being liked. Rather, it has everything to do with being attractive (in the broadest sense). Thus, I propose a new definition for the words "popular" and "popularity:"

Popularity: *noun*, 1) A hierarchical social phenomenon associated primarily with grade school; 2) The disproportionate receipt of preferential treatment in the form of input of energy.

Popular: *adjective*, A label given to people who have (or seem to have) achieved popularity.

THE BEAUTY PAGEANT

In *Queen Bees and Wannabes*, Wiseman describes an exercise she does when presenting in schools. She asks the girls she works with to "describe the characteristics and appearances of the girl everyone wants to be, the girl with high social status". Next, she asks the girls to describe all of the characteristics and appearances of a girl who they think will have low social status. Around all of the positive characteristics, she draws a box that she calls the "Act Like a Woman" box. Wiseman does a similar activity with boys. She calls it the "Act Like a Man" box.[61] Both are shown in Figure 6.5.

If popularity was about being well liked, then why is status dependent on the attributes listed in the "Act Like a Man" and "Act Like a Woman" boxes? If popularity was about being nice and kind to everyone as suggested on countless self-help websites, how do Queen Bees and Kingpins get away with being aggressive, arrogant jerks? There is an excellent reason why students give the responses that they do. Even if they cannot write a book about it, they know intuitively that social status is dependent on being attractive and not being liked. Furthermore, I want to highlight the fact that it is not just descriptions of physical appearance that are listed in the box. Clearly, students agree on an intuitive level that attractive is a broad term which encompasses *many* attributes.

---

61 Wiseman, 2002, p. 39 & 178

Implicitly, they are using the same definitions of "popular" and "popularity" as those I have proposed.

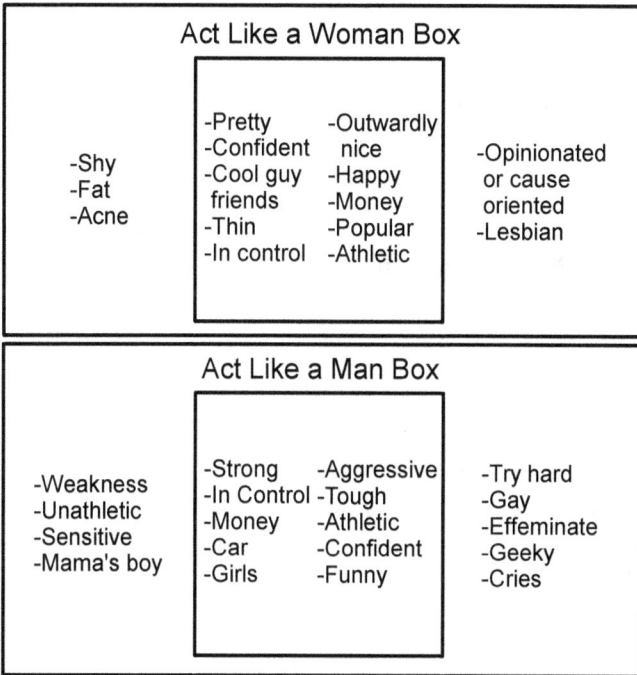

Figure 6.5 *The "Act Like a Woman" box and "Act Like a Man" box Rosalind Wiseman creates based on input from the students she interviews.*

Year after year the same characteristics lead to high social status; therefore it doesn't matter how many times educators, self-help websites, and movies say that popularity is dependent on being nice to everyone. It is simply not true: popularity is dependent on being attractive to peers and this is what students are responding to.

POPULARITY IS NOT EARNED THROUGH
SOCIAL MANIPULATION

A major myth that often appears in the popular media is the notion that popular students earn their social status through strategic acts of social manipulation and aggression. The following quotations demonstrate the point:

- "Getting popular requires strategy and calculation, that affection be shown selectively, that some be left behind, that others be attended to in private, and that the rules change from day to day." *Odd Girl Out*, Rachel Simmons, p. 160.
- "We had a popularity plan." *Cliques*, Aislinn Hunter, p. 84.
- "No one ever became popular overnight. Popularity is something that must be earned by paying dues, just like in a social club. So don't make the mistake of acting as if you think you're better than other popular people who have been at the game longer than you have. They've earned their popularity through hard work and commitment and deserve your respect. Once you've earned your popularity, they will repay you in kind." *How to Be Popular*, Meg Cabot, p. 198.

If popularity really did depend on picking and choosing friends selectively, there could be no Hollywood Protagonists among us. These amazing people are defined as being both popular and universally accepting.

The truth is that the achievement of popularity is a passive process mediated almost entirely by Factor #2, how the group relates to the individual. Students who are lucky enough to be born attractive need to do little except sit back and wait as input of energy propels them to the top of the social totem pole.

FOOD FOR THOUGHT:
RIDING THE POSITIVE VIBE

Maybe a student is not "that guy/girl" but has at times found themselves atop the Hierarchy of Attraction. They may never attain the adjective "popular" but that doesn't mean that they can't expect to benefit from input of energy. So long as they know what to look for, no one has to acknowledge them as "popular" for them to catch the positive vibe of popularity and ride it to its natural conclusion. Look for it: if everything a student seems to do/say is somehow "right" and ends in opportunities for future interaction, they're riding the positive vibe for at least one, glorious, moment.

UNPOPULAR/POPULAR IS ONLY ONE THIRD OF THE STORY

Recall from Chapter 5 that feelings of attraction are dissociable from feelings of liking. As such, it is possible to be attracted to someone without actually liking them. In practice, this means that "bitchy" girls and "asshole" boys who are attractive can still benefit from input of energy even if no one *likes* them (hence why students are often guilty of Queen Bee worshipping). Even if they feel terrible doing it, they cannot help themselves. Attractive students hijack the motivational centre in their brain and compel them to input energy independent of liking.

The distinction between attraction and liking is also part of the reason why being *perceived as popular* is only one third of the story. If you look at the next page, you see that there are two more axes that need to be considered on Figure 2.5: how much a person is *liked* and how much a person is *disliked*. These two axes also play a major role in determining where a student ultimately lands in the social landscape.

CHAPTER 7

LIKING AND DISLIKING

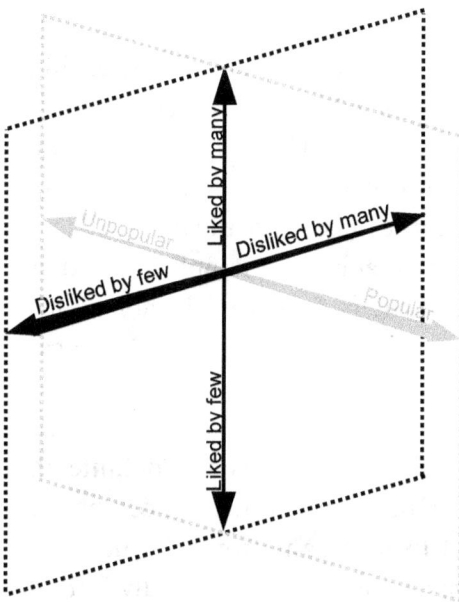

Figure 7.1 A modified version of Figure 2.5 emphasizing axis number 2 & 3, liking and disliking

D o you remember the thought experiment you did in Chapter 4? For a moment, think back to the hallway and the attractive stranger I suggested you imagine crossing paths with, rays of light emanating from his/her perfect form. As already discussed, the natural human response in this situation is to input energy and seek proximity. Unfortunately for would be suitors, this is only half the battle. Once interaction occurs both people must decide how much they like each another. Imagine the following two scenarios:

Scenario 1: Jay is an average boy. He's 145 pounds, 6 feet tall, and not especially handsome. Although motivated, his hobbies are more intellectual than athletic. He's somewhere in the middle of the Hierarchy of Attraction. In contrast, Sasha is a vivacious blonde who's athletic, assertive, and hangs out with the popular clique. In short, she's high in the Hierarchy of Attraction. As would be expected, Jay and most of the other boys are attracted to Sasha. One day, Jay decides to act on his attraction and strikes up a conversation with her the next time they make eye contact. Unfortunately for him, Sasha is a total snob to anyone who is not in her own clique and so she dismisses his friendly "Hi!" with a sneer and a cold shoulder. Jay's only consolation is that she treats nearly everyone like this. In time, the majority of the boys will learn that interacting with Sasha is generally an unpleasant experience but, unfortunately for them, they won't be able to help themselves from getting "sucked in" every time she smiles at them—Jay included.

Scenario 2: There is another girl at the school named Meghan. Like Sasha, she's upbeat, pretty, and definitely in with the popular clique. Once again, attraction compels Jay (and all the other boys) to make an effort. The next time he sees her in the hallway, he shoots her a friendly "Hi!" In contrast to his interaction with Sasha, this time the response he gets is different. Unlike Sasha, Meghan responds with an equally pleasant "Hi!" She's not attracted to Jay but decides to reward his efforts with quick and pleasant chit chat. In response, Jay feels great about himself! He leaves the conversation with his head high and his chest out.

What Jay doesn't know is that Meghan treats everyone in the same pleasant way. Unlike Sasha, she's a genuinely agreeable girl. In time, the student body will learn that interacting with her is always a joy. With every pretty smile, they like her more and more.

PERSONALITY

Popularity is mediated by how the group relates to the individual (Factor #2 of the Three Factor Model). In contrast, how much people *like* or *dislike* the individual is mediated almost entirely by how the individual relates to the group (Factor #1). As mentioned in the previous chapter, this is a question of personality.

The field of personality research is still developing and no theorist has yet to propose a fully unified theory. Nonetheless, significant progress has been made since 1936, when Gordon Allport and Henry Odbert counted all 17,536 English words that can describe it. Today, there is widespread consensus among psychologists that personality can be narrowed down to five major dimensions: openness to experience, conscientiousness, extroversion, agreeableness, and emotional stability.[62]

THE BIG FIVE

Trait #1: Openness to Experience
(Imagination, Intellect, Perceptiveness)

Are you a boundary pushing adventure seeker or a sensible conservative? Openness to experience refers to how willing a person is to accept or consider new ways of thinking or understanding. This can be in regards to art, music, religion, food, travel, etc. People who are open to experience

---

62 Digman, 1990

generally like to try new things and consider a wide range of perspectives. Creativity is often associated with openness to experience.

Being closed minded is the opposite. These people prefer the status quo and are unlikely to deviate from established norms. Anything foreign, like ethnic food, is usually lost on them as is variation to the dominant political view. Closed minded people are less likely to appreciate things like art, poetry, and music.

Trait #2: Conscientiousness (Orderliness, Decisiveness, Reliability, Industriousness)

People at the negative end of the conscientiousness continuum are stereotypical burnouts: happy to be "stoned" all the time with as few concerns as possible. They're satisfied avoiding responsibility and generally end up with minimum wage employment. Employers and teachers can't expect much from people with a lack of conscientiousness because they lack drive and dependability.

In contrast, people *with* conscientiousness are hardworking and are driven to do things right. Even when faced with obstacles, they persist and continue with what they are doing. They pay attention to detail and are dependable. If taken too far, conscientiousness can become an impediment to success in the form of obsessive perfectionism. Somewhere in the middle of the conscientiousness continuum is a happy medium.

Of the big five personality traits, conscientiousness is the best predictor of success in school and the workplace. Improved organizational skills and the ability to control impulses are qualities especially suited to achieving mainstream success.

Trait #3: Extroversion (Sociability, Inhibition, Assertiveness, Adventurousness)

When you have the choice, how do you spend the majority of your time: with other people or by yourself? If you're the type of person who is energized by other people, you're most likely extroverted. Extroverts enjoy active involvement in groups and generally see things clearer when they can bounce ideas off someone else. In addition, extroverts are usually active "go-getters" and people persons. They have large networks of friends that they dutifully maintain. Adjectives to describe them are gregarious, assertive, and talkative.

Introverts are the exact opposite. If your idea of a good time is silently contemplating the universe by yourself, you are likely an introvert. These people shy away from crowds and prefer quiet, secluded spaces, but this does not necessarily imply shyness. Introverts can have highly developed social skills even though they prefer solitary activities.

Trait #4: Agreeableness (Warmth, Affection, Gentleness, Generousness, Modesty, Humility)

Agreeableness is the tendency to be caring and compassionate with others. Agreeable people have a strong desire to maintain group cohesiveness and are willing to compromise their own desires in order to preserve harmony. Other adjectives that describe agreeable people include sympathetic, pleasant, generous, and helpful. They avoid conflict and sincerely enjoy seeing others succeed. They aren't paranoid or suspicious and generally have a positive view of human nature. Agreeable people are usually a joy to interact with because they know how to avoid conflict and contention. Often they will forfeit an argument instead of pursuing it.

The opposite of agreeableness is to be miserable, suspicious, and venomous. These people are usually married to their ideas and set in their ways. Lack of agreeableness can lead to serious problems in children. They have a tendency to interpret ambiguous actions by others as intentional acts of aggression, making them likely to respond aggressively to innocent or accidental provocations. This causes a self-perpetuating loop of aggressive responses.

Trait #5: Emotionality (Emotional Stability, Neuroticism, Irritability, Insecurity)

Emotionality is the tendency to experience frequent and prolonged bouts of depression or other negative emotions. It is characterized by debilitating indecision in everyday situations. People who are emotionally labile tend to interpret ambiguous situations as abnormally threatening or negative and break down easily as a result. They are quick to give up challenging tasks as too difficult or impossible and this constant stress and self-doubt leads to social maladjustment.

The opposite of emotionality is emotional stability. People who are emotionally stable have well-tempered emotional reactions and don't experience wide swings of mood. To them, occasional failure is just a part of life. They aren't dissuaded from applying themselves in the future.

BEING LIKED AND DISLIKED

Think back to the two scenarios that opened this chapter. Based on Jay's interactions with Sasha and Meghan, it should be clear to you that how the individual relates to others (Factor #1) and how the group relates to the individual (Factor #2) are both important. Initially, it is attraction that compels Jay and the other boys to strike up friendly conversations. The two interactions have this in common. Constant input of energy puts both Sasha and Meghan into the "popular" half of Figure 2.5. The difference between the two girls, however, comes in their responses to Jay. In contrast to Sasha, who is manipulative and snobbish to anyone but her own clique, Meghan is a genuinely pleasant person to everyone. As a result, the popular clique will like Sasha while the rest of the student body will dislike her. On Figure 2.5, this moves her into the front, top right quadrant—the Queen Bee. Everyone, including the popular clique, likes Meghan; this moves her into the front, top centre quadrant—the Hollywood Protagonist.

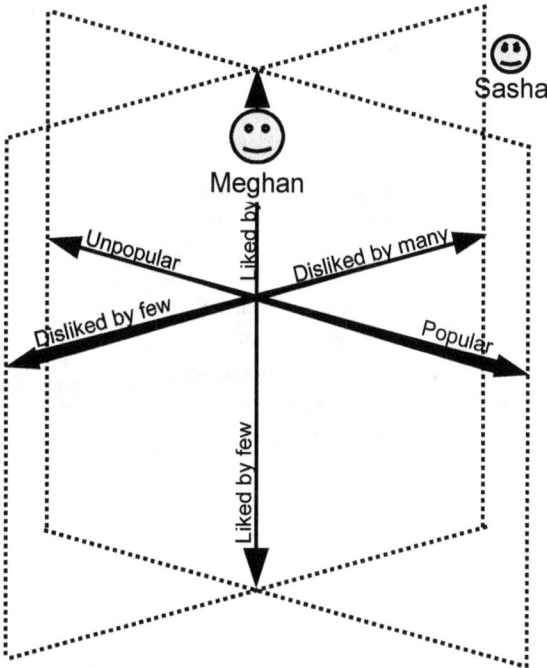

Figure 7.2 Modified version of Figure 2.5 showing where Meghan and Sasha would likely sit.

As you can see from these examples, it is primarily attractiveness that drives the popular/unpopular axis, whereas it is mainly personality which drives liking and disliking. In short, where an individual sits on Figure 2.5 is interplay between what they are and who they are as shown with table 7.1. As you can see, the eight prototypical students described in Chapter 2 have been redefined using a combination of *who* and *what* traits.

Table 7.1				
What Traits (Factor #2)		Who Traits (Factor #1)		Student Type
-Physically attractive		Aggressive, sociable, extroverted	=	Queen Bees & Kingpins
-Athletic		Agreeable, extroverted, unaggressive	=	Hollywood Protagonists
-Wealthy	+	Agreeable, introverted, unaggressive	=	Dumb Blondes & Hopeless Models
-Edgy or mature				
-Large social network		Aggressive, disagreeable, Machiavellian	=	Sidekicks
-Physically unattractive		Aggressive, sociable, extroverted	=	Wannabes
-Not athletic		Agreeable, extroverted, unaggressive	=	Resigned Socialites
-Middle class	+	Agreeable, introverted, unaggressive	=	Happy Loners
-Unexciting				
-Small social network		Aggressive, disagreeable, Machiavellian	=	Misfits

There are four important things to note about Table 7.1:

1.   Personality traits are not absolute. No one is completely agreeable or completely disagreeable. Instead, personality is a matter of degree and only a very few people are found at the extreme ends of any of the big five personality dimensions.

2. The qualities listed in the *What* column are not definitive. Recall that what makes someone attractive is entirely dependent on the context and therefore the *What* qualities that make someone attractive can change. In junior high and high school, a place where the majority of students are surging with sex hormones, physical attractiveness is important. If you were analyzing a businessman's luncheon, wealth would be more relevant.

3. A person does not need all of the *What* qualities I listed to fit a particular student prototype. For example, an incredibly athletic boy does not necessarily need to be extremely handsome in order to benefit from input of energy.

4. Each of the eight student prototypes described is a pigeon hole that approximates reality. The number of traits that define *what* a person is multiplied by the number of traits that define *who* a person is will certainly equal a really, really, big number. Remember from Chapter 3 that every individual is unique. Theoretically, this means there is an infinite number of subtle variations in student type—I only described the eight broadest!

Even though Table 7.1 is inadequate because it defines only eight prototypes, it serves a specific purpose. It demonstrates that if you want to understand the nuances of grade school social dynamics, it is not enough to focus on Factor #1, or how the individual relates to the group. You must also consider Factor #2, how the group relates to the individual. Where a student sits on Figure 2.5 is a complicated back-and-forth between these two factors.

IDEAS FOR BEING LIKED, DISLIKED, OR SOME COMBINATION OF THE TWO

I want to keep this section brief because you probably already have a good idea about what makes a student liked or disliked. For a more detailed discussion than what I provide here, I suggest the timeless classic *How to Win Friends and Influence People*, by Dale Carnegie.

Ideas for Being Liked by Many, Disliked by Few

If a student wants to be liked by many and disliked by few, they must start by ensuring that all of their interactions with others are pleasant, enjoyable, and not awkward. Making people feel rejected or somehow lesser is exactly what they do *not* want to do. I like to think of it in terms of treating others with respect. I use the word respect because it's easy to define other concepts in terms of it: kindness is respect for someone's feelings; courtesy is respect for someone's person; consideration is respect for someone's possessions; and so on. That beint said, no simple rule exists. A range of interpersonal skills is necessary if a student wants to be liked by many, disliked by few.

The Hollywood Protagonist I dedicated this book to had the most pleasant way about her. I remember once standing with her and a group of our peers. I asked the group if there was a pay phone anywhere in the building because I didn't have a cellphone at the time. Although we were just acquaintances, she was the first to answer. Holding out her cellphone she said to me, "I don't know, but there's a free phone right here." Because we were so loosely affiliated, I was almost too shocked to accept. I was not popular and this was not the kind of courtesy I had come to expect from girls in the popular clique. From what I can remember, all of my interactions with this girl had the same pleasant and unassuming overtones. When we passed in the hallways, she acknowledged my presence. When I tried to be funny, she looked at me without scorn. She would ask me how my day was and didn't make a point of pushing me from her social circle. Alas, I wasn't special—she treated everyone like this. In my mind, she is the best example when it comes to making others like you.

Ideas for Being Liked by Many and Disliked by Many

The Hollywood Protagonist I just described had a friend who was a classic Queen Bee and the perfect example of how to be simultaneously liked and disliked by many. Just like in the movies, she would smile at you when you were useful to her and cast you out as soon as you were not. In one class, she went so far as to divide up the seating arrangement along imaginary lines to ensure that a clear boundary existed between people who were "cool" and those who were not.

I shouldn't make it sound as if this Queen Bee was entirely loathsome. When it was your turn to be in her good graces, life was good. She was sociable, funny, and, at times, a joy to be around. The problem was that she played favourites as if manipulation was a hobby. The popular clique was always in her good graces, but the rest of the students could be promoted and demoted as she willed. She was a master manipulator whose antics always left a bad taste in my mouth.

It's not just popular students who can be liked and disliked simultaneously. One of my high school peers can serve as example. Allan desperately wanted to be part of the popular clique and he was ever ready to ditch people he judged a liability. After graduating from high school, it didn't take long before he drifted into obscurity. None of his high school friends were keen on keeping in touch. It's not as if Allan wasn't connected. His participation in various sports gave him ample opportunity to mingle with different social circles. His problem was the same as the Queen Bee's. Because he was constantly playing favourites, some people liked him and others did not.

Ideas for Being neither Liked nor Disliked

It is difficult to think of students who are neither liked nor disliked. By definition these people are not highly visible. They generally mind their own business and are happy with the friends they have. They don't headline controversial statements, engage in highly visible demonstrations, or make a point of acting exclusively. Instead, they go about their daily routine content to take what comes to them. Unlike Queen Bees and Kingpins, they don't proactively seek to undermine other students nor do they stand up for victims. If a student wants to be neither liked nor disliked, they should keep their head down and try not to instigate or get involved with day-to-day drama.

Ideas for Being Disliked by Many

Of all four categories, it's easiest to think of the ways in which a student can be disliked by many. Basically, treat everyone poorly and aggressively and, in general, act as an all-around vile person. When I was young, my brothers and I were playing in a neighbourhood playground. While I was on the swings minding my own business, a stranger my age approached me and asked how I had spent my summer. I responded by saying that I had been to a particular summer camp to which he responded, "Me too!" I asked him how he had gotten there and his response was, "I jumped from tree to tree like a monkey!" Instead of pressing the issue I decided to let it go and wandered off.

I was playing in the sand by myself when this kid started throwing small pebbles my way saying, "It's not safe to play here anymore!" Not keen on making friends with him, I stood up and simply said, "Fine," and left him sitting there by himself. The sad part about this story is that even at a young age I could tell that this kid just wanted someone to play with, but he had no idea how to make friends. His social skills were terrible and I had no desire to play with him.

Another good way for students to ensure no one likes them is by being socially awkward *all* the time. One boy in my school made himself a rope belt—that didn't go over well. Another girl would perform Ukrainian dance (complete with the outfit) by herself at school dances—that didn't go over well either. Neither was attractive enough to get away with these deviations from the social norm, so you can imagine the snickers that pervaded the school at their expense.

It is not necessary for a student to be rejected to be disliked by many. Although it is rarer and more subtle, even so called "popular" students can be equally disliked. Think of the sidekick who is always poking her head out over the Queen Bee's shoulder. She has one powerful ally, the Queen, but everyone else cannot stand her. This is beautifully demonstrated in the movie, *Mean Girls*. After a small riot breaks out at the school, all of the girls are gathered in the gymnasium. Under the direction of Ms. Norbury, they engage in a reconciliation activity designed to ease tensions. In turn, each girl stands atop a small platform and reads an apology to the group. Then, each girl is supposed to turn and fall backwards into the crowd where she is to be caught and let down gently. When it comes time for Gretchen Wieners (the movie's token Sidekick) to take her turn, she confidently steps onto the platform and says, "I'm sorry that people are so jealous of me. But I can't help it that I'm popular." After her conceited apology, she turns around—ignorant to the fact that the crowd has dispersed—and falls to the floor with a loud thud. Implied in this scene is the fact that being popular doesn't guarantee being liked.

I don't think that the point needs to be stressed further. If a student wants to be disliked by many, they need only be awkward and/or treat everyone poorly. It's not complicated.

CHAPTER 8

THE SITUATION

How the individual relates to the group (Factor #1) and how the group relates to the individual (Factor #2) are enough to explain Figure 2.5. But these two factors alone are not enough to explain every social outcome that a student might encounter. To get the full picture the situation must also be considered (Factor #3).

The power of the situation to influence social outcomes is demonstrated by the fact that personality—the core essence of who a person is—changes depending on the situation they are in. If you have ever filled out a personality inventory, you'll know that it is very difficult to place yourself at any extreme of the big five personality dimensions. Consider, for example, whether or not you are "open to experience." I bet that depending on the situation you find yourself in, how "open" you are changes. Maybe you're willing to try extreme sports but have an aversion to ethnic food. Or maybe you love ethnic food but are unwilling to try extreme sports. Your personality can change because it's not just internal characteristics that drive your behaviour—the situation plays a major role.

Have you ever known someone who's a jerk in public and nice in private? Their duplicity is easily explained if you consider the situation as an important driver of behaviour. At school, their behaviour is likely being driven by the desire to appear tough or superior to their peers. In private, where they don't feel the need to manage the impressions of others, their friendly nature shines through. In the above example, the same person shows two different behaviours solely because of changes to the situation. The same can be said of sympathetic bystanders who don't intervene when a student is being bullied. Even if they would help the victim under different circumstances, the situation of school prevents them from stepping up.

The situation is somewhat of a wild card. Although Factors #1 and #2 are generally more important, the situation cannot be ignored. In fact, the phenomenon that is popularity would never exist were it not for the specific "situation" present in a modern school system.

THE GRADE SCHOOL CONTEXT

Attraction and liking, the two psychological forces responsible for producing popularity, are not unique to adolescents. Adults, elderly, and young children also experience these feelings. Consider, for example, the use of status symbols like luxury cars or expensive jewelry amongst adults. These items serve to communicate to the world that a person is rich, connected, and successful. In essence, their purpose is to influence how the group relates to the individual. People purchase status symbols because they know that these objects change how others relate to them (Factor #2).

If liking and attraction are not unique to adolescents, then why is popularity so closely associated with grade school? Human psychology doesn't fundamentally change after graduation, but the situation does. Popularity can only reach fruition as a by-product of the grade school context and as a result of a particular set of circumstances. All humans respond to feelings of attraction with input of energy and all humans like some people more than others—this never changes. What does change is the situation: compared to the rest of life, the grade school context is special for several reasons.

CIRCUMSTANCES THAT MAKE GRADE SCHOOL UNIQUE

Circumstance #1: A Limited Pool of Potential Relations

A challenge facing the modern education system is getting millions of students educated in both an effective and efficient manner. Efficiency necessitates that the curriculum be standardized into grades so that children can transfer between institutions and receive a comparable education anywhere in the country. Efficacy necessitates that children be schooled in reasonably sized classes of approximately 15 to 30 students. The net result of the need for efficacy and efficiency is a relatively stable group of students that move together through a progression of subsequent grades. As such, most students spend their entire grade school careers interacting with the same group of students.

This has important implications for grade school social dynamics. Under such circumstances, a student's reputation carries momentum and follows them year after year. For students who are popular, this is a benefit. At the outset of each year, they don't need to re-establish their social dominance. For others, such as Misfits, the implication is a perpetual stigma. After their name becomes synonymous with unpopular, it becomes incredibly difficult (if not impossible) for them to break free from a cycle of social failure. By virtue of how the school system is designed, students are perpetually stuck with the same peers—peers who are not likely to spontaneously change their interpersonal opinions from one year to the next.

In the adult world, beginning immediately after high school graduation, things are much different. Unlike grade school, where the students are pulled from a small geographic area, universities and colleges are filled with people from across the country and all over the world. The majority of the time, it's unlikely that a student will be friends with or even have previously met many of their classmates. Each semester a shuffling occurs and every classroom they enter is likely to be filled with people they don't know. As a result it is difficult for people to gain a reputation that follows them endlessly. It doesn't matter whether they become popular or unpopular in a particular setting because every semester they begin with a clean slate.

Entering the work world after high school and working a series of menial jobs is similar. Every time a new graduate starts a job, the process of getting to know their co-workers starts over again. Consequently, every new job represents another opportunity to reinvent them self socially.

Circumstance #2:
A Large Need for Interpersonal Esteem

In his seminal book *Motivation and Personality*, the psychologist Abraham Maslow explicitly describes the intrinsic human need for esteem as:

> *[T]he desire for reputation or prestige (defining it as respect or esteem from other people), status, fame, glory, dominance, recognition, attention, importance, dignity, or appreciation. [...] Satisfaction of the self-esteem need leads to feelings of self-confidence, worth, strength, capability, and adequacy from being useful and necessary in the world. But thwarting of these needs produces feelings of inferiority of weakness and helplessness.*[63]

More than any other time, adolescence is when people spend time with friends and therefore it's not surprising that they have a magnified need for interpersonal esteem. The friendships they make at school dominate their lives. Without friends for social back up, malicious peers can easily make their lives miserable. Without question, peers play an important role in the formation of adolescents' general self-concept and emotional stability.[64]

The need for esteem is so important to adolescents that they are willing to give up other goals and aspirations in order to achieve it.[65] The psychologists Kathryn LaFontana and Antonius Cillessen probed how far students between the ages of 6 and 22 were willing to go in order to retain social status. They presented the students with simple social dilemmas that forced them to choose between popularity and five other common priorities: friendship, obedience to rules, personal achievement, altruistic behaviour, and romantic inter-

---

63 Maslow, 1987, p. 21
64 Hay & Ashman, 2003
65 LaFontana & Cillesen, 2009

ests. Here is an example scenario given to students in grades
9 to 12:

> *Imagine that you are invited to a party. Everyone who is anyone*
> *is going to be there. You ask if you can bring your best friend,*
> *but you are told that your friend is not welcome to come. You*
> *really want to go, but you know your friend wants to go too.*
>
> *1. How likely are you to tell them that you can't go because your*
> *friend can't come?*
>
> *2. How likely are you to go to the party anyway without your*
> *friend?*

What LaFontana and Cillessen found was that the desire
for popularity peaks around grades 10 and 11. At this age,
students tend to prioritize status over other common goals
(sometimes to a surprising extent) demonstrating that the
need for interpersonal esteem is of major importance to students in grade school.

After graduation, things change. Dating relationships become longer and more serious and eventually lead to marriage. Good friends move away and new friends are made.
Social circles become more flexible and expand beyond the
small geographic area served by a grade school. The need for
esteem is a core part of the human experience but it no longer dominates day-to-day life. One probable reason why is because adults have far too many other things to worry about:
bills, mortgages, food, work, children, housecleaning... The
list goes on and on.

Circumstance #3: The Influence of
Hormones and Sexual Desire

If money makes the adult world turn, certainly, it is sex
that turns the world of adolescents. Puberty, a monumental step in human sexual development, further complicates

the drama that is grade school social dynamics. The release of various hormones primes sexual interest and creates the physiological need for sexual expression. As a male, I feel comfortable admitting on behalf of the male population that yes, we think about sex all the time. For girls, it is less socially acceptable to admit it—but don't be fooled. Girls are not immune from the sexual impulse either. In her book, *Queen Bees and Wannabes*, Rosalind Wiseman shares a question that boys often have of girls, "Do girls think about sex like boys do?" Her answer, quite simply, is "Yes".[66] Here is a quote from a non-fiction publication of high-school memoirs that demonstrates the point. Speaking to her friends, this author puts words to her sexual frustration:

> *"Yes, just like you guys, I too would like some ass. Not just any ass, but a tight, luscious... um, right. But let's try not to let the lack of ass get us down. Be strong, girls!"*[67]

A glance at the cover of any teen girl magazine highlights this idea.

With the need for sex pounding below the surface, finding a boyfriend or girlfriend becomes an important preoccupation in grade school. Not only do romantic relationships provide a culturally approved venue for sexual experimentation, they also confer social points and help students climb the social totem pole. I agree with Rosalind Wiseman when she states that a girl's social status is, to an extent, "tied to her relationship with boys" and that "the driving force for almost all boys is the same — getting girls and getting respect from other boys".

The surging interest in sex has noticeable implications for grade school social dynamics. All of a sudden, the desires of adolescents change and alter the collective definition of

---

66 Wiseman, 2002, p. 186, 235, 183
67 Baskin, Newman, Pollitt-Cohen & Toombs, 2006

attractive. During elementary school, attraction is based on things like who is the most fun and exciting to be around. Around grade six, the definition of attraction changes. Suddenly, beauty becomes a foremost consideration. If the Queen Bee from grade 1 to 6 is less physically attractive than her peers, a changing of the social order is likely when she and her friends move from elementary to junior high.

There is no question that adults remain interested in sex. The continuing presence of prostitution throughout history is perhaps the best evidence of this fact. Interest in sex does, however, decrease with age. For the student reader who doesn't believe me: ask your parents how many times a week they have sex these days in contrast to when they were first married... Or, if that's awkward, just look at Figure 8.1.[68] The point is that because the sexual impulse dampens with age, the importance of physical beauty as a predictor of attractiveness wanes over the course of the lifespan.

Frequency of "Sex Last Month" vs. Age for Married Couples

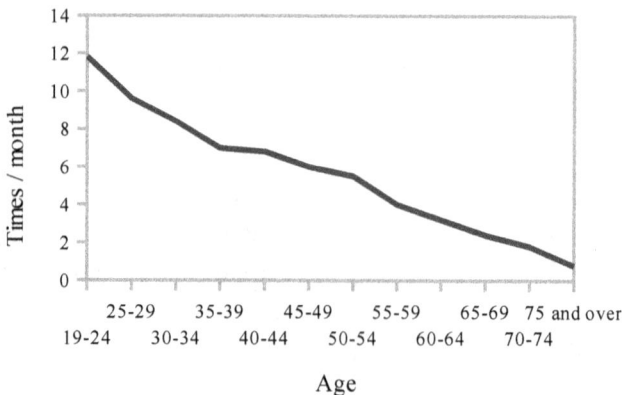

Figure 8.1 A graph showing the declining frequency of sex as couples age. Adapted from Call, Sprecher, & Schwartz, 1995.

68 Call, Sprecher & Schwartz, 1995

Circumstance #4:
Opportunities for Daily Interaction

School is a full-time job for children and adolescents. It generally runs five days a week for approximately 7½ hours per day. Students see each other on a daily basis for extended periods of time. For this reason, if a student is unlucky enough to get expelled from their clique it can seem like the end of the world—in a way, it is. So dominant is school in the life of students that it is not difficult to appreciate why they equate it with being their "whole world." In short, constant daily interaction reinforces the importance of friends and social status which puts even more power in the hands of the social elite.

Circumstance #5:
The Limited Perspective and Maturity
of Young Children/Adolescents

Young children and adolescents have limited perspective and wisdom. Having never really travelled, provided for themselves, and/or experienced what it is like having friends move off in hundreds of different directions, it's not possible that they have a fully developed understanding of life. Even from a biological perspective, it's not until late in high school that the human brain even begins to approach full development.

Back in high school, for example, I had no idea that time slips by so rapidly and I couldn't appreciate the incredible number of people I was destined to meet in the future. Without question, my interest in understanding popularity back then was driven partially by a lack of foresight and wisdom. I simply could not appreciate the bigger picture—life beyond grade school.

FOOD FOR THOUGHT:
IT'S NOT TRIVIAL

Relative to adult problems, the social problems of students may seem trivial. Even I, at times, write as if grade school is just a passing moment in the grand scheme of life.

Grade school is not, in any way, trivial. Even if a student's problems seem small to adult observers, to the student they're not. For an adolescent trying to fit into a world turned by sex, being struck by a flare of acne can be equivalent to a business man losing all of his investment capital. Although transient acne might seem miniscule in comparison to thousands of dollars lost, the individual experience of frustration may be equivalent.

APPROXIMATING THE GRADE SCHOOL CONTEXT

Grade school is unique because it is the only time in life when all of the five circumstances mentioned come together at one time. Although everyone experiences feelings of attraction and liking throughout their lifespan, never again will they have to deal with popularity in the same way. Without the five specific circumstances discussed, the phenomenon that is grade school popularity cannot form. Too many obstacles—such as the constant shuffling of classrooms at university—prevent it.

There are, however, other instances in life where the grade school context is approximated. These situations provide excellent proof that the behavioural forces underlying popularity are innate and enduring throughout the lifespan. If ever you find yourself in a situation that approximates the grade school context, you can expect the phenomenon of popularity to rear its ugly head. A good example of this is medical school and to this I can attest.

Most medical curricula in North America are four years in length and coincide with the standard academic year. Grade sizes are similar to those of high school, ranging from around 100 to 250. Students move pedantically through a curriculum and remain with a relatively stable group of peers throughout the degree. The majority of first year students are in their early 20s, when an interest in sex is still peaking.[69] If you read the following two blog entries, you'll see that popularity re-emerges as a key concern in the life of medical students:

> "In medical school you can find the nerds, the jocks, the popular kids, and the bullies. They're just called different names. For example, bullies have graduated to being called gunners. The really mean ones have an even cooler name: snipers. [...] Even the class elections, where interesting promises and platforms can be found aplenty, seem like popularity contests. It's just tough to grow up."—W. J.[70]

> "Hi all—I am going to be a [first year medical student] for the 2010–2011 school year. A main concern I have is establishing good relationships with my classmates/getting to know them well enough that they remember my name and can at least have a good conversation if I meet them on the streets. [...] So I am worried about the following: How important is integrating yourself into your class? I don't want to be the loner on the weekend who doesn't go to bars with his med school peers (only been to one once in college). Or is everyone too busy studying to do this?"—Anonymous[71]

69 Barr, Bryan & Kenrick, 2002
70 W. J., 2009
71 Anonymous, 2010

In the first quote, W. J. suggests that "it's just tough to grow up." Although I agree that even medical students are not fully matured, the re-emergence of popularity in medical school has more to do with the situation than some sort of lingering immaturity amongst the students.

If you ever attended a summer camp in your youth, you probably remember noticing that cliques started to form and certain campers emerged as popular. This is because camp, like medical school, approximates the grade school context. The same is true of many other situations in life, such as university dorms and office environments. I've never tested it, but I would wager that elements of high-school social dynamics make their way into retirement homes as well.

APPLYING THE THREE FACTOR MODEL TO SITUATIONS THAT APPROXIMATE GRADE SCHOOL

I have a friend taking a master's degree in biology. Together, she and I volunteered at our local hospital. One day while cleaning the toy room, she told me about a workplace bully that everyone—including her—continued to treat nicely. Like most workplace bullies, this girl wasn't physically violent but was emotionally abusive. During her colleagues' presentations, she regularly made a point of trying to make them look incompetent by asking the most obscure and difficult questions. Behind their backs, she was equally unforgiving and gossiped persistently.

Because situations like this intrigue me, I wanted to understand why people like my friend tolerated this bully. After all, none of the other students liked this individual. Even the person everyone *thought* was the bully's closest friend turned out to hate her just as much as everyone else.

In order to understand the dynamics of the story, I used the Three Factor Model described in Chapter 6. According to the details my friend had already given, I was able to get a sense of the situation (Factor #3): the bully was working in the biology department at the university along with several other Master's and doctoral students under the supervision of a professor. Because advanced degrees take at least two years to complete, my friend's peer group was relatively stable and saw each other on a daily basis.

To get a full picture of how the bully related to others (Factor #1), I asked some probing questions about her. Apparently, she was easily offended and got angry quickly. Her biggest assets were intelligence, skill in the laboratory, and connection to the professor. Unlike my friend who was *completing* her Master's degree, the bully was a post-doctorate fellow (someone who has completed their PhD and is now working as a paid researcher).

In this situation, it's easy to see where the bully gets her power. Because she is good at what she does, the professor is pleased with her work and therefore motivated to keep her as an employee. This connection gives the bully privileged influence. For the students in the department whose most pressing concern is grades, keeping the professor pleased is a top priority. The bully is attractive by virtue of this close rela- tionship and in depth knowledge of biology. Students like my friend know that keeping on good terms with her will help them get a good grade. So, instead of confronting the bully directly, they put on a friendly façade whenever they have to deal with her (Factor #2) and dislike her only in secret. If the situation ever changes, and the bully loses her privileged position, she would be wise to watch her back.

CHAPTER 9

FRIENDSHIP AND THE GENESIS OF CLIQUES

The social landscape of schools might change at the rate of glaciers but they are never totally static. The following is a story adapted from the book *Odd Girl Speaks Out*. It follows the plight of a girl named Leslie as she is slowly expelled from her clique:

Throughout the beginning of grade seven, Leslie, Zoe, Rebecca, and Kayla were the best of friends. Every Friday they would shrug off invitations from other girls to hang out with each other instead. They were the quintessential Popular Clique—"teasing people about anything [they were] capable of teasing them about".

One day, out of nowhere, Leslie noticed that Zoe was acting weird around her. The change was so sudden it caught Leslie off guard. She and Zoe had never clicked 100% but in grade seven they had become much closer. Zoe's behaviour proved to be long lasting. It was as if Zoe had suddenly decided that she didn't like Leslie. Over the weeks and months that followed, Leslie was at a loss to explain Zoe's cold behaviour.

Every time she tried to confront her, Zoe responded by saying, "Leslie, you know what you did." This sudden change
bothered Leslie because "Zoe was the type of person that you
want to be friends with. Her personality drives you toward her
in a way that if she were mad at you, you would be on your
knees for forgiveness. Every school has one of [these] kinds
of girls". Even though Leslie continuously tried to apologize,
Zoe never forgave or forgot.

Zoe's cold shoulder soon turned into purposeful acts of
exclusion. Every week she would invite Kayla and Rebecca to
her house while purposefully leaving Leslie out. One night,
Kayla and Rebecca were at Zoe's house with some boys while
Leslie was home alone. She recounts the painfully cheerful
answering machine message that left her in tears. Whenever
she called, she got an away message ending with, "Loveeee…
Zoe, Kay and Bec."

In time, Rebecca and Kayla started acting strange as well.
As grade seven came to an end they became increasingly uninterested in her. By the time summer came, her best friendships had faded beyond repair. When she returned to school
for the first day of grade eight, none of her previous clique
was excited to see her. Even Kayla, who had stood by her for
the longest, gave her a look that said it all. "It told me not to
go near her, I would embarrass her, or she was not allowed to
talk to me anymore". It wasn't long into eighth grade before
Leslie was forced to accept the undeniable: she had been expelled from her clique.[72]

While doing research for this book, I came across story
after story like that of Leslie's. So many girls, it seems, suddenly become slated for expulsion from their clique. Or a
friendship that was once so strong becomes fractured as
the popular clique pulls one friend into their group while

72 Anonymous, 2004a, p. 132, 133, 136

purposefully leaving the other behind. I cannot claim to be an expert on adolescent aggression like Rachel Simmons or Rosalind Wiseman, but I can offer a possible explanation as to why the majority of these stories occur between the ages of 10 to 14 (around Grade 6), and why they are so inexplicable to those affected.

FRIENDSHIP

Friends are an important part of life. They provide companionship, social security, personal safety, help, acceptance, entertainment, inspiration, and much more. Simply put, life wouldn't be the same without them.

As we get older, the quality and nature of our friendships change. For young people, the definition of friendship is simple. They likely believe that any pleasant interaction between them and someone else is enough to constitute a friendship. By the time children are 6 to 8 years old and entering elementary, the most important features of friendship become the exchange of favours (like sharing a snack) and joint play. At this age, petty disagreements can quickly turn friends into non-friends.

As people reach adolescence, the definition of friendship becomes more sophisticated. By age 15, close friendships are defined by mutual trust and attachment. The scope of benefits provided expands to include companionship, emotional stability, help, and mutual affection. The sharing of interests, perspectives, thoughts, and intimate feelings within a mutually affectionate environment becomes the norm.

Friendship is a complicated concept. Not all friendships share the same purpose or depth. It is important to note that it is not an "all or none" phenomenon. Relationships that range from acquaintances to BFFs (Best Friends Forever) can all be considered friendships.

THE SPECIFIC *CAUSES* OF FRIENDSHIP VERSUS *PREDICTORS* OF IT

When you look out into a group of strangers, you can never know exactly who will become friends with whom. There are countless reasons why any two people might form a friendship: perhaps their parents were acquainted and they grew up together; both are the only two males interested in choir at their school; or maybe shared religion puts them together on a weekly basis. Parents, choir, and religion are all examples of specific *causes* and it would be impractical to try and write a comprehensive list of every possible reason why two people may come together as friends.

For the purposes of theory, more useful than long lists are rules in general and unlike the specific causes of friend-ship (which are endless), there are only three predictors of friendship: mutual proximity, mutual similarity, and mutual attraction. As complicated as friendship is, it's possible to look into a group of strangers and make some very educated guesses about who will click with whom.

Predictor #1: Mutual Proximity (Being in the Same Place at the Same Time)

The social landscape of school is constantly being influ-enced by who is in the same place at the same time. Even if these encounters occur completely by chance, they are still im-portant. Throughout elementary and junior high, my school was divided into two groups: French Immersion and English. I was in French Immersion and we spent almost every class separate from those in English. No surprise then that there was more rivalry than friendship between us. It wasn't until high-school that we were finally mixed and friendships be-tween the two groups emerged. Although we didn't know it at the time, our friendships had more to do with proximity than any substantial differences between us!

Being in the same place at the same time causes friend-ships through three different mechanisms:

1. If two students are in the same place at the same time, they are going to experience similar circumstances and events. These shared experiences ensure that they can relate to each other. Put simply, if the conversa-tion dies they won't have to resort to talking about the weather. Multiple shared experiences will give them something to talk about.

2. Being in the same place at the same time creates op-portunities for bonding as two students work together towards a common goal. When it comes to friend-ship, the importance of bonding over shared goals cannot be overstated. This phenomenon is so strong that Hollywood has based several successful movies on it. The 1995 film *Toy Story* is a famous example of the classic "buddy movie." The plot is based on the unlikely pairing of an old toy cowboy with a fancier new toy astronaut. Although their relationship is tenu-ous at first, a friendship slowly develops as they work together to find a way back home. "Buddy movies" are all dramatized versions of the fact that working togeth-er leads to bonding which leads to friendship. If you ever had the opportunity to backpack solo through another country, you probably discovered that you're rarely solo for long. Thanks to this phenomenon, it is incredibly easy for just about any two travellers head-ing in the same direction to become friends. As they

struggle towards their next destination, a friendship develops.

3. Friendship cannot develop without interaction. Proximity—face-to-face or facilitated by technology— is a practical necessity. True, it is possible to maintain a friendship for long periods of time without regular interaction, but this is only because at some point in time there was regular interaction and the relationship had a chance to develop.

Simple proximity is such a powerful promoter of friendship that it can make friends out of people who otherwise never would have been. In grade 11, I spent a month with three classmates learning French as part of an exchange program. Over the course of the month, we spent a lot of time together and became excellent friends—we ate dinner together, went to movies together, and hung out on a regular basis. What's interesting about this anecdote is that in all the years prior, none of us had been close and, shortly after returning home, we went back to our respective cliques. Obviously proximity was the dominant catalyst of our friendship in this case.

Predictor #2: Mutual Similarity (Across a Range of Characteristics)

Mutual similarity refers to a huge range of personal characteristics including similarity with respect to attitudes, beliefs, physical appearance, interests, and life circumstances. If you consider the definition of friendship, it is easy to see why similarity is an important predictor of it. Close friends provide companionship, emotional stability, help, and mutual affection. This means the sharing of interests, perspectives, feelings, and intimate thoughts all within a mutually affectionate environment. It is similarity that facilitates this in important ways.

First, let's consider similarity with respect to personal interests. How people spend their free time is a reflection of their interests hence why:

- People who are interested in fashion browse fashion magazines and/or enjoy shopping.
- People who are interested in sports play them and/or follow professional teams.
- People who are interested in music play instruments and/or join ensembles.

In each case the fulfilment of personal interests requires being in a particular place at a particular time, meaning that people who share interests will often be in close proximity. Members of a school's musical ensemble are an excellent example. All of the students who enjoy singing end up in the choir, the students who like musical instruments end up in band, and so on and so forth. The pathway is this:

Similar interests → proximity → friendship

In the same way that shared interests put two people in the same place at the same time, so to do shared beliefs (like religion) and attitudes (like caring about school): all of the students who share a particular religion are more likely to be members of the same congregation, and students who misbehave will find each other in detention.

Similar beliefs → proximity → friendship

Similar attitudes → proximity → friendship

In short, similarities in interests, attitudes, and beliefs lead to proximity, and proximity is a predictor of friendship.

In addition to resulting in proximity, similarity also facilitates compatibility. Imagine two students talking and getting to know each other for the first time. In this situation, an infinite number of subjects can be discussed and there are no specific rules about what each should say. Potentially,

they could talk about nearly anything at all: school, relationships, music, the colour of their shoes, the meaning of life,
or nothing at all.

With no obvious rules to guide them, interacting with
each other is like playing a game of darts. Their goal is to
"hit the target," so to speak. They need to say the things that
will spark the interest of their peer and lead to an enjoyable
conversation. If they say the right thing, they "hit the conversational target." If they say the wrong thing, they leave
the other unsure how to respond. Under such circumstances,
what they say is guided by personal interests, attitudes, and
beliefs. The more similar they are to each other, the more
likely they are to respond positively and relate to each other.

Imagine a homosexual boy who notices the bodies of
his male classmates automatically and without thought—he
can't help it, he's gay. It just happens. If this same boy were
talking with a religiously conservative, anti-gay classmate, do
you think he should say, "Did you notice Tanner's cute abs today in the locker room?" Assuming he did, do you think that
his "conversational dart" would "hit the target" and spark an
enjoyable conversation? I can guarantee no. Such a comment
would be conversational suicide. Still, this boy did in fact
notice Tanner's abs—it happened. This fact, however, is an
intimate thought that he is not likely going to be comfortable
sharing with someone whose views on homosexuality differ
substantially from his own. Instead, he'll seek a peer with
whom he can relate. In this scenario:

Similarity in belief →
the sharing of intimate feelings →
friendship

The similarity/dissimilarity between two people doesn't
have to be so blatant. Imagine a girl who really likes shopping and so she brings up the subject as she walks and talks

with a new female companion. If the companion likes shopping too, the conversation will progress. Both of them will know about stores, accessories, and brand names, which can all be topics of enjoyable conversation. In fact, if the conversation is pleasant she may even suggest that the two of them go shopping together. In this scenario, her personal interest in shopping has guided her "conversational darts" and she has "hit the target." The two girls have discovered something over which they can bond. In this scenario:

Similarity of interests →
proximity (shopping) →
friendship

Imagine the opposite situation. The new female companion is a complete tomboy and detests shopping. Instead, she likes soccer. In this situation, the comment about shopping "misses the conversational target" and the tomboy is unlikely to relate. The correct "dart" to throw was something on the subject of soccer and now that the girl who likes shopping has "missed the target," the conversation will be less fluid and enjoyable. The suggestion to go shopping is unlikely to be well received and thus:

Dissimilarity →
missed opportunity for shared experience →
missed opportunity for bonding

Do you remember when you were younger trying in vain to explain something to your parents or a teacher only to give up in frustration and exclaim, "Ughhh... you just don't understand!" As social beings, having someone empathize with us is a rewarding feeling so we naturally seek out people who *can* relate. "Hitting the target" when you're interacting with another person is not just about what you say. It's also about what you do. For example, everyone has a bubble of personal space and it is not a good idea to get inside this bubble when you're talking to them. Some people are "touchers" (that is, they like to put their hands on you during conversation) and some people are not. Pairing a "toucher" and a "non-toucher" together can be awkward to say the least. I, personally, am a non-toucher and when someone puts their arm around me during conversation, I am never entirely sure how to react. In fact, when someone I already dislike gets inside my bubble they "miss my target" and I end up disliking them a little bit more.

The next time you are talking with someone, imagine that you are playing a game of darts. Everything you do/say is a dart that you throw. If you "hit the target," the conversation continues smoothly and naturally with no awkward pauses or stops. If you do/say the *wrong* thing and "miss the target," you get an awkward pause or semi-enthusiastic response. With this analogy in mind, compare and contrast the conversations you have with really good friends to those you have with non-friends. You will be amazed at how easily you do *and don't* "hit the target" depending on who you are talking to. Behind the easy conversation we enjoy with our friends are a significant number of important similarities that guide the "darts" that we throw. The more similar we are to someone else, the easier it is to hit the "hit the target." In short:

Similarity in attitudes, beliefs and interests →
being "on target" →
easy and enjoyable conversation →
friendship

Don't misinterpret the previous section and think that if you "miss the target" on occasion it's the end of the world. Successful friendships are built on hundreds of thousands of miniscule interactions over a long period of time, which contributes to the importance of underlying similarity: two student must be consistently "on target" with each other for the friendship to prosper easily. With no well-defined rules to guide them, the more similar they are to each other, the easier this will be.

FOOD FOR THOUGHT:
MISSING THE TARGET

Once, I greeted a very attractive acquaintance by smiling and saying, "Hi—how goes the struggle?" She stopped and said, "I'm sorry, but what do you mean?"

"You know, life. Stress. Problems..." I said.

"I don't think life's a struggle."

Target missed.

Predictor #3: Mutual Attraction (In the Broadest Sense)

Let's face it: no one is terribly motivated to be close friends with someone who is, for lack of a better word, pathetic. The television show *South Park* parodies this. In "The Entity," the cousin of a main character joins South Park Elementary and this boy, named Kyle Schwartz, is so pathetic that his cousin is forced to bribe other students not to make fun of him. In addition to whining perpetually, he cannot do basic playground things like catch a ball or tolerate minor annoyances like "cold dry air."

People like Kyle Schwartz find it difficult to make friends because friendship is a "two way street" meaning that both people must be motivated to maintain the relationship. *South Park* is only a caricature of real life, but people like Kyle Schwartz do exist. I met a guy once who wanted to go home after a movie because his feet had gotten tired. How your feet can get tired after watching a two hour movie I don't know but, unbelievably, this was his rationale for not wanting to stay and talk. I later confirmed that it wasn't just me who wasn't motivated to get to know this guy. The other three people in our group were equally unimpressed.

In contrast to being pathetic, students are motivated to be friends with those who are efficacious (i.e. good at what they do). Friends are an important source of personal esteem and so, in an intangible way, their failure is our failure and their glory is our glory. "Groupies" are notorious for basking in the reflected glory of their star. The next time you are watching an interview with someone famous, look for members of his/ her entourage trying to get as close as possible in an attempt to be associated.

Like mutual proximity and mutual similarity, mutual attraction also predicts friendship because people who are attracted to each other (1) seek proximity and (2) emphasize the similarities between them. Examples of people seeking proximity are obvious and can take the form of texting, sitting together, making joint plans, etc. Just watch as two friends cross a gymnasium in order to sit with each other— that's mutual attraction in action.

In contrast to seeking proximity, catching someone trying to emphasize similarity is a little more subtle and difficult to notice. The easiest way to witness this phenomenon is by watching a Wannabe try to get in with the popular clique. Listen and see how easily they adopt the dominant opinion, preference, or attitude. I remember once my brother demonstrating this beautifully. We were sitting with a large group of people and he decided to toy with the unsuspecting boy sitting across from him. He pointed to a blatantly ugly car and said, "That car looks sweet, don't you think?" The poor boy, oblivious to having been set up, immediately agreed.

FOOD FOR THOUGHT:
FRIENDSHIP AS A MIRROR

"How physically attractive am I?" and, "Where in the social totem pole do I fit in?" are two questions that students might want to answer for themselves. Unfortunately they cannot possibly judge themselves fairly, and it may be difficult to ask their peers. To get around this problem, a student can take advantage of the fact that similarity predicts friendship. Asking the same question of their friends can give them a decent idea of what the answer would be for them (e.g. "How physically attractive are my friends?") It's a not a perfect measure, but it will give them some idea.

Friendship is a Self-Sustaining Cycle

The three predictors of friendship all contribute uniquely to the process:
- Mutual proximity (face-to-face or facilitated by technology) is a practical necessity.
- Mutual similarity ensures compatibility and the ability to relate.
- Mutual attraction is what motivates two people to invest the necessary time and effort into the relationship.

In real life, you will notice that none of the three predictors is independent of the other two. In scientific jargon, each is said to be *correlated*. In other words, each factor causes the other two and it is impossible to know which came first.

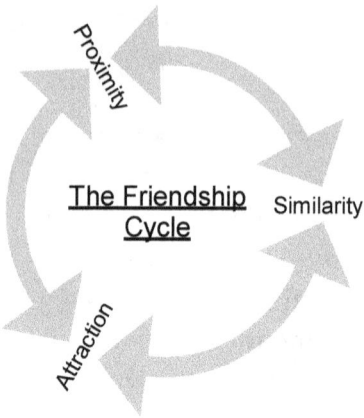

Figure 9.1 The Friendship Cycle

With adequate motivation—i.e. attraction—friendship is a self-sustaining cycle. When all three elements are in place, two people move from being total strangers to potentially best friends. The more attracted they are, the farther along the continuum they move. This is depicted in Figure 9.2.

Figure 9.2 As the Friendship Cycle turns, individuals move from acquaintances to close friends.

At the negative extreme of the friendship continuum are simple strangers who have never met. At the other extreme are individuals who are so close that their behavior becomes pathological. There is a psychiatric disorder known as *Folie à Deux* which translates in English to *Madness of Two*. In essence, it is a shared psychosis which develops between one "normal" individual and another who has an underlying psychiatric disorder. The relationship is so close that the delusional state of one individual is passed on to their otherwise healthy partner.

If you consider Figures 9.1 and 9.2, the treatment for *Folie à Deux* should be obvious. A psychiatrist breaks the cycle by severing proximity between those involved and, in time, the "normal" individual returns to their senses. Without proximity, the cycle cannot turn and the pathological similarity which has developed dissipates.

WHERE DO CLIQUES COME FROM?

It turns out that the same predictors of individual friendship also apply to the formation of cliques: hence why I have chosen to discuss both in the same chapter.

Mutual Similarity

When a large group of strangers comes together for the first time, everyone is in a "friendly" frame of mind. In the beginning, there is a lot of tolerance for lame jokes and odd personality quirks but this grace period doesn't last long. Everything that a person says or does is being recorded in the minds of their peers and if the group is to remain together for a long time, the stakes couldn't be higher. The first impression that a person makes is what people judge them against. Unfortunately, peers never tell each other when they are being socially inept. It's not realistic for a student to expect honest and helpful criticism, so what are they to do? Unless they are trying purposefully to isolate themselves, *what else can they do but be themselves*? How can they know beforehand that their jokes aren't going to be funny or their conversation awkward?

It is because social interaction is so ambiguous that similarity is so important in the first days and weeks of a large group coming together. A student's interests, beliefs, and attitudes are what will guide the things they do/say and thus determine the extent to which they are "on target." The more off target they are, the more likely they are to be perceived as lame, odd, or difficult to relate to. If a student starts talking about Japanese Anime with the wrong group, they're not going to get an enthusiastic response from their peers. It sounds like it should be obvious, but I've witnessed misplaced talk of anime! Assuredly, you too have witnessed hopelessly "off target" social blunders at some point in time.

In the first days that a group is together, no one really knows who they belong with so different groups transiently and haphazardly come together. I cannot emphasize enough the importance of these first encounters to the long term outcome. People quickly learn who they can and cannot relate to and it motivates their future behaviours:

Similarity → *being on target* →
the ability to relate → *enjoyable conversation* →
liking → *seeking proximity during times of*
unrestricted movement →
the beginnings of a friendship and a clique

Mutual Proximity

Most school curricula are a combination of core subjects (math, social, language arts, science), options (shop, home economics, drama), and extracurricular activities (sports, band, choir, student politics). This means that there are lots of ways in which an individual can complete a high-school diploma depending on personal interests and natural ability.

As a result, the more similar two individuals are to each other, the more likely they are to end up in the same place at the same time. For example, all academically gifted students will end up in advanced placement programs. The obvious consequence is not difficult to appreciate:

Similarity amongst a group →
proximity amongst the group →
shared experiences and bonding amongst the group →
formation of a clique

The mechanisms through which proximity promotes the formation of a clique are the same as those that promote individual friendships:

1. Experience of similar circumstances and events.
2. Opportunities for bonding
3. Fulfilment of a practical necessity.

Mutual Attraction

From the beginning, interpersonal attraction influences the formation of cliques within a group of students. Before a single word has been spoken, a large amount of information is already exchanged. Think back to the picture of Johnny Depp playing a piano. Just by looking at this picture, the viewer was able to infer a significant amount of information about him. When a large group comes together, the same process that occurred between you and the picture also occurs amongst the group. Instantly the Hierarchy of Attraction comes into existence and starts to direct input of energy. Naturally, the most attractive students have a strong tendency to pick each other as preferred friends first and so it is not surprising that cliques tend to be made up of people who are more or less equally attractive (in the broadest sense).

Interpersonal attraction → input of energy →
interaction → opportunities for friendship →
genesis of a clique

THE "PUSH" AND "PULL" OF CLIQUES

Similarity, proximity, and attraction are what guide the formation of cliques but where do they develop their iron clad borders and stark divisions? Once a clique is formed, there are two forces that prevent members from escaping or joining: one extrinsic and one intrinsic.

Sitting with people you know and like is simply *better* (for lack of another word). It's fun and comfortable to sit with friends, for obvious reasons, and this natural desire to return to the safety and security of a familiar group can be described as the "pull" of cliques. It originates within the individuals themselves and motivates them to return.

The "pull" of a clique is not enough to guarantee clique membership because, like friendship, attraction must be mutual. The group must want the individual as much as the individual wants the group. If there is a mismatch between the clique and the individual, it manifests as a "push." The best examples of this "push" in action can be witnessed when a Wannabe tries to break into a clique that is uninterested in them. Without a word being spoken, each member of the clique knows to do things like avoid eye-contact, ignore the individual's comments, and otherwise make them feel awkward. This hostility can be so subtle that it is imperceptible from a distance. Regardless, it is terribly apparent to the individual. If the individual has been outright rejected by a brazen clique, this "push" might even be manifested as open hostility. In contrast to the "pull" of cliques, which originates from within the individual, the "push" originates from the group.

Together, it's the "push" and "pull" of cliques that makes them impenetrable fortresses of exclusivity and unstoppable by teachers and/or administrators. As soon as students are given opportunities for uncontrolled movement (e.g. lunch, recess, evenings, and weekends), students naturally gravitate towards their respective cliques because they are intrinsically and extrinsically motivated to do so. Even if restrictive rules are put into place, such as assigned seating, cliques will persist. It never ceases to amaze how industrious even young students can be when they are properly motivated. Until every student is sincerely motivated to be friends with everyone equally, groups of friends will find ways to congregate preferentially and cliques will remain an inevitable part of grade school.

FOOD FOR THOUGHT:
A FADING SMILE

I watched, from across the room, a known Wannabe try and break into a clique that had congregated around an object of interest. He came up behind two members, got their attention, and then told a joke that made him smile from ear to ear. They didn't return his smile or pick up the conversation. Instead, they turned back around to face the object of interest and continued talking amongst themselves. The Wannabe's smile, so sincere at the beginning, faded slowly as I watched from a distance.

CLIQUES HAVE CULTURE

Like friendships, cliques are self-sustaining and follow the same cycle depicted in Figure 9.2. In and out of school, members choose each other as preferred companions and playmates:

Clique membership → attraction →
out of school invitations →
proximity → shared experiences →
bonding → friendship →
re-affirmation of clique membership → etc...

Once established, cliques last for years because of the pathway depicted above and, when applied to groups, the process depicted in the friendship cycle has a very interesting result. The combination of mutual attraction and repeated proximity leads to a similar set of beliefs, attitudes, and mannerisms. In other words, cliques develop a shared culture that comes to characterize them.

The phenomenon of clique culture can be readily apparent. A particular expression, mannerism, style, or tone of voice takes hold of the clique and to the outside observer the end result can be quite humorous. As soon as they get together, previously unique individuals suddenly dissolve into clones of the same person.

Manifestations of clique culture aren't always as obvious as a particular mannerism. Important attitudes and beliefs are also transmitted and reinforced by the clique. If you ever have the opportunity, I suggest that you listen to the discussions of different cliques and pay attention to how they talk about certain subjects. You will be amazed at how much variation exists with respect to attitudes and opinions concerning sex, alcohol, morality, dating, and school work. I personally have spent time with a group of students who nod their heads at the belief that "sex should be restricted to marriage" but I've also spent time with students who talk openly about their partners from the night before! I've spent time with opera vocalists who simply banter as they change into their outfits but also with fiercely heterosexual hockey players who compare penis size while changing. Culture shock is not just experienced by international travellers: if a student has the chance to flip-flop between cliques, they are likely to experience the same phenomenon. Cliques have incredible influence on their members and it's not possible to spend countless hours with the same group of people and not be influenced by the dominant culture created.

FOOD FOR THOUGHT:
HEAD BOBBING

A group of campers I knew began making a particular facial expression over the course of a week. The first to do it was a prominent member of the oldest boy's cabin. By Wednesday morning, a number of his friends had picked up the habit and would smile and bob their chins back and forth anytime they wanted to feign stupidity. By Friday evening, their clique looked like a flock of pigeons anytime they did something wrong.

CLIQUE ASSIMILATIONS
AND EXPULSIONS

When young students are tossed into the fray of grade school, they are faced with a daunting task. Rosaline Wiseman uses a frank analogy to illustrate. School, she says, is a foreboding ocean and cliques are like life rafts floating listlessly on the waves. Students are stuck with the same group of students year after year and their survival depends on staying in the life raft. Failure to make friends quickly can result in an isolated and miserable existence. Floating alone in the water leaves them vulnerable to bullying and ensures a dismal social life. "To girls," Wiseman writes, "the life raft of the clique can truly feel like a matter of life and death"[73]. Boys are not immune either. They too must find support among peers lest they be swept away.

When a large group of strangers comes together for the first time, there is guaranteed to be growing pains as students jostle for their spot in a life raft. Everyone must go through the process of getting to know each other before stable cliques can emerge. It takes time for the social landscape to solidify. Most students spend time with a variety of groups before settling into a clique.

The "push" and the "pull" of cliques make the whole process a lot like speeding dating. A student's motivation to be part of a clique must be reciprocated if their bid for membership is to be successful. A clique that is not motivated to let them join will slowly but surely "push" them from their activities. If, on the other hand, members of a clique want the student as a friend but the student remains uninterested, their lack of enthusiasm will eventually lead the clique to give up trying. For students, the process of finding the right clique can be trial and error.

Once the initial phase of a group getting to know each other is complete, the social landscape solidifies and cliques become like fortresses of exclusivity. This does not, however, guarantee that change is not possible. As exemplified by

---

73 Wiseman, 2002, p. 39

this chapter's opening anecdote, clique membership doesn't always last forever.

Unlike the growing pains of a new group getting to know one another, any disruption to the status quo is guaranteed to be emotionally charged. In clique expulsions, the sudden feelings of being ignored and left out are inexplicable and painful for the affected individual. What used to be his/her group no longer wants to be associated with him/her, with no explanation of what went wrong. In the case of clique assimilations, the person(s) being left behind is often hurt when the assimilated individual is forced to choose between their old clique and one that is more attractive.

In both cases, the cliques and friendships involved are well-established. Therefore these disruptions cannot be attributed to the short term "growing pains" of the group getting to know each other. A more robust explanation is required. Recall that once mutual similarity, mutual attraction, and mutual proximity are properly aligned, friendship is a self-sustaining cycle. It does not, however, continue indefinitely. Things change, people change, and circumstances change. The cycle of friendship can be altered by life events, genetics, twists of fate, parents, variations of fortune, acts of God, and anything else that significantly affects mutual similarity, attraction, and/or proximity.

During clique expulsions, something causes the cycle to falter. An example is an individual abruptly moving to another city. The lack of physical proximity breaks the cycle immediately and the departing individual can no longer be part of the clique, regardless of how integrated they were prior to leaving. The opposite process occurs during clique assimilations. Something happens to set the cycle of friendship in motion between an individual and the members of a clique. For example, a new girl moves into the city. If she is both attractive and similar to her new peers, the friendship cycle starts to turn from the moment she enters the classroom door.

A common theme in stories such as Leslie's (getting expulsed from a clique) is that the student in question doesn't understand what happened or what went wrong. All they have is the memory of great times with what used to be "their clique" and the undeniable fact that they have now been kicked out. Clique expulsions are inexplicable because the cycle of friendship can slowly stop turning as a result of something unknown to the individual or even the perpetrators. During this time, those involved start to sense a rising tension in the air. The critical moment comes when mutual attraction is lost, because this is when calls and invitations stop coming. To the individual expelled, the situation is particularly painful because they maintain the same attraction—for them, nothing has changed.

"But why," you might question, "do clique expulsions and assimilations peak around the ages of 10–14?" The answer lies in human biology; specifically, the onset of puberty. This monumental step in development has major implications for grade school social dynamics. People discover new interests, learn what they are good (and bad) at, and start to care about sex and dating. These important changes set off a number of chain reactions that cause some cycles of friendship to grind to a halt while simultaneously kick-starting others. Consider the following example: an active boy develops a congenital heart problem after puberty that significantly affects his athletic ability. In this case:

Puberty →
changes that result in a dissimilarity of athletic potential →
different preference for extra-curricular activities →
being in different places →

differing experiences between him and the athletic boys →
less common ground →
less likelihood of him eventually becoming a "Jock"

Other examples are easily imagined: consider a physically attractive girl who is reserved prior to puberty and has gone more or less unnoticed. Even if her relative beauty remains unchanged, the newly raging hormones of her male peers will ensure that she no longer flies under the radar. Prior to puberty, the definition of attractive is weighted towards someone who is fun to play with. After puberty, being attractive has more to do with sexual appeal. All of a sudden, this previously reserved girl is going to be inundated with input of energy thanks to her new position in the Hierarchy of Attraction. The popular clique will take note and the pathway to assimilation will look as follows:

Puberty → *a change in the definition of attractive* →
a changing Hierarchy of Attraction →
new patterns of input of energy →
new experiences for the previously reserved girl →
common ground between her and the popular clique →
mutual attraction → *clique assimilation*

In both examples, the biological changes associated with puberty lead to a disruption of the social order.

At any point in time, any major life event can have a similar effect on the friendship cycle. Puberty remains special, however, because it is the one time during grade school that every single student is guaranteed to undergo significant change. Under such circumstances, changes to the established social order are inevitable.

In the case of Leslie, the girl whose story opened this chapter, it is impossible to know exactly what disrupted the friendship cycle between her and her friends based on the details she gives. Many explanations are possible: perhaps

Zoe has discovered a new found interest in sex/dating but Leslie's religious convictions prevent her from engaging fully in the activities Zoe has begun to suggest to the clique. In such a case:

Dissimilarity of religious beliefs →
differing willingness to engage in various activities →
inability to relate → loss of attraction →
loss of friendship → clique expulsion

Wiseman's brilliant analogy of cliques as life rafts highlights the fact that cliques can be the result of strategic alliances and not just mutual liking. It is also possible that Zoe is just an unscrupulous Queen Bee who has who suddenly felt empowered to act on a long-time desire to see Leslie expelled. Perhaps puberty has solidified Zoe's position atop of the Hierarchy of Attraction and now she is going to leverage this fact in the following way:

Puberty → changing Hierarchy of Attraction →
input of energy directed at Zoe → social power and influence →
empowerment to act on a long-time grudge towards Leslie →
clique expulsion

Leslie (and Zoe for that matter) may never be fully aware of what disrupted the cycle of friendship. Social problems are notoriously convoluted and rarely the result of superficial disagreements or feuds (see chapter 11, question 10). If Leslie decides to resist her new social reality, how she might go about uncovering the cause of her expulsion, and what she can do about it are the subjects of the next chapter.

CHAPTER 10

BREAKING IN
AND PAINFUL
SELF DISCOVERY

When I was in grade 12, I went on the class ski trip which spanned a weekend. As you can imagine, the cliques were out in full force the entire time. Everything from our hotel accommodations to our seats on the bus were self-selected. Lunch tables, dinner tables, tour groups, hotel rooms, and even the buses were divided up along clique lines. It was there, in the context of posh hotel set in a beautiful mountain resort that I experienced a situation which beautifully illustrates the challenge someone like Leslie will face trying to break back in.

My most vivid memory from that weekend is Saturday night. At dinner, the hall was awash with whispers and speculation. One of the girl cliques had planned an exclusive escape to the hotel bar across the street and away from the formal party planned at the hotel where we stayed. From my seat at dinner, I watched the quiet group huddles and strategically timed forays into the hallway for water breaks. Secret plans were brewing.

After the meal, I returned briefly to my hotel room. As I walked down the long hallway lined with rooms, I noticed three female members of the aforementioned clique coming towards me from the far end of the hall. I took one look at their dresses and heels and knew that they were on their way out. As we passed in the hallway, I smiled at them and they smiled at me. I continued on to my hotel room and they continued on to the front lobby and exit.

Imagine now that the three girls coming towards me were Zoe, Rebecca, and Kayla and that I was Leslie. The moment in the hallway wouldn't have been an insignificant blip in time. It is precisely these moments that define the impenetrable nature of cliques. The key point is that Leslie would know that they had planned an exclusive outing and, because the dinner was awash in whispers, they would know that Leslie knows. In this situation, Leslie would be desperate to get an invitation and the clique would have a golden opportunity to extend it in the hallway.

I was not a member of their clique and they did not extend the invitation to me. Had I been Leslie, the friendly smile I did receive would actually have been a tremendous act of exclusion. How could someone like Leslie plan to overcome this?

THE PROBLEM

In moments like this, Leslie would have been plagued primarily by two questions: what went wrong and how do I fix it? These, and similar questions, are the perpetual bane of countless students. Wannabes are, after all, defined by their ambitions of clique assimilation. Even beyond Wannabes, I suspect, every student has found themselves in a situation where, no matter how hard they try, they just don't fit in or are dissatisfied with their position in the social landscape and want to change it.

There are ways for an individual to purposefully take charge of their social destiny and affect change. That being said, I don't believe that it is always advisable for a student to identify a clique and then try to break in. As discussed later, this is not necessarily *impossible* but it's not necessarily *possible* either. The road to premeditated assimilation can be long, painful, and ultimately end in failure.

Regardless, this chapter is included because I doubt many students will be satisfied with the clichéd, but excellent, advice of, "Be patient. School doesn't last forever." They are almost certain to ask questions like, "How do I break in?" I leave it to the discretion of parents and teachers, with their superior wisdom and tact, to help students identify practical aspirations and avenues for personal growth.

BREAKING IN...

As described in the previous chapter, the cause of clique assimilations and expulsions are significant events like puberty that alter the friendship cycle. If the cycle is set in motion, the result is assimilation. If the cycle is disrupted, the result is clique expulsion. If a student wants to purposefully break in, their task is to actively set in motion the friendship cycle between themselves and the chosen clique.

A CYCLICAL PARADIGM: PLAN → ACT → REFLECT → REPEAT

There is absolutely no way that I, or anyone else, could supply students with a comprehensive list of rules to govern every situation they may encounter. Social success requires constant attention to detail and there is no way to adequately address all the possible circumstances a student will face. All anyone can do is elaborate on general principles. Ultimately, it is the student who makes their own plan.

Breaking into a clique is not a linear process because relationship building does not have a perfectly defined ending. The student's goal is to get the friendship cycle turning. One cannot expect to implement changes, go to school the next morning, and ride a wave of success. Instead a student must approach the challenge as a repetitive process of planning, acting, and reflecting over many months and years.

TASK 1: PLANNING (ANALYZING AND UNDERSTANDING CURRENT CIRCUMSTANCES)

As described in Chapter 6, there are three factors that ultimately determine a student's place in the social landscape:

1. Who they are (how they relate to others).
2. What they are (how others relate to them).
3. The situation they are in.

Any barrier preventing them from joining a clique will fall into one of these categories.

Analyzing the Situation

Of the three factors, the easiest to analyze is the situation. A student can simply ask: "When am I in the same place at the same time as the chosen clique during regular scheduled activities?" Classes like language immersion, options, and advanced placement, as well as extracurricular activities like sports, drama, music groups, and religious activities, are especially important. A student needs to determine if the members of the clique are more often with each other than with them during the average day. If the only time they and the clique are in the same place is at lunch and/or recess, then the situation is a barrier.

Lack of proximity →
lack of bonding opportunities →
fewer opportunities for friendship →
outsider status at lunches/breaks and evenings/weekend.

If the situation is a barrier, the student can consider stopping their analysis. Lack of proximity is often enough to keep someone on the outside looking in. Imagine if, every day after school, the student rides home on the bus while members of the choir are at school singing. Anytime something interesting happens at choir—a secret is shared or a funny accident happens—the student on the bus will not be able to relate the next day and this will hinder any attempt at being part of the group.

Analyzing What "You" Are

Friendship is a two way street. The chosen clique must want to be friends with someone as much as a particular student wants to be friends with the clique. If the clique does not think someone is attractive, then another barrier has been identified:

Possession of valued characteristics →
attraction → *input of energy* →
opportunities for friendship.

A student looking to break in must answer the question: "Do I have the skills, abilities, or characteristics valued by the clique's culture in order to make me attractive?" In other words, honestly reflect on whether or not they, and their chosen clique, match in terms of *what they are*. Some questions to ask are:

1. "Who are the members of the clique I want to join?"
2. "What do I think of them?"

3. "Why do I think of them like this?"
4. "Can I say the same for me?"

If the answer to the final question is "yes" then *what they are* **is not** likely a barrier. If the answer is "no," then *what they are* **is** likely a barrier. For example:

1. Let's say the clique of interest is the "Party Girls" and...
2. ...the student perceives them as being party animals...
3. ...because they always go to parties and get drunk on weekends.
4. So, the student asks, "Do I party and get drunk on weekends?"

If the answer is "yes," then *what* they are **is not** likely a barrier between them and the clique. If they don't, a barrier between them and the Party Girls has been discovered.

As a student goes through this exercise, they should appreciate that the members of a clique are not defined by just one thing. As a second example, let's imagine that the student is analyzing the "Sports Guys" and they perceive them as being two things: athletic and "players." Their analysis might look as follows:

1. They want to analyze the Sports Guys and...
2. ...they perceive them as being "athletic..."
3. ...because each of them plays many sports.
4. So, the student asks them self the question, "do I play many sports?"

Then, continuing with their analysis:

1. The student is still analyzing the Sports Guys and...
2. ...they also perceive them as being "players..."
3. ...because each of them is always "hooking up."
4. So, the student asks them self the question, "Am I always hooking up?"

As the student analyzes *what they are* it is important to consider as many dimensions as possible. The more dimensions they include, the more accurate their analysis will be.

A student cannot pretend to be something they are not because *what they are* is based on objective facts; in others words, things that can be seen or counted such as sports played, number of girls/boys dated, height and weight, academic scholarships, etc. Students are observant of their peers and if they don't see it they won't believe it. Even if a student learns to swagger like a tough guy, swear like a tough guy, and snub school like a tough guy, no one is going to perceive them as a tough guy unless they have actually started and finished fights. Other examples are easily imagined:

- If the student is not a member of several sports teams, their peers will not think of them as athletic.
- If the student is constantly studying, their peers will think of them as a "keener."
- If the student is consistently at the top of the class academically, their peers will think of them as "genius."

Objectivity is the key to analyzing *what*.

Analyzing Who "You" Are

Who students are is based on how they treat other people, act in public, and relate to others. It is their personality, beliefs, attitudes, and interests. For a detailed discussion, see Chapter 7.

There are two ways that *who* a student is can be a barrier between them and the clique. Either:

1. Their interests, beliefs, and attitudes differ substantially from those of the clique (which makes them off target with the things they do/say).
2. They're unpleasant and/or annoying.

If a student suspects the first, they probably like the *idea* of being in the clique more than the actual act of belonging. If they suspect the second, here are some things they can watch for:

- They get one word responses from people with no engagement or enthusiasm in their replies.
- They use a particular phrase or expression repeatedly.
- They talk too loudly.
- People avoid eye contact with them when they try to contribute to a conversation.
- They tell a joke and no one laughs, so they tell it again, and again, and again, until they get a pity response.
- They say things primarily to convey a particular persona: "Don't you guys *love* working out, fixing cars, or not caring about school?"
- They do or say things to get attention.
- They automatically and enthusiastically agree with everything someone says without actually expressing their own opinion.
- Any discussions they have always end in argument.
- The subject of conversation changes after they finish making their comment.
- They interrupt people continually.
- Their only contribution to a conversation is a request for clarification concerning a story or the comment just made.
- They don't let someone's verbal jab or insult against them go without retaliating.
- Their jokes are never funny amongst a certain crowd.
- They talk loud enough so that someone who is standing near but not in the conversation can hear what they say.

- They've never admitted that they're wrong.
- They flip flop between conversations.
- Their stories have no punch lines.
- They are never quiet.

These examples are just suggestions. Each student must use their own judgment if they suspect that they are being unpleasant or annoying. As a rule of thumb, anyone who is worried about how they relate to others can just stop talking and listen to the people around them—it's the safest way for them to avoid saying something stupid or obnoxious. Steven Covey, author of *The Seven Habits of Highly-Effective People*, devotes an entire habit to what he calls, "seeking to understand before seeking to be understood." In short, he emphasizes the importance of listening.

Analyzing the "who" question is difficult for three reasons:

1. When it comes to *who they are*, not everyone is created equal. When the late rapper Tupac wears a backwards bandana, sags his pants low, and folds his fingers into a "W" to signify "Westside," people think that he looks cool. If I—a university educated white boy from suburban Canada—was to do the same, people would think I looked ridiculous, and rightfully so. The same is true of everything anyone does/says. It is biased by *what they are*. In other words, when a Queen Bee does something, it doesn't mean that if a Misfit were to do the same the response by peers would be equivalent. Unlike *what they are*, *who they are* cannot be analyzed through direct, objective, comparison.

2. The second challenge that makes judging *who "you" are* difficult is that peers are rarely going to be upfront if something a student did was lame, stupid, or annoying. Even best friends are only going to be candid

under certain circumstances. Unfortunately, peers will gladly talk about others behind their back and laugh about their quirks long before they will say something to their face. Everyone is guilty of not being upfront at times, so the challenge for students is to self-reflect on what personal quirks and nuances make them annoying, lame, or "tools."

3. The final challenge that makes judging *who* notoriously difficult is the simple fact that as humans it is not possible to be impartial observers of ourselves. The human ego can be fragile, and we're motivated to preserve it as much as possible by thinking the best of ourselves.

The conscientious individual is always analyzing *who they are* to a certain extent. However, for students looking to identify barriers between them and a clique, analyzing *who they are* can be dangerous. As soon as a student starts to believe that the things they do/say are somehow "wrong," they can very easily fall into a self-perpetuating cycle of self-doubt. Regardless, *who they are* is always one third of the social puzzle and so it is important to think about. I suggest that students avoid the trap of perpetual self-doubt by following a process of exclusion. Only after they have ruled out the situation and *what they are* as barriers between them and the clique should they conclude that *who they are* might be.

TEMPORARY TATTOOS, REALLY?

Everything that we do and say is being judged and we don't get a lot of chances before we "strike out." A friend of mine once told me a story about how this "loser" was trying to pick up girls using temporary tattoos at a dance. Written in between the lines of his anecdote was the fact that this silly attempt at input of energy had been decoded and judged—simple as that.

I was climbing one afternoon with a good friend and mutual acquaintance and, as we left the climbing wall, I couldn't help but think to myself, "Man, this [mutual acquaintance] is annoying. I really hope my friend doesn't invite him to hang out this evening." As soon as it crossed my mind, it struck me:

1. How could the mutual acquaintance ever know what I was thinking?
2. How many times have I been the annoying one and ignorant of the fact?

A Student Should Not Be Surprised if They Think It's All Three:

If after self-assessment a student has the sneaking suspicious that *what they are, who they are*, and the situation are all barriers between them and the clique, they should not be surprised. As discussed in Chapter 6, all three factors affect each other. If one is out of sync, the other two are likely to be as well. After all, friendship is a cycle. Consider:

A student likes soccer (who they are) →
they join the soccer club (the situation) →
become an athlete (what they are) →
they make the soccer team (the situation) →
they learn the culture of soccer players (who they are)→
they gain the ability to relate to the soccer clique.

Or:

A student has avascular necrosis of the hip (what they are) →
they develop an aversion to sports (who they are) →
they don't join any sports teams (the situation) →
they don't develop an athletic body (what they are) →
girls find them less attractive (what they are) →
they can't banter about sexual encounters (who they are) →
they lose the ability to relate to the "Bros" in class.

TASK 2: TAKING ACTION (PURPOSEFULLY GETTING THE FRIENDSHIP CYCLE TURNING)

After identifying potential barriers, the student must act to remove them. The following seven steps are an example of how they might.

Step 1: Discover Shared Interests

The cycle of friendship has three potential entry points: similarity, proximity, or attraction. Catalyzing attraction happens to be the final step (as will be discussed later) and starting with proximity is a poor choice because trying to get too close too soon will surely end in the student being branded a "Wannabe." This leaves similarity as the best point of entry.

There are likely several ways to determine what shared interest(s) coordinate the clique. I suggest the following two: 1) consider when the members of a clique are all in the same place at the same time (e.g. football practice); 2) listen for recurring topics of conversation. The student's job is to take an interest in the same.

CAUTION: A student should never advertise their new found interests. Advertising too soon will tip off their peers and make them a Wannabe. The social landscape changes over months and years and a rapid change to *who they are* will give them away.

Step 2: Get Good at Whatever it is that Coordinates the Clique

Step two is developing expertise and/or becoming competent at the shared interest. If it's school, they ought to start studying; if it's choir, start singing; if it's professional sports, start watching the sports channel. The purpose of becoming competent is threefold:

1. On occasion they are going to end up in the same place at the same time as the clique and, when this happens, they will have something to talk about.
2. Being good at something is synonymous with being efficacious and this makes them attractive.
3. Being good at something has practical requirements that set them up for Step #3, seeking proximity.

Step 3: Achieve Proximity

Imagine a student discovered skateboarding as the clique's coordinating interest. They take an interest in skateboarding and start to practice in the alley behind their house. Next they expand where they are comfortable skateboarding and eventually become confident enough to go to the local skate park. There they will likely meet members of the clique. The pathway looks like this:

Shared interest → practice → proximity

Another example: a grade 7 girl discovers that volleyball is one of the activities that coordinate the popular girls' clique. She purchases a volleyball and starts practising at home. She doesn't advertise her new found interest and grade 7 passes uneventfully. Over the summer she continues practising, and by the time she returns for grade 8, she has developed significant skill. The social landscape stays frozen until the day when her gym teacher notices her new talent and invites her to try out for the volleyball team. All of a sudden she is in the same place at the same time as the popular clique and no one can claim that she's a Wannabe—it was, after all, the teacher's idea that she try out. Again, the pathway is as follows:

Shared Interest → *practice* →
proximity + *attraction via efficacy*

These are overly optimistic and simplified examples but they demonstrate the point.

Step 4: Continuous Improvement

Even after a student achieves proximity they must continue improving their skill. Remember efficacy is attractive and the better they are the more success they will have at motivating peers to seek friendship.

Step 5: Learn the Culture

Different cliques have different cultures, therefore once proximity is achieved, a student must internalize the dominant culture. The best way for them to achieve this is simply by listening with an open mind. Clique members will make their attitudes, beliefs, and values known through the things that they do and say and it is the student's job to read between the lines in an effort to understand and absorb. Specific attention should be paid to attributes considered attractive by the clique. Remember, it is the student's job to motivate their peers to seek a reciprocal relationship and this depends on possessing valued characteristics.

When learning culture, emphasis should be placed on having an open mind. If a student thinks that the clique will mold itself to their attitudes, beliefs, and values, they're wrong. It is the student who must be willing to see things differently and step out of their comfort zone. The clique cannot be expected to come to the student because, as will be discussed shortly, they already have each other.

Step 6: The Student Must Ensure They Are Neither Obnoxious nor a "Tool"

I knew a girl who possessed the qualities valued most by the Popular Girls with whom she shared a cabin but couldn't—much to her frustration—break in. Hers was a case where the problem was uniquely *who she was*. Admittedly, this girl could be unpleasant: she interrupted everyone and flip-flopped between conversations. You couldn't tell a story without her interrupting you or turning to someone else mid-sentence. Talking to her was a constant challenge and behind her back everyone agreed that she was not a pleasant person to be around. It was frustrating for me to watch her flounder socially because she had so much potential. If she could have learned to listen and be patient, she could have broken into the Popular Girl clique easily. Her situation is not common but I share the anecdote because I want to highlight the importance of Factor #1: *who a student is.*

Unfortunately, I cannot include a list of the intangible skills that make someone pleasant and/or agreeable. Any such list would be inadequate because social skills are learned *implicitly*; that is, below the level of consciousness. Only the basic principles of "good social skills" can be learned from sources like a book and the rest must be learned by doing.

My favourite analogy to illustrate what I mean by *implicit* learning is playing the piano. Look at the music depicted in Figure 10.1.

In the beginning, new piano students must painstakingly interpret each note. After years of diligent practice however, they can recognize larger and more complex patterns. Instead of seeing many individual notes like in Figure 10.1, they perceive only a few larger patterns, such as those depicted in Figure 10.2.

This ability to organize details into manageable patterns unconsciously is what allows experienced piano players to

Figure 10.1 *An excerpt from Chopin's Scherzo No. 2 in Bb minor op.31*

Figure 10.2 *The same excerpt with markings showing how a professional piano player might interpret the score.*

read music quickly. In time, it is amazing how proficient they become.

Social situations are like piano music in several important ways. The social world is made up of hundreds of tiny details that combine to form complex patterns that must be interpreted. Just as there are infinite ways to arrange musical notes on a page, there are infinite ways to arrange social cues. People must learn to quickly recognize complex patterns and respond appropriately.

Like piano, the only way to learn is to practice. A student must put them self into social situations again and again and learn from their mistakes. Ironically, the advice I am currently writing is, for the most part, useless. The most I can hope to do through a book is convey vague generalities such as this:

> *Be friendly: Popular people are on friendly terms with pretty much everyone. [...] They're on good enough terms that they can hold a short, friendly conversation with anyone in the room. There's no reason you can't do that too.*[74]

Even if this statement is true, it's unhelpful. The "devil is in the details" when it comes to social skills and trying to produce simplified generalizations will always result in clichés.

Step 7: Wait for It, Then Reciprocate

Unlike the previous six steps, the final step—the moment of truth—is achieved passively. All a student must do is be open to it when it comes and that's it... they're in. The cycle is turning. They have been successful.

I like to refer to the seventh step as the "mind control step" because at times breaking into a clique is equivalent to just that. Friendship is a two way street and a student cannot *force* a group to accept them; ultimately, it is the group who makes the decision to call, respond, make eye contact, text, invite, etc. In essence, the student must evoke specific behaviours from others indirectly: i.e. mind control.

FOOD FOR THOUGHT:
GETTING THE "WAVE IN"

Whenever I see a clique welcoming someone in, I always imagine the clique as a ground crew waving in a landing plane with their orange batons. The student is called over, noticed when they enter the room, asked questions, and otherwise attended to. Once a student gets the "wave in," it is shared culture that will guide the things they do/say and keep them on target.

Once, while at a bar, I stole the attention of an attractive girl from a peer and proceeded to dance with her for the rest of the evening. "I am SOOOO mad at you," he kept saying to me—a large smile on his face—as he, his clique, and myself sat in a restaurant and ate later that evening. He wasn't mad at all. I was getting the "wave in" from him and his clique for having achieved a culturally valued accomplishment.

RETURNING TO LESLIE AND THE POSH MOUNTAIN RESORT

By the time Leslie arrives at the mountain resort, she's far too late to be thinking, "How do I break into the clique?" The process of her clique expulsion began long ago. Out of the seven steps I just described, it's only the final step, the mind control step, that occurs in the hotel hallway. Leslie cannot force the three girls to include her in their plans. *They* must decide by *their own volition* to include her. Her problem is that the friendship cycle faltered long ago and there's really nothing she can do in the moment. If she begs to be included, she's a Wannabe. If she accepts her fate, she misses out on an exclusive outing.

Moving forward, how Leslie might reverse the process of expulsion and set the friendship cycle turning again is exactly what I have described in this chapter. Breaking in is a slow process that begins months in advance. Getting the invite is only the last in a long string of events that leads to success.

TASK 3: REFLECTION (WHAT CAN BE EXPECTED)

Six easy steps to success: simple in theory but is it practical? No, almost never. Theoretically, free will allows individuals to reinvent themselves whenever. In practice nothing is more difficult.

The seven steps I just described are truly inadequate. Behind each is an untold mountain of effort and emotional investment. If breaking in sounds like it should be easy, it isn't. The changes I propose go to the very core of *who* and *what* a student is. In short, there is a reason why this chapter ends the way it does. If a student decides to attempt a targeted assimilation, I can guarantee that they will encounter some combination of the following challenges along the way:

Challenge 1: The Wannabe's Paradox

The student who decides they want to be part of another clique is faced with a fundamental dilemma: imagine that they want to be part of the Skateboarders clique (a.k.a. the Skaters). The clique does not include the student in their activities because the members of the clique do not perceive him/her as one of them. Remember, it is not the student who decides *what they are*. It is their peers who do. Whether or not the student perceives them self as a Skater is irrelevant. The only thing that matters is what their peers think. In this case, the student is NOT A SKATER because their peers DO NOT perceive them as such. If they did, the student wouldn't have a problem in the first place.

Said differently, the moment a student thinks to them self, "I wish I was part of that clique," they are forced to admit that the clique does not perceive them as a member. This is a problem because in order to break in, the clique must do exactly that. No one can force them to invite the student out, include them in group chats, or otherwise welcome them into their group. The student is thus confronted with a dilemma: the definition of a Wannabe is someone who tries to be something they are not, yet the only way for them to learn is to try! Said differently:

- The student has decided to try and be a Skater therefore they must admit to themselves that they are not.
- The student knows they are not because if they were they wouldn't have a problem.
- The only solution to their problem is to try.
- But if they try to be a Skater, they are by definition a Wannabe.

In one sentence, if the student tries, then they are *not*, but the only way to *be* is to try—this is the Wannabe's paradox. If the student decides to head down the path of clique assimilation, he/she is guaranteed an intense period of emotional turmoil because they necessarily start off as a Wannabe. If their peers catch on—and they certainly will if the student doesn't take their time—there will be no mercy. In the beginning the student is "damned if they do, damned if they don't."

Challenge 2: Time and Timing

The only way to learn a clique's culture is to participate in the same activities and be around them as frequently as possible. The best way to do this is to choose the same classes and participate in the same extracurricular activities. Unfortunately, it's not as if a student can wake up mid-semester and decide that this is what they are going to do.

Imagine that two weeks into a semester, a student discovers that all of the girls in a particular clique chose Drama as their option. The student, on the other hand, chose Home Economics. Now they have a problem: while the clique they envy is bonding and getting to know each other, they are with a different group. By the time the student realizes this, it's most likely too late to change their option—the schedules have been made. This scenario demonstrates the problem of timing and highlights the importance of inherent similarity. Had the student shared similar interests with the clique from the beginning, all of them would have chosen the same option to begin with.

When it comes to extracurricular activities, in addition to *timing*, a student can also face the problem of *time*. The person they are today is not going to change in a night, a week, or even a month. Becoming *who* and *what* they are was a process that took years.

With that in mind, imagine a grade 8 student and their clique of envy, the basketball players. The student wants to join but unfortunately the basketball team—like all competitive teams—is an exclusive club that only accepts students with a certain level of skill. Basketball, like piano, volleyball, singing, painting, or any other skill, is something that

requires time. Routine practice over the course of years is the
only way to get good. It's not possible to suddenly decide to
join the basketball team. Joining the basketball team represents only one step towards the ultimate goal of assimilation,
yet it can take years to achieve. This is a problem of *time*.

In his book *Outliers*, Malcom Gladwell argues that it
takes approximately 10,000 hours to become an expert at
something.[75] That's approximately three hours every day for
ten years. The student does not need to become an expert
in everything that they do but they should appreciate that
purposeful changes to *who* and *what* they are do not occur
overnight. High school is generally three years—not a long
time in the grand scheme!

Challenge 3: Parents and Preachers

Imagine a student has joined Home Economics with all
of the members of the clique they envy. In this scenario, they
don't face problems of *time* or *timing*. Two or three times a
week, the student interacts with the clique, yet even in this
scenario it's no guarantee that they won't face barriers. The
student has the perfect opportunity to learn the clique's culture but forces outside of their control may prevent them
from internalizing it.

Consider what would happen if the student came from a
conservative, religious, family and the clique's favourite topic
of conversation is sex and dating. Day after day, they talk and
giggle about awkward moments dating and exploring their
boyfriends. They are open to the student joining their conversation but the student cannot. Their parents don't allow
them to date, so they truly don't know what it is like to go to
a movie and dinner, stay up late and talk on the phone, or try
awkwardly to get under each other's clothes. Even if they are

---

75 Gladwell, 2008

motivated to internalize the clique's culture of dating, their parent's rules get in the way. In fact, their parents have made their rules precisely because they *do not* want their daughter to internalize a culture of serial dating and easy familiarity. As a dependent adolescent, there may be little the student can do to change their parent's minds and therefore they cannot contribute equally to their favorite clique's conversation.

Contentious issues such as alcohol, curfews, suitable movies, violent video games, and dating are often regulated by parents and/or religious belief. If a student's parents subscribe to a different culture than the clique, the student is faced with another obstacle to full integration.

Challenge 4: Genetic Potential

Cheerleaders are often thin, basketball players often tall, and power lifters often stocky. Certain genetic attributes lend themselves to certain activities and sports are an obvious example of this. In fact, any activity that is competitive selects for a particular set of characteristics. The spelling team selects for superior memory, the choir for vocal talent, and various sports teams for physical prowess. All of these groups represent exclusive clubs only open to a select few. Not everyone has an equal capacity to join. If a student is bound to a wheelchair, they cannot be part of the school's mainstream volleyball team, end of story.

The point is that everyone is limited in the things that they *can* and *cannot* do. If it is an exclusive extracurricular activity coordinating a clique, there is no guarantee that a student can join. Lacking necessary physical attributes is enough to prevent participation in spite of necessary drive and motivation. Once again the link between similarity and friendship is obvious:

Dissimilarity in genetic potential (what) →
*participation in different extracurricular activities
(the situation)* →
missed opportunities for bonding (the situation) →
*less opportunities to develop specific friendships
(clique membership)*

In contrast:

Similarity in shape and size (what) →
*participation in similar extracurricular activities
(the situation)* →
opportunities for bonding (the situation) →
*more opportunities to develop specific friendships
(clique membership)*

Challenge 5: It's Not Always Obvious What Coordinates a Clique

I've put a lot of emphasis on extracurricular activities as essential to the coordination of cliques. Sometimes, however, it is not always obvious why certain people group together. The student looking to break in will not always be able to point to specific activities and say, "those are what coordinate the clique." Even if a group of students never meets outside of the classroom, subtle similarities can still push them to group preferentially.

Imagine a week long summer camp where there are 25 male campers. Three of these campers come from families where both parents are physicians. Having two parents that are physicians sets children up for a host of experiences and situations that are unique. All three boys are likely going to know what it's like to live in a large house; to have their parents constantly working; to always shop for designer clothing; to enjoy expensive vacations; and other such stereotypes. Without having spent any time together participating in extracurricular activities, there is a good chance that these three boys will "clique" together. The fact that all three come from similar situations at home increases the likelihood that they can relate and be "on target" with the things they say and do. As an outsider, there isn't much a student can do to overcome their dissimilarity if they come, for example, from a rural farm family. The reality is that they simply cannot go back in time and learn what it's like to have two parents who are physicians.

Now, imagine that instead of coming from double physician families, all three boys share the privilege of being ridiculously good looking. In grade school—where sex makes the world turn—this is not an insignificant similarity. As described in Chapter 4, these three boys are all going to be the constant recipients of input of energy. Like having two parents who are physicians, this is going to give them a tremendous amount in common. If the student, unlike them, isn't Hollywood beautiful, they cannot expect to be as "on target" when it comes to talking about attention from girls. Again, the principle is always the same:

Being ridiculously good looking → *similar experiences* →
"being on target" → *friendship* →
clique membership

In both scenarios no extracurricular activity is coordinating the clique, but to the outsider it might seem that all three boys were immediately and inexplicably drawn to each other.

Challenge 6: Peers are Smart, They Can't Be Fooled

It can be uncomfortable integrating into a new culture. Unfortunately for the outsider, breaking into a clique requires that they not only learn the clique's culture but live it. Peers will not be fooled if a student tries to pretend to be something they're not.

One of my favorite opportunities to witness faked cultural integration is when students are sharing attitudes towards alcohol. Drinking is portrayed in the media as "cool" and mature. It is idealized and glorified in music and television as a staple of the high-school/college culture but not every student drinks to the same extent. Many students, especially from religious and/or conservative families, do not agree with the excessive or even moderate consumption of alcohol. Yet because few students want to risk being "uncool," they keep their personal attitudes private. As such, I have witnessed non-drinkers actually condone and facilitate the consumption by others. Outwardly, they absorb and reflect the dominant culture despite the fact that inwardly they believe something different. They know when to yell "chug, chug, chug!" and are willing do everything associated with drinking except... drink.

If this accurately describes the student looking to break in, they should not think that their friends are fooled. When the clique decides who they want to drink with on a Friday night, the student should not expect to be atop the list. Students cannot pretend to absorb a clique's culture—they must embrace it. Peers are astutely aware of what each does and *does not do*. They are not easily fooled.

Another example of faking cultural integration is students outwardly expressing indifference towards school and then privately studying for extended hours. They "talk the talk" of a slacker but are constantly spotted flipping through their notes, arguing about exam marks, and asking questions in class. Again, no one is fooled by their charade. Peers are astutely aware.

A student should never feel the need to advertise a particular image or persona by saying certain things. What I mean is that:

- If a student is physically fit and goes to the gym often, they do not need to talk about protein powder, different exercises, and so forth. Their peers will see their biceps and be convinced that yes, they're huge.
- If a student is a ladies man, they don't need to share stories or boast. Their peers will see the attention they get from girls and be convinced that yes, they get women.
- If a student is intellectually gifted, they don't need to leave their report card face up or joke about how easy an exam was. Their peers will see the ease with which they finish assignments and be convinced that yes, they're bright.

When it comes to breaking into a clique, a student cannot pretend to be—they need to be. If a student "talks the talk" but does not "walk the walk" their peers will not be fooled. Remember, it is not the student who gets to decide *what they are*. It is their peers and peers base their judgments on objective facts.

Challenge 7: The Clique Doesn't Need the Student the Way They Need the Clique

Cliques are fortresses of social safety. In Rosalind Wiseman's words, the clique is a safety raft floating in a treacherous sea of social exclusion. Presumably, a student looking to break in is either floating listlessly in the ocean or looking longingly at another life raft. What they want is for their clique of interest to reach out a hand and pull them aboard.

Challenge seven is that the clique doesn't need the student the way the student needs it—if they did, they would have welcomed them aboard already. I like Wiseman's analogy because just like survivors in a lifeboat, the presence of another student comes at a certain cost to the clique. Remember that being friends with someone is an investment of time and energy and that they, unlike the student, already have each other. If they let the student float off into the horizon, it comes at no significant cost to them.

One potential downside to welcoming a new student in is that the risk of privileged information leaking out goes up with every additional person who knows it. Recall that the sharing of secrets is very common among friends. During a game of poker, a car ride, the lunch hour, etc., it is very common for a clique to banter about personal information. The implication for the student, an outsider trying to break in, is that the clique needs to trust them enough that they can carry on with their normal discussions. Unless they want the student to be "in the loop," they are a potential burden every time the clique wants to talk confidentially.

Overcoming the seventh challenge is analogous to the "mind control" step described earlier. The only way to motivate members of a clique to be welcoming is by being attractive. A student will know that they have failed to overcome the seventh challenge if they discover that they're always the one attempting to achieve proximity (i.e. texting, calling, giving invitations, etc.).

Challenge 8: Old Friends

Clique assimilations are proof that breaking into a clique is possible. If the student overcomes all of the previous seven challenges I have outlined, there is still one more: old friends. Unless their old clique is also assimilated, the student is forced to choose between growing apart from their old clique and denying them self a new and exciting opportunity. Emotions are guaranteed to be involved either way and at least some drama will ensue. Best case scenario, the student is socially adept enough to successfully balance their relationship with both groups. Worst case scenario, they fail to break into the new clique and their old friends get wise to the fact that they tried to switch groups. In some ways, old friends are the gambling chip a student places on the table if they decide to "take the plunge."

...& PAINFUL SELF-DISCOVERY

If a student is considering trying to break into a clique, I hope that the eight challenges I described in the last half of this chapter has dissuaded them. It takes years to mold a student into the person they are and there are good reasons why they fit into the social landscape where they do. Breaking into a clique is not *impossible* but it isn't necessarily *possible* either.

I knew a guy who was athletic, physically attractive, and intelligent. With respect to *what he was*, he embodied the characteristics valued most by the beer drinking football players with whom he spent a lot of time. Nonetheless, he fell through the cracks because he refused to internalize their culture. It seemed like such a simple fix. His behaviour puzzled me until I learned—much later—that his mother had been an alcoholic.

I was discussing social dynamics with a good friend of mine and I asked her, "If you wanted to join the popular girls from our grade, what would you do?" She replied, "Well, for one thing, I could giggle a lot more." Her answer struck me because, although in a sense it was true, it missed the point. Superficially, my friend wasn't as "girly" as the girls I had compared her too so giggling more would enhance a superficial similarity but faking a true change in personality isn't possible—peers are too smart. Change at a fundamental level is required and unless my friend actually began to interpret the world in the same way as the clique, she would "miss the target" every time she went to giggle.

If a student is destined to be assimilated into the clique of their choice, they will know it because it will seem effortless. If they continuously have to force them self along the path I laid out in the first half of this chapter, I suggest that they consider the possibility that they're fighting a losing battle. Not everyone has the potential to be everything and if the student reflects on the eight challenges discussed in this chapter, they may discover that this includes them. It is painful self-discovery, but the reason why they are not part of a certain clique might be that, fundamentally, they are not one of them. They cannot purposefully set the necessary friendship cycles in motion because they do not share the key qualities that coordinate the clique. If this is the conclusion they come to, there is nothing else to say. Certain things cannot be changed. Life is unfair and sometimes, that's just the way it is.

CHAPTER 11

SOME QUESTIONS
ANSWERED

1. "Why is popularity inevitable in every generation and around the world?"
2. "Why do popular students get away with being arrogant jerks?"
3. "Why are Hollywood Protagonists seemingly so rare?"
4. "Why not stop the popular students from being so exclusive?"
5. "Why are the popular students always in the right place at the right time?"
6. "How do I get him/her to notice me?"
7. "Why can't Wannabes ever be cool?"
8. "Why do girls say they're looking for someone who respects them and then date the guys that don't?"
9. "Why do people ditch old friends to join a clique they don't even like?"
10. "Why can everything I do/say be used against me?"
11. "Where do feelings of righteousness come from when one person is obviously being a bitch?

12. "Why are popular students at risk for early exposure to drugs, alcohol, and sex?"
13. "What's the motivation to gossip?"
14. "How do you know if someone likes you?"
15. "Why do girls and boys get sucked into the beauty myth?"
16. "Why do adults and teachers say that the secret to popularity is being kind to everyone when obviously it's about being good looking?"
17. "Why do popular students talk as if being popular is a 'cold, meaningless, existence'?"
18. "Why do girls sometimes act dumb when they are around boys?"
19. "Why doesn't being smart make you popular?"
20. "Why does sex always complicate things?"
21. "How do I know I've internalized the clique's culture?"
22. "How can I experience popularity in five minutes or less?"

QUESTION 1:
"Why is popularity inevitable in every generation and around the world?"

"I've been to seven different schools in seven different states and it's always the same."—Jason Dean, a character from Heathers

This quote was true in 1988 when *Heathers* was produced, and it is true today. Every generation has its high school movie; each is complete with stereotypical characters as timeless as the plot lines. Why is this? How does popularity rear its ugly head year after year?

The answer cannot be cultural because the phenomenon of popularity is a global phenomenon. One night while having dinner with my family, I asked my parents, "Were there popular kids in your school when you were growing up?" Both emphatically said, "Yes," despite the fact that they were decades older than me and grew up in different parts of the world. My mother is Caucasian and grew up in a predominantly Christian suburb of Vancouver, Canada. My father, on the other hand, is Middle Eastern and from the predominantly Muslim country of Iran. He grew up on a farm outside of Tehran. Even so, both of them knew what I was talking about and were able to relate to what I was saying. Amazingly, the same patterns of social behaviour had been observed by my mother, my father, and even my younger brother, who was in school at the time. What gives?

Popularity is inevitable for three reasons. First, the five facts of life that underlie the Hierarchy of Attraction are timeless and universal, hence why I refer to them as "facts of life" (see Chapter 3). Unless everyone becomes exactly the same or statistics cease to exist, the Hierarchy of Attraction will exist in every social group. Remember, without short people there can be no tall people. Without dumb people there can be no intelligent people. Without ugly people there can be no beautiful people. In short, without unattractive people there can be no attractive people! This statement is as true today as it was when my parents were growing up.

The second reason why popularity is a constant across generations and around the world is because the psychological processes that underlie it are hardwired into the human brain. Input of energy is an evolutionary adaptation innate in all humans. In fact, the experiences of attraction, liking, and attachment are not exclusive to humans. What is the peacock's famous tail other than a beautiful demonstration of attraction and input of energy in action?

The third reason for popularity's timeless universality is that all around the world, educators face the same challenge. Administrators and teachers must effectively and efficiently move a large number of children through a standardized curriculum. The end result is always the recreation of the grade school context described in Chapter 8.

Popularity is not, by any stretch of the imagination, dependent on contemporary inventions such as the Internet or cellphones. Instead, popularity is the timeless by-product of statistics, human nature, and context. Whenever the Hierarchy of Attraction, the innate psychology of humans, and the grade school context are combined, the social phenomenon that is popularity will result.

FOOD FOR THOUGHT:
A PRIMITIVE EMOTION

I was listening to a lecture on the brain when the professor asked, "Can someone give me an example of higher cognitive functioning?"

"Love," a student responded.

"Love, ha. Love is not a higher cognitive function. It is a primitive emotion."

QUESTION 2:
**"Why do popular students get away
with being arrogant jerks?"**

For the record, not all popular students are arrogant. Real life examples of Hollywood Protagonists do exist. Queen Bees and Kingpins, on the other hand, have an uncanny ability to stay atop the social totem pole despite arrogant and cruel behaviour. How do they do it?

The answer lies in the distinction between *liking* and *attraction*. Recall from Chapter 5 that these two feelings are distinct and dissociable. Not only can a student feel one without the other, but they can also experience disconnect between the two. In other words, the student can be attracted to someone they dislike and not attracted to someone they like. Just like compulsive drug seeking behaviour, attraction can compel them to do things that they consciously dislike. The practical implication is that even though a popular student is a jerk, attraction can motivate their victims to repeatedly forgive them. Attractive students are able to get away with bad behaviour because peers keep coming back with more input of energy.

Being attractive is like having a social safety net. To understand what I mean by a "safety net," imagine a stereotypical Queen Bee named Claire. Like every Queen Bee, she parades through the school as if she owns it. To her, friends are just minions and average students are untouchable. One day the popular clique decides that "enough is enough" and together they make a pact to ignore Claire.

Even if the popular clique succeeds in enforcing their agreement on each other, the situation is inherently unstable. Even if all of the boys who know Claire dislike her, they will not be able to repress their attraction to the qualities that made her Queen Bee in the first place. As a result, Claire's isolation will last only until one of the boys can no longer resist the temptation. Realizing that her moment of emotional distress represents his best opportunity to catalyse a relationship, one boy or another will rebel against the popular clique and rush gallantly to her rescue. Unbeknownst to him, all of the other boys are likely to be thinking the same thing and planning to do the same. The sequence of events that will follow is predictable: boys will input energy, male-male rivalries will occur, other girls will become attracted to Claire's renewed social power, and ultimately she will regain all or part of her social status.

Consider this excerpt from the book *Odd Girl Out*. It's a conversation between Rachel Simmons (the author) and Michelle, a member of the popular clique that has just revolted against their Queen Bee, Erin:

> *"But let's assume," [Simmons says], "that Erin would do anything to be forgiven, that she'd promise to be a better friend.*
>
> *"We knew her. We knew that she wasn't going to be. We were all sick of it and we just wanted to get away from it."*
>
> *"What would you rather happened?" [Simmons asks].*
>
> *"Well, she was suffering, but she was getting friends. We wanted her to see what it was like. I mean, subconsciously, we wanted her to see what it was like to not have anybody there, because she needed to".*[76]

Just like in the hypothetical example of Claire, even if Michelle and her popular clique successfully ignored Erin themselves, they found it impossible to isolate her fully. Because she was once popular, we can assume that Erin had attractive qualities that ensured there was always someone willing to give her another chance. Later in the story, Simmons explains that "[Erin] hung out with seniors, got invited to parties, and managed to appear as cool as she had been". In essence, despite the fact that she was ditched by her old clique for being horribly unpleasant, Erin's attractiveness acted as a social safety net.

---

76 Simmons, 2002, p. 94 & 98

No matter how aggressive or awkward they may be at first, attractive students almost always get a second chance. Unattractive students aren't so lucky. If they are aggressive or awkward it leads almost immediately to rejection. Without a social safety net to catch them, they don't get repeated opportunities to practice their social skills.

QUESTION 3:
"Why are Hollywood Protagonists seemingly so rare?"

Although it may be difficult to believe, being wanted by everyone all the time is not always easy. Consider the following lyrics taken from Eminem's song, *The Way I Am*:

> *But at least have the decency in you to leave me alone*
> *When you freaks see me out in the streets*
> *when I'm eating or feedin' my daughter*
> *Do not come and speak to me.*
> *I'm racing, I'm pacing, I stand and I sit*
> *And I'm thankful for every fan that I get*
> *But I can't take a shit in the bathroom*
> *Without someone standing by it.*
> *No I won't sign your autograph*
> *You can call me an asshole*
> *I'm glad cause I am*
> *Whatever you say I am*

Certainly most celebrities can relate to what Eminem is saying. No matter where they go or what they do, people want to talk to them, be near them, take pictures with them, and so forth. Eventually celebrities can become fed up with the attention and stop caring about other people's impressions.

A similar situation occurs with attractive students. No matter where they go, somebody is always sending input of energy their way. Not surprisingly, they begin to lose patience even if they are genuinely nice people because it becomes too difficult to please everyone. What would you do if you were called to go to a movie every night of the week by seven people you didn't care for? If you accept, you have to go to a movie with someone you don't like. Unless you patiently decline each invitation with tact and courtesy, you risk being called a stuck up jerk.

A scene from the movie, *Sixteen Candles*, demonstrates this well. Minutes before her bus stop, the main character Samantha Baker is approached by a boy known only as "Ted the Geek." After getting her attention, he slides into the empty aisle seat next to her and corners her in the window seat. Their conversation is as follows:

Ted: *How's it going?*

Samantha: *How's what going?*

Ted: *You know things, life, what not.*

Samantha: *Life is not whatnot, and it's none of your business.*

Ted: *Hmm... So you goin' to the new faces dance tonight, or...*

Samantha: *That's also none of your business.*

Ted: *[Sniffing the air around her neck] Are you inhibited about dancing in public? I mean, you don't have to dance. Maybe you could just stand there with me and my dudes and just be you, and...*

Samantha: *Sounds major.*

Ted: *[Sniffing the air again] So, I mean, what's the story? I mean, you got a guy, or...*

Samantha: *Yes, three big ones, and they lust wimp blood. So quit bugging me, or I'll sic them all over your weenie ass.*

Ted: *You know, I'm getting input here that I'm reading as relatively hostile. I mean, it's just...*

Samantha:	Go to hell.
Ted:	Whoa... Very hostile. Come on, what's the problem here? I'm a boy, you're a girl. Is there anything wrong with me tryin' to put together some kind of relationship between us?
Samantha:	[Getting up to leave]
Ted:	[Pulling her back down] Look, I know you have to go. Just answer one question...
Samantha:	Yes, you're a total fag.
Ted:	[Laughing innocently and wagging his index finger at her] That's not the question... Am I turning you on?

Be honest, if you had to constantly deal with guys like "Ted the Geek," would you eventually get tired of being bubbly and pleasant to them?

QUESTION 4:
"Why not stop the popular students from being so exclusive?"

Acts of exclusion are, by definition, a passive type of aggression. They do not require action on the part of the perpetrator. Physical and verbal bullying, by contrast, are active forms of aggression because the perpetrator must act to have an effect. Punching someone in the back of the head is active, whereas failing to laugh at someone's joke is passive—the perpetrator has literally done nothing by failing to laugh. Consequently, passive aggression is incredibly difficult to anticipate or notice. Think about it: if a student punches another in the back of the head, a teacher can see what they have done. If, however, the same student fails to laugh at someone's joke, a teacher cannot be mad at them because, after all, they haven't *done* anything. In order to punish them, they would have to prove that their failure to laugh was both intentional and purpose-fully cruel—something that is impossible to do.

Consider an example from the movie *Mean Girls*. During Math class, Cady, the female protagonist, decides to ask the most popular boy, Aaron, a question. After answering her question, Aaron invites Cady to a party. With the charm of a senior heart throb, he gives her the details so she can at-tend. Inviting Cady to the party was not, however, the only course of action Aaron could have taken in this situation. Think about it. What else could he have done? Replace Cady with someone you think Aaron is likely to find *unattractive*. Be honest, do you think that in this new scenario Aaron would have been so quick to invite the girl you have imagined? For a teacher watching the interaction between Aaron and the *un-attractive* girl, Aaron's failure to invite her to the party would be an invisible act of exclusivity. So long as he respectfully answered her question, he has done nothing wrong. In fact, to any observing teacher he has been a model of exemplary behaviour by respectfully helping a peer.

Failure to Act is one of the most powerful social weapons there is. When a student enters a library, for example, they are free to choose any seat available. If they choose the fur-thest possible seat from an unpopular student, no teacher can tell them to do otherwise. After all, there are no rules governing where students must sit in the library. Likewise, when a student walks into a library and finds a popular stu-dent already sitting, there is no reason for a teacher to inter-vene when input of energy compels the student to seek prox-imity. Without doing anything wrong, the student's choice to sit away from the unpopular student yet close to the popular student has reinforced the social order of their school.

Some school teachers have tried and failed to prevent stu-dents from "failing to act." Valentine's Day at an elementary school is an excellent example. If students are left to their own devices, how do you think the valentines would be distributed? Obviously, students atop the Hierarchy will receive a disproportionate number of valentines whereas those at the bottom will be almost completely left out. Years of weepy children on Valentine's Day has taught teachers this valuable lesson. As a result, they often implement the "one valentine per student" rule.

But students are smart. Never underestimate the ingenuity of motivated human beings — even children. To the less popular student, the student body gives the ugliest and most dishevelled of valentines such as a chewed up tennis ball (true story). A less audaciously terrible valentine might say only "To:" and "From:"— nothing more. To the class sweetheart, in contrast, they give the most beautiful and thoughtful: the type that carry a poetic salutation and are complete with a little bag of candy. Theoretically, the rule has worked because every student has received a valentine. In practice, the rule has not made much of a difference.

Rules and/or discipline cannot stop students from acting exclusively and enforcing the boundaries of their cliques. A motivated student, guided by their instincts, will always find ways to preferentially direct their input energy. In short, popular students cannot be "stopped" from acting exclusively.

QUESTION 5:
"Why are the popular students always in the right place at the right time?"

Have you ever noticed that popular students always seem to be in the right place at the right time when it comes to things like finding dance partners? The reason why is simple: it's not because they're lucky, it's because they're benefiting from input of energy.

In the movie *The Sisterhood of the Travelling Pants*, the character Bridget Vreeland is attending a soccer camp coached by the attractive Eric Richman. After communicating her interest by showing off for him during games (a.k.a. input of energy), she makes a final effort to capture his heart one fateful evening. Wearing a pair of beautifully form fitting jeans and a button up shirt tied in the middle over a colourful blue bra, she walks suggestively by his window late one night. Noticing her, he gets out of bed and follows her to the moon swept beach. There, she gives herself to him and he takes her virginity.

Eric is motivated to get out of bed and pursue Bridget because he finds her attractive. Think about how this would have played out if Bridget was replaced by someone Eric did not find attractive. Do you think he still would have gotten out of his nice, warm bed and followed her to the beach? He no doubt would have rolled over and reminded himself that relationships between coaches and players are strictly forbidden.

It's only an illusion that popular students are lucky enough to always be in the right place at the right time. It's not because they're luckier in choosing where to be at what time—it's because they're benefiting from input of energy. Others are constantly making a special effort to be around them at key times.

QUESTION 6:
"How do I get him/her to notice me?"

My most secret desire is that one of them will notice me, look at me like they're seeing me for the first time. Like in the movies, I'll be standing around with my friends in the school hallway,

*then the crowd will part and Pete or Cory will walk over and say
"Hey." Just like that. — Aislan Hunter*[77]

In the book *How to Be Popular*, Meg Cabot suggests that if girls
like Aislan want to get noticed, all they need to do is smile.[78]
I have to disagree. A student who asks, "How do I get them
to notice me?" is really asking why the popular students are
always in the right place at the right time. With respect to
Aislan, I would argue that both Pete and Cory noticed her a
long time ago. Unfortunately for her, they're simply not interested and failing to act in response to her overtures.

If a student wants to get noticed, they have to be attractive to the person they're pursuing. As always, I use the word
"attractive" in the broadest sense. An interpersonal attraction
can develop for numerous reasons. Regardless, a word of caution to students: some things aren't meant to be. Even though
it's easy to imagine what a student can do to become more attractive in general, it is impossible to know what they need to
do in order to be more attractive to one person in specific.

QUESTION 7:
"Why can't Wannabes ever be cool?"

Every class has Wannabes. They're the students that surround
the popular clique and beg to be accepted. They'll do anything to gain social status, including automatically agreeing
with the opinions of popular students and mimicking their
behaviour. They're quick to do favours, and even though
they're routinely left out of the popular clique's activities
they continue to cling tenaciously to whatever relationships
they have with its members. Despite their best efforts, they

---

77 Hunter, 2010, p. 89
78 Cabot, 2006, p. 137

just can't get it right. What's the deal? Why can't Wannabes ever be cool?

Wannabes often wear the same clothes and engage in the same activities as popular students but never really attain the adjective "cool" because it's not based on anything objective. There is nothing inherent in a particular object or action that makes it "cool" and this is why the definition changes so easily from generation to generation.

As explained in Chapter 4, people's perceptions of "cool" are easily influenced by attraction. Consider, for example, what happens when an innovative hairstyle appears on television. If a popular student mimics it, input of energy compels their peers to perceive it as "cool." In contrast, when a Wannabe mimics it, they are likely to be perceived as "trying too hard." Whether or not something is perceived as "cool" is dependent on a student's prior social status and not the object or action itself. This is why Wannabes and Misfits are never considered "cool" even if they mimic the style or behaviour of popular students perfectly.

In *How to Be Popular*, Meg Cabot gives the following advice to students seeking popularity:

> *Examine those in your social circle who are more popular than others. Study them. See where they go. Observe what they do and how they behave. Analyze what they wear. Listen to what they talk about.*
>
> *These people are your role models. Without "copying them" (no one likes a copycat!), try to be more like them.*[79]

To a certain extent, I agree with Meg Cabot because she is advocating the internalization of clique culture—something that I emphasized in the previous chapter. I would like to add, however, that unless a student is attracting their own

---

79 Cabot, 2006, p.63

input of energy, mimicking the culture of the popular students makes them a Wannabe—not popular.

QUESTION 8:
"Why do girls say they're looking for someone who respects them and then date the guys that don't?"

In a scene from the movie *Carrie*, the beautiful Chris Hargensen arrives at a party with the bad boy, Billy Nolan. They've just had a fight and the mood is tense as he parks the car. Billy opens the car door and quickly steps out, but she pulls him back, saying "Don't be in such a hurry."

"I'm hurrying away from you, you know that!" he responds angrily, "You're a right pain in the ass."

Despite Billy's temper, Chris manages to pull him back into the car and calm him down with a suggestive twist of her lips around his finger. They start kissing, but when Billy gets impatient and tries for too much too soon, she pushes him away and shouts, "Dumb shit!" Billy Nolan responds by slapping her.

"I thought I told you never to call me that! You know, you are totally fucked up! That's it, I'm convinced," he yells.

Why do girls date boys like Billy Nolan? In her work with students, Rosalind Wiseman has actually asked girls this question. Plain and simple, their answer is, "We are confused".[80] Although they might not be able to explain the neuroscience, their answer is actually correct.

Girls who fall into this trap are experiencing a "confusion" at the fundamental level of biochemical neural impulses. Recall that there is a difference between *attraction* and *liking* and that unconscious desire influences human behaviour.

---

80 Wiseman, 2002, p. 186

When you ask someone to describe what they're looking for in a boy/girlfriend, their answer will likely contain some combination of the following adjectives: respectful, courteous, thoughtful, kind and/or considerate. In general, these are the qualities that cause us to *like* a person. What students don't realize is that what they are *attracted* to is often more important than what they *like* and the true cause of their behaviour. Recall from Chapter 5 that *attraction* works its magic deep inside the brain along the mesolimbic pathway—the same circuit that controls the experience of wanting. This "wanting" circuitry is so deeply rooted that it can influence behaviour without conscious awareness. When this "wanting" circuitry is turned on, the individual may experience an insatiable desire to attain the object of interest without being able to explain why. Think back to the example of the heroin addict who no longer enjoys the drug but continually craves it. When it comes to interpersonal relationships, the implication is that we can be *attracted* to a person even though we don't *like* them.

If we analyze Billy Nolan, perhaps we can uncover what motivates Chris to date him despite the fact that he is a "dumb shit." For one thing, Billy has a rebellious persona: he drives recklessly, dabbles in drugs and alcohol, and owns his own car. To top it off, he is portrayed by a young John Travolta. Does this description sound familiar? If you can't picture Billy Nolan, swap his image with that of Johnny Depp playing piano as discussed in Chapter 3. Can you guess what these two men have in common? In an episode *The Simpsons*, Bart answers the question best. Speaking about Jimbo Jones he says, "What do you like about him? He's just a good-looking rebel who plays by his own rules." His female audience swoons in response.

The reason girls date attractive jerks is because even if they *dislike* the person, *attraction* motivates them to overlook this feeling. Recall from Chapter 4 that one facet of input of energy is biased interpersonal judgements. Attractive boys get away with being jerks because they are constantly being forgiven for their missteps.

Don't think that this phenomenon is exclusive to girls chasing boys. The same is true when boys bend over backwards to please the Queen Bee. Even if they don't *like* her, *attraction* compels them to behave otherwise.

QUESTION 9:
"Why do people ditch old friends to join a clique they don't even like?"

The answer to this question also lies in the distinction between attraction and liking. More than once, I came across stories of two best friends being torn apart as one friend is mercilessly sucked into the popular clique and the other friend left behind. For the friend offered membership, the choice is irresistible because the clique is incredibly attractive. Just like in individual relationships, however, attraction does not necessarily guarantee liking. The confession of an anonymous author demonstrates the point. Speaking about her old friend, she says:

> So here I am hating the only person who really wants to hang
> with me. The group I do hang with is made up of me, a pretty
> annoying guy, another girl, and her boyfriend, who happens to
> be one of the two guys I'm in love with.[81]

For girls stuck in this anonymous author's situation, the choice is difficult. On one hand, the popular clique is

irresistibly attractive even if some of its members are disliked. On the other hand, a true friend must be sacrificed
in order to stick with them. Just like drug addicts, students
often make the wrong choice.

QUESTION 10:
"Why can everything I do/
say be used against me?"

In social conflicts the currency of success is the hearts and
minds of peers, which can be easily swayed and biased. If
a student is in a situation where everything they do/say is
used against them, it's because in social conflicts nothing is
necessarily factual, logical, or objective. The only thing that
matters is who the majority of their peers side with. As long
as their adversary is benefiting from input of energy, peers
will side preferentially with the adversary whether or not
their jabs against the student are justified, unjustified, right,
wrong, upside down, or backwards.

If a merciless Queen Bee, for example, decides to call another student a "slut," they cannot retaliate by calling her a
"slut" even if her number of sexual encounters outnumbers
their own. The Queen Bee is benefiting from input of energy,
therefore bystanders will habitually side with her. As soon as
the motivational part of their brain is hijacked, all of their
rational will be lost. Attraction compels them to ignore logic.
Rosalind Wiseman succinctly states, "Breasts are power".[82].
Winning a relational war with someone who is attractive is
almost impossible because the student body is rarely, if ever,
motivated by feelings of justice and equity. The unfortunate
reality is that even if a Queen Bee or Kingpin is completely
unprovoked in their aggression, it doesn't matter. They can

---

82 Wiseman, 2002, p.67

start petty conflict after petty conflict and tear a less prominent student apart mercilessly while still enjoying the support of their peers.

If a student has been unfortunate enough to be targeted for clique expulsion, they probably have some appreciation for what it is like to have everything used against them. First, the student may notice that the perpetrator begins to laugh mercilessly at the mistakes they make and that they have become the target of every hurtful joke. If the student becomes fed up and decides to confront their tormentor directly, they will likely be accused of taking it poorly. The perpetrator may retreat behind a retort such as, "I was only joking." If the student continues to confront the perpetrator, they will likely be accused of being too clingy and further ignored for being "too sensitive."

Behind the petty insults and disagreements is the fact that the perpetrator's ultimate goal is to exclude the student from the group. Nothing will suffice until the student is no longer part the clique. All of the jabs are just manifestations of a deeper, more sinister goal.

QUESTION 11:
"Where do feelings of righteousness come from when one person is obviously being a bitch?"

One of the most uncomfortable psychological positions to be in is known as "cognitive dissonance." It occurs whenever an individual cannot reconcile their beliefs and attitudes with their own behaviour. The human mind is designed to keep us happy and content and so instead of confronting our own hypocrisy, humans reflexively engage in a process of mental justification when faced with cognitive dissonance. In plain language, people lie to themselves in order to justify their own behaviour and they do it without even knowing it! As discussed in Chapter 4, all humans are excellent liars, so feelings of self-righteousness are an innate human reflex.

In the novel *How to Be Popular*, the protagonist Stephanie Landry demonstrates how the process of mental justification can take place. At several points, she explicitly expresses the antagonism she feels towards her arch rival Lauren Moffat. "It's Lauren Moffat I want to see go down. And WILL see go down if there is any justice in this world!" she tells the reader on page 181.

Stephanie has good justification for hating Lauren. After all, Lauren is her principle tormentor and the cause of her bad reputation at their school. Regardless of whether Stephanie is correct is ultimately irrelevant. In her mind, she feels justified for engaging in various acts of underhanded aggression. A perfect example comes when, after becoming part of what she calls the "A-crowd," Stephanie blames the "B-crowd" girls' aggression on jealousy.

> *And I was one of them. I was an A-crowder, one of the beautiful, popular people. I had made it. And everyone knew it. I could feel their gazes on me—Courtney Pierce and Tiffany Cushing and all those other girls who, B-crowders at best, had still taken every opportunity to say, "Don't pull a Steph Landry" within my hearing. They were jealous. I knew they were jealous.*[83]

The sad irony is that every girl, including "the bad guy" Lauren Moffat, feels equally justified in their own aggression and therefore won't hold back when it comes time to retaliate. How do you think someone like Lauren Moffat explains Stephanie's constant antagonism towards her? She'll prob-

---

ably think something along the lines of, "Stephanie's just a jealous B-crowder at best."

What a student needs to know is that even if it is apparent to everyone else, total jerks/bitches often believe that they are justified in their actions—they are sincerely clueless as to their own wrongdoing. As Rosalind Wiseman writes,

> Girls will almost always blame their behaviour on something or someone else. Let's say your daughter is accused of spreading a rumour. Instead of admitting her guilt, she'll demand to know who exposed her as the information source, as if the snitch were the person who's really at fault—conveniently forgetting that she was the one who gossiped.

The practical, take home message, is twofold. One, a student can assume that their adversaries feel justified in what they are doing and two, they are probably not 100% innocent either. In the words of an anonymous Queen Bee: "I'm never mean to people without a reason".[84] Neither is anyone else.

QUESTION 12:
"Why are popular students at risk for early exposure to drugs, alcohol, and sex?"

People underestimate how much the situation can influence behaviour.[85] Even the most disciplined and good intentioned students can be undone by situational factors such as peer pressure. Being at a party where everyone is drinking can be incredibly difficult. The same is true of drugs and sex.

Corporate marketers know that in order to influence the behaviour of consumers, they must consider what are called the "Four Ps of Marketing." These are *product, promotion, price,*

---

84 Wiseman, 2002, p. 112 & 122
85 See Wilson, 2002, p. 71

and *place*. *Product* refers to the object or service being sold. *Promotion* refers to the advertisements used to sell the product. *Price*, obviously, refers to the cost and *place* refers to the distribution or availability of the product. By altering any one of the "Four Ps," marketers can influence sales. For our purposes, the most relevant "P" is place. Marketers know that by making their product more accessible and by widening its distribution, consumers will buy more even if the product, promotion, and price remain constant. This is why Coca-Cola uses vending machines: increased accessibility means increased consumption. The same is true of drugs, alcohol, and sex. The more accessible they are the more likely students are to experiment with them.

Popular students are generally the most attractive. As a result, input of energy ensures that they have constant access to places where drugs, alcohol, and sex are prevalent—namely parties. Quite simply, when everybody wants you, there is an abundance of invitations to events where experimentation is likely to occur. Receiving numerous invitations is analogous to coming across vending machine after vending machine. Under these circumstances, even if nothing else changes, the consumption of drugs, alcohol, and sex will increase.

Think about the opposite situation: imagine a student who does not receive any invitations and instead spends Friday night knitting with her mother. Under these circumstances, she's unlikely to experiment because her access to drugs, alcohol, and sex has decreased.

QUESTION 13:
"What's the motivation to gossip?"

In addition to being places of learning, schools can be a lot like soap operas. Everyone is interested in the latest intrigue, including such juicy tidbits as who hooked up with whom, who wasn't invited to a party, and so on. If a student is the holder of privileged information, they possess something others want and they become attractive, at least momentarily, as a result. As expected, this means that they get to benefit from input of energy. Juicy gossip, therefore, can be a resource just like physical attractiveness. Consider the following quote:

> *Gossip is like money. We exchange it, sell it, and lend it out. It's what we have of value.—Jane*[86]

In the game of popularity, the more resources a student controls, the more attractive they become and the more input of energy they receive. In addition to its uses as a weapon, gossip can be used as a way to climb the Hierarchy in the short term.

QUESTION 14:
"How do you know if someone likes you?"

By now, you should know that the word "like" is ambiguous in the context of the above question. Liking is the personal experience of pleasure so unless a student can read someone else's thoughts, it isn't possible for them to know how much they are liked. I suspect that the real question most students want to ask is, "How do you know if someone is *attracted* to you?" Answering this is much easier.

If a student wants to know if someone is attracted to them, the trick is to look for patterns of behaviour that demonstrate input of energy directed at them. In Chapter 4, there is a detailed list of the different forms that input of energy

86 Wiseman, p. 121

takes: attempts at proximity, subtle changes in body language, indirect changes in verbal communication, the quality/content of conversation, helping behaviour, attitudinal changes, social influence, and cognitive intrusion. If someone is attracted to a student, they can expect to notice these patterns of behaviour.

The reason a student must look for *patterns* is because one or two instances of input of energy are insufficient evidence of an underlying attraction. There are many times when someone can be momentarily attracted to someone else; for example, when a juicy piece of gossip is known or there is a need to borrow money. Being romantically attracted, in contrast, represents a whole other level of feeling. In this case, the student is looking for convincing evidence of a stable underlying attraction. If someone is romantically attracted to them, they should be able to find evidence of input of energy over a longer period of time. To know for sure, the responses of their person of interest must be consistent and predictable. In other words, a pattern.

Whenever a student is looking for input of energy, it's useful for them to keep in mind a simple rule of thumb I like to use: "talk is cheap but behaviour rarely lies." People are often shy and don't want to let the world know what they are truly thinking or feeling. They'll say things to purposefully mislead their peers in order to maintain privacy. Luckily for students, behaviour is significantly more difficult to fake. If a student pays attention to what people actually *do* and not just what they *say*, the feelings of even reserved students can be read.

In a scene from the movie *Ten Things I Hate About You*, Patrick Verona (a classic heart throb) takes a seat at the bar during a live concert. While pretending to mind his own business, the girl he's been pursuing, Kat, comes up behind him and angrily says, "If you're planning on asking me out again, you might as well get it over with!" In this scene, Patrick knows that what Kat says really doesn't matter—it's her behaviour that counts. Imagine that Kat had "failed to act" and *not* come up behind Patrick. Instead, after noticing him she simply walked away (after all, walking away was an option). Kat tries to hide her true feelings by adding an annoyed tone to her voice but it is no use. She sought proximity voluntarily and behaviour rarely lies.

I use input of energy (or lack thereof) to guide my interactions with others all the time. Several years ago, there was a girl in my organic chemistry lab that I really wanted to get to know. The problem was I didn't know if the feeling was reciprocal. To find out, I did exactly as I have suggested. A couple of times in casual conversation, I mentioned how the *24 Hour Study Lounge* had become my favourite place to study. I would joke that it was my "second home." Then, over the next couple days I watched to see if she started coming to the 24 Hour Study Lounge more often than before. When I noticed the frequency of her visits increase, I grew bolder in our interactions during lab. When late on a Friday afternoon she came in and sat down once again, I decided that I'd seen enough. I waited between five and ten minutes before confidently approaching her and asking, "Do you ever go look at the art over by the stairwell? I've been sitting here studying for too long, would you like to go look at it with me?" Apparently she did—who knew?

FOOD FOR THOUGHT:
A SLIPPERY SLOPE

Few things could be more fraught with bias and misinterpretation than trying to understand what somebody thinks of us or the things we do. As great as it is to accurately predict the feelings of another person, it's a very slippery slope if a student gets into the habit of always "reading between the lines." Once, I found myself walking home with two of the "cool" kids and, during our conversation, one of them started saying something about "three good friends" hanging out together. Because I didn't consider myself one of them, the first thing out of my mouth was, "Who are you referring to?"

"Well," he replied, "there are only three of us here..."

QUESTION 15:
"Why do girls and boys get sucked into the beauty myth?"

Books like *The Beauty Myth* vilify the media and blame it for causing girls to chase an unrealistic standard of beauty. The problem with these arguments is that they ignore human nature. Within every human infant is the tendency to prefer physically attractive faces[87] and this predisposition carries throughout life. Putting all the blame on the media is naively simplistic. The relationship between society and the media is better understood as reciprocal:

---

87 Ramsey et al., 2004

society responds positively to beauty because of innate psychology →
advertisers take advantage of this to sell their products →
mass media reinforces a culturally defined concept of beauty →

society's innate psychology is reinforced →
advertisers take advantage →
and so on...

In *Queen Bees and Wannabes*, Wiseman puts words to her frustration that girls participate in what she calls "the beauty pageant" generation after generation.

> *Your daughter knows that the girls in the magazines are air-brushed and probably have fake boobs, but it doesn't stop her from comparing herself to them and feeling inadequate. Girls know that if Barbie were life-size, her body would be so out of proportion that she wouldn't be able to walk. Girls know that magazines, TV, and movies are in the business of making girls feel insecure so they'll buy their products. They know companies are advertising in all three so that girls will buy their products. Yet in spite of their awareness and sophistication, they still get sucked in.*[88]

It's not that people are getting "sucked in" to the beauty pageant. In fact, the desire to be beautiful is a logical response to the patterns of behaviour in the social environment. Even though students cannot put words to their feelings, somehow they know that beautiful people benefit more from input of energy than others. As a result, they are intuitively aware of how important it is to be physically attractive without ever having studied psychology. If writers such as Naomi Wolf want to destroy "the beauty pageant," they need to change humanity's collective and innate response to beauty. There is

---

88 Wiseman, 2002, p.81

no question that the media influences and perpetuates culturally defined conceptions of beauty but it is naive to think that the problem will go away if corporations and their "evil advertisers" are abolished.

QUESTION 16:
"Why do adults and teachers say that the secret to popularity is being kind to everyone when obviously it's about being good looking?"

First of all, *popularity is not about being good looking* — it's about being attractive in the broadest sense of the word. Attraction is not synonymous with beauty and I cannot emphasize this enough! Similarity, socioeconomic status, and efficacy are also important. Old wrinkly men and brutish looking athletes would never manage to attract lovely young women if money and efficacy didn't count for something.

Second, popularity is only a third of the story. Being popular is not the same as being liked. Adults tell you to "be nice to everyone" because they are confusing the consequences of *liking* with those of *attraction*. By basing their advice on the wrong definition of popularity—being well liked—they're unknowingly focusing on axes 2 and 3 of Figure 2.5 (liking and disliking). What they don't realize is that being nice to everyone makes you well liked but it does not necessarily make you popular.

QUESTION 17:
"Why do popular students talk as if being popular is a 'cold, meaningless, existence'?"

Yeah, being popular was all I ever wanted, but who knew that behind all the smiles were cold, empty hearts? So this was what it was like to be truly popular.—Demi Chang[89]

Almost everyone would do anything to be part of the popular crowd, but once people get there they talk as if it's some sort of terrible curse. What's the deal?

Popularity can feel cold and superficial because when everyone wants an individual all the time, talking with peers can be like interacting with "yes men." Even friends can seem superficial and phony because the popular student is never entirely sure what the true motivations of their "friends" are: perhaps peers are just using the student to be popular themselves; maybe its sex that's on their mind. It can be difficult to know for sure.

QUESTION 18:
"Why do girls sometimes act dumb when they are around boys?"

Helping behaviour is one of the forms that input of energy takes and it's a favourite among boys looking to impress an attractive girl. Acting dumb facilitates male overtures by giving boys an opportunity to be helpful and thereby demonstrate efficacy. Interpersonal relationships are an intricate dance and "acting dumb" is one demonstration of this.

QUESTION 19:
"Why doesn't being smart
make you popular?"

Popularity is dependent on being attractive and being attractive is dependent on holding the keys to other people's wants and desires. In grade school, getting good grades is not the highest priority for most students—neither is getting married. Being intelligent might make a student a good study partner, but this is a paltry asset when the majority of students are more interested in the immediate and tangible. Intelligence is a good predictor of future employment and socioeconomic status, but this is of little consequence to adolescents. Unfortunately for those who score high with respect to intelligence, other qualities like physical attractiveness are more relevant in grade school.

QUESTION 20:
"Why does sex always complicate things?"

Sex couldn't be more intuitive. The percentage of young lovers who grope their way to success on the first try must be close to 100%. Sex and sexual arousal, it turns out, are actually incredibly complicated. Consider the following two descriptions, pertaining to males and females respectively:

> "Physiological sexual arousal in males involves the regulation of penile hemodynamics that is dependent on signal input from central and peripheral nervous systems, and on a complex interplay between neurotransmitters, vasoactive agents, and endocrine factors. Within the penile sinusoidal tissue is a central artery and veins that exit and drain the erectile bodies. The

*smooth muscles that line the sinusoidal spaces and the central
artery are tonically contracted during the flaccid state."*

*"Physiological sexual arousal in women begins with increased
clitoral length and diameter, and vasocongestion of the vagina,
vulva, clitoris, uterus, and possibly the urethra. Comparable
to the penis, the corpora cavernosa of the clitoris consists of a
fibroelastic network and bundles of trabecular smooth muscle.
Pelvic nerve stimulation results in clitoral smooth muscle relaxa-
tion and arterial smooth muscle dilation."[90]*

Who knew that sex was so complicated?

As illustrated in these quotations, the experience of sexual arousal involves a cascade of hormonal and neurological
events—and that's just arousal! The act itself is also incredibly
complex when analyzed in detail. During sex, natural chemicals of all sorts surge through veins and arteries of partners
and permeate every part of their bodies. Even orgasm, the
final explosion of pleasure that caps the sexual experience,
has its own physiological signature.

Of particular importance to the current discussion is the
hormone oxytocin. Oxytocin is a special type of hormone
because it acts as a "neuro-modulator." This means that once
it gets inside the brain, it affects the way an individual thinks.
Unsurprisingly, this can have a major impact on cognition.

One of oxytocin's major functions is the formation of
pair bonds between individuals. This can be the bond between mother and child or between romantic couples. One
of the ways oxytocin achieves this is by altering memory of
events. Adam Guastella, Philip Mitchell, and Frosso Mathews
demonstrated this by administering oxytocin to 69 male
volunteers and then presenting them with a slide show of

90 Meston & Frohlick, 2000

happy, angry, and neutral faces.[91] What they found was that participants who had oxytocin administered were more likely to remember the happy faces. Based on these results, they speculated "that oxytocin could enhance social approach, intimacy, and bonding in male humans by strengthening encoding to make recall of positive social information more likely." In other words, oxytocin makes you focus on and remember the good times.

Research on how oxytocin works is still emerging but one thing is already certain: this hormone is one of the primary chemicals responsible for the modulation and creation of attachment relationships. It turns out that during sex (and especially orgasm) the brain loves to flood the body with oxytocin. As a result a person is literally out of their right mind in moments of sexual pleasure. Even if what they had in mind was a one-night-stand prior to the encounter, physiologically their body is laying the foundation for a long term relationship with whoever happens to be with them at the time. The morning after, the person and/or their partner might find it inexplicably difficult to move on. Physiology can't tell the difference between protected and unprotected sex meaning that by default it assumes a goal of procreation. Child rearing is a long term endeavour and the body has evolved ways of locking partners in for the long haul even if they had something else in mind.

Oxytocin is just one way that the body primes people to form attachment relationships with their sexual partners:

> [S]exual arousal (and orgasms) deactivate a region in the frontal cortex that overlaps the deactivated region observed in romantic love. This is perhaps not surprising, given that humans often take "leave of their senses" during sexual arousal, perhaps

even inducing them to conduct which they might later, in more sober mood, regret.[92]

In plain language, interpersonal judgements of sexual partners become less critical in the moment. As such, faults and foibles which would have prevented a long term relationship prior to sex might suddenly seem irrelevant in the morning light.

As intuitive as sex is, it's not something to be taken lightly if one or both partners are planning on moving on. With so many cascading physiological and psychological effects, sex complicates things. There are good reasons why two long-time friends who agree to be "more than friends" might find it impossible to go back to the way things were—their brains fundamentally altered after just one night of reckless abandon.

QUESTION 21:
"How do I know I've internalized the clique's culture?"

A student who decides to internalize another clique's culture may be curious to know how they can tell when they have changed at a fundamental level and that *who they are* is different. The trick to knowing change has occurred is by considering specific events from the past. If a student thinks to them self, "In that specific situation, I can't believe I thought that way. I never would have done/thought that now," they'll know that there has been change to the core of *who they are*. Personality is guided by interpretation of the world. A different interpretation of an event is evidence of fundamental change.

---

92 Zeki, 2007

QUESTION 22:
"How can I experience popularity in five minutes or less?"

If a student wants to experience popularity, all they need to do is attract input of energy and then appreciate it for what it is. The first step is to become attractive. As discussed in Chapter 3, this means holding the keys to someone else's wants or desires. An easy way to do this is by going to a store where the staff is paid on commission, such as a big box electronic retailer. In this context, shoppers hold the keys to the employee's primary desire, getting paid. As such, consumers can expect to be the recipients of input of energy.

Once there, the student can start by meandering down any aisle. Unless it's very busy in the store, it shouldn't take more than five minutes before a sales rep approaches. Once they have the rep's attention, the curious student can make a game out of asking for favours such as requesting a catalogue, holding bags, or taking a computer down from the top shelf. So long as it's within reason, it doesn't really matter what specific favour(s) are requested. The rep will do it because input of energy compels them to (those who are really desperate for cash might even do it with a smile!). If the student wants a direct comparison, they can try telling the sales rep a bad joke that none of their friends at school thought was funny. If the sales rep laughs, that student has just experienced what it's like to be popular.

It can be argued that it's not attraction which compels a sales rep to help the student but rather an employment contract. I would agree that calling it "attraction" is a stretch especially if the employee is not being paid on commission. The point, quite simply, is that the experience is similar to being popular. Even if the sales rep doesn't *like* the student, they will still put up with them because they want to get paid. When a busty Queen Bee stares down a school hallway full of adolescent boys it's a comparable situation—they might not *like* her but they still put up with her because they want to get laid.

CHAPTER 12

PRACTICAL
ADVICE AND
CONCLUSIONS

E ven years after graduating from high school, I cannot help but sigh. How fantastic it would have been to live out the high school dream as "that guy:" the one whose smile melted every girl's heart; the one who could do and say nothing wrong; the one who swaggered confidently through the halls high-fiving friends along the way. Studying and writing about popularity has taught me that I'm not the only one who has felt this way. Let there be no doubt, concern with popularity dominates the minds of grade school students.

Nothing about the theory of popularity that I have proposed is overly complex or conceptually difficult to understand. In fact, the most common criticism I receive in regards to my theory is that "it's all so obvious." If this was the case, why is it that overly simplistic explanations and muddled snippets of advice are still common in the media and on the Internet? An excerpt from Wikihow demonstrates:

> *What do all popular people have in common? Do they all wear the same clothes? Have the same hair? Say the same things? Of*

course not. There are popular people all over the world, enjoying their social status at school, work, and wherever they go. They don't all look or act like each other—but they do all share one very crucial characteristic: people skills.[93]

One of my primary motivations for writing this book was the lack of coherent and meaningful advice available for people seeking explanations. Broad over-generalized statements like the one above overlook important considerations and have convinced me that it's not "all so obvious." If people skills were all that mattered, why do Resigned Socialites never become popular?

Popularity is not, in fact, dependent on having excellent social skills and being liked by many. Instead it is the result of students atop of the Hierarchy of Attraction receiving a disproportionate amount of input of energy. Popularity is less about being well liked than it is about being attractive.

That being said, to focus solely on attraction would be as much of a mistake as focusing solely on being well liked. As depicted in Figure 2.5, it takes three dimensions to fully represent the social landscape: 1) how much the individual is liked; 2) how much the individual is disliked; and 3) how attractive the individual is. A majority of advice is unsatisfactory because it unknowingly focuses on only one-third of the puzzle: being well liked. Being kind and respectful, smiling at everyone, and being true to yourself are all excellent ways to be liked, but this is not synonymous with being popular. Of course, it is worth reiterating that being very popular is not synonymous with being well liked either.

---

93 Wikihow, 2013

IF I WAS TO DO IT OVER AGAIN, I WOULD...

...USE A MORE ACCURATE DEFINITION OF "POPULAR" AND "POPULARITY."

Definitions of "popular" and "popularity" based around "being well liked by many" are wrong. More accurate definitions are as follows:

Popularity: *noun,* 1) A hierarchical social phenomenon associated primarily with grade school; 2) The disproportionate receipt of preferential treatment in the form of input of energy.

Popular: *adjective,* A label given to people who have (or seem to have) achieved popularity.

...ACCEPT THOSE THINGS I CANNOT CHANGE.

There is no question that physical appearance matters. Time and time again, it is cited as the most important determinant of attraction in junior high and high school. Not surprisingly, this research got me thinking, "How physically attractive am I?" Although I don't care to answer this question definitively, I have some appreciation for what the answer might be based on objective observations.

No matter how hard I try, I can never get my glasses to sit level across my face because one of my ears is slightly lower than the other. Although this asymmetry is not glaringly obvious, it's important because symmetry is a major determinant of physical attractiveness.

Theoretically, if it really bothered me, cosmetic surgery is available. However, surgery is not a feasible option for grade school students. Even if it was, nothing is perfect. Small imperfections are inevitable and other asymmetries would certainly become apparent. The reality is that my appearance will never rival Johnny Depp's—such is life.

So where does this unfortunate fact leave me with respect to popularity? Like everything in life, the answer is that it depends. If I am at a bar where the majority of women are looking for a one-night-stand, my position in the Hierarchy of Attraction decreases because physical attractiveness is the primary determinant of desirability. Under such circumstances I would be naive to believe that popularity is an achievable goal for me.

Under different circumstances the outlook for me is not necessarily bleak. Currently I am studying medicine and when I finish I can expect to earn a respectable income. If I attend a conference of small charities and not-for-profit organizations sometime after graduation, do you think my asymmetrical ears will make any difference? Of course not. Representatives from charities and not-for-profit organizations are looking for donations and it's my income that they're interested in. They couldn't care less about my ears! In this situation, socioeconomic status would propel me to the top of the Hierarchy and I could expect to experience the joy of input of energy being disproportionately directed my way.

When it comes to the Hierarchy of Attraction, sometimes a student just doesn't have "it." Even if I could go back in time and relive grades 9 through 12 knowing what I do now, I couldn't expect to be "that guy" even though I wrote a book on popularity, I simply don't embody grade school's most attractive qualities and there's little I can do about that.

If a student is unattractive to their peers but desperately wants to be popular, the unfortunate truth is that they won't achieve it no matter what they do. Even though this might be unsatisfactory advice, it's always commendable to accept what cannot be changed. I am not suggesting that reading this book was a waste of time for parents and educators looking to counsel students seeking popularity. Even though the label "popular" might be currently outside a student's reach, they can still do a lot to improve their social standing and the suggestions that follow are all practical strategies they might try.

...MAKE AN EFFORT WHERE I CAN.

Trying to form an unbiased opinion of them self by acknowledging both strengths and weaknesses is unlikely to be an overly enjoyable experience for most students. No one is perfect and upon self-reflection they're guaranteed to find imperfections. More frustrating than the imperfections can be the fact that there is nothing they can do: life has dealt them a certain hand.

As unfair and frustrating as this might be to a student, I will never suggest complacency or apathy. Even if they may never be the best, brightest, or most beautiful, they should still make the effort. Everyone is always free to improve their circumstances—even if it means doing nothing more than being optimistic.

In the library where I write this, I swear there lives a hermit. He is about 5 foot 8 inches tall and probably weighs about 115 pounds. His hair and beard are medium length, unkempt, and scraggly. Every day he wears a pair of short, navy blue sweat pants and a loose fitting pyjama style shirt. Regardless of the season he wears massive hiking boots. Altogether his choice of clothing combines to create a synergistic attack on all things fashionable. Because his pants are too short and have ankle elastics, about an inch of his socks show above his massive boots. When you see him it's difficult to keep a straight face. Obviously some things this man cannot change—his height, for example. However, it goes without saying that he could most certainly trim his hair and beard and wear more sensible clothing.

If, after a personal assessment, a student is forced to accept that being "popular" is not a realistic aspiration for them in grade school, they shouldn't throw up their hands in despair. Even though they may not embody the qualities that lead to mainstream popularity, giving up and dressing in sweat pants and massive hiking boots will not help. A student can always attend to the little things while keeping in mind that it becomes much easier to find their social niche after high school.

With respect to popularity, it is always advisable to make an effort. In everything a student does, they can try to be engaged, competent, and a well-regarded participant. The qualities that make people attractive are often those that require time and effort to obtain: talent, physical prowess, socio-economic status, and so on. Anything that everyone can do (like play video games) is generally not going to move them up the Hierarchy of Attraction. In contrast, if they can speak two or more languages fluently, they're part of an exclusive club. It takes considerable effort to learn a language so it's not surprising that crowds swoon when a Hollywood star suddenly lets loose something other than their native tongue.[94]

...APPRECIATE THAT THE SOONER I "FIND MYSELF" AND ACCEPT, THE SOONER I'LL SUCCEED SOCIALLY.

Wannabes all share a common problem: they want to fit into the social landscape where they don't and they won't (or cannot) accept this. These students want to have the "right" friends so that they fit in with a very specific group of people. This is, after all, the definition of a Wannabe.

Although Wannabes make up only a small portion of the student population, I think that their social troubles can teach everyone a valuable lesson. Just about every student— I suspect—has been unhappy with their social position at some point in time and wanted to shift their place in the social landscape. As described in Chapter 10, purposefully altering the social landscape is an extreme undertaking because it requires a fundamental and sincere change to *who* and *what* the student is. Not only will they be faced with the Wannabe's Paradox, but they'll also face some combination of the other seven challenges I described in Chapter 10. As a result, anytime a student is unhappy with their social position, they have to choose a course of action somewhere between the following two extremes:

1. They can wait and let fate take its course: the social landscape shifts slowly but it does change over time. It's possible that a student's current problems disappear if they patiently wait them out. An unexpected change in context, for example, might suddenly thrust them into a totally new position in the social landscape. The upside to patiently waiting is that it is, without doubt, the safest and easiest thing to do. It requires that they do nothing but accept their current circumstances and then roll with the punches.

2. If the latter is untenable, a student can try instead to transform into something different and fight their way into a different social niche. The upside to fighting is that there is opportunity for tremendous personal growth and social advancement. The downside, of course, is that they are guaranteed a lengthy period of emotional turmoil of unimaginable intensity.

Changing *who* and *what* they are is a tremendous undertaking with no guarantee of success. It's an emotional gamble of obscene proportions. If successful, life can be good. If not, I promise them that they will be paralyzed by waves of depression as they crash up against things they cannot change.

Neither of the aforementioned extremes is a good choice, so I suggest the following healthier way to strike a balance between the two:

1. The student should take some time to meditate and ponder what they want to be in three years. They can chose a longer or shorter time frame if they'd like but it shouldn't be anything less than one year. They should really try to focus on their own personal interests and aspirations: what do they really enjoy doing and want to do even better?

2. Whatever their personal interest is, they should set a lofty and long-term goal that is non-social in nature. For example; "I want to make a particular sports team;" "learn to play an instrument;" "get a prestigious academic scholarship;" "become an architect;" etc. The goal must be both meaningful to them and realistic given their current circumstances.

3. Before they set out to achieve their goal, a sincere mental note should be made to make interpersonal relationships a priority in their life. It seems to me that all of the Hollywood Protagonists I know value their friendships to an incredible extent. They spend the necessary time and energy in order to cultivate their relationships and this doesn't go unnoticed by their peers.

4. As they strive toward achieving their goal, the student must take advantage of the varied and interesting

social situations that come their way as a natural side effect. By trying to get a scholarship, for example, they might find them self on various student committees where opportunities to hone social skills abound.

5. As opportunities come their way, a constant effort to be conscientious should be made because they are being judged all the time. Social skills cannot be learned from a book. They must learn by doing and it's a constant process of planning, action, and reflection.

6. After one year of striving towards their goal, they can re-assess their position in the social landscape. So long as they stepped out of their comfort zone to achieve a goal different from their status quo, I guarantee that their place in the social landscape will have shifted.

It is not difficult to understand why the above pathway to social success works if the cycle of friendship and the genesis of cliques is considered. As the student focuses on achieving a goal which is non-social in nature, they inevitably discover three things:

1. They meet people as a natural consequence of striving towards something.

2. They are very similar to the people they meet.

3. They start to get really good at whatever it is they do.

In other words, as a by-product of trying to achieve a goal that is non-social in nature, the student will set in motion friendship cycles they never could have predicted. Without making a conscious effort to do so, they'll have achieved the three predictors of friendship—proximity, similarity, and attractiveness—with a whole new group of people!

Let me give an example: let's say that the student has always wanted to do photography. So, taking my advice they decide that in three years, they want to be an excellent photographer. Over the course of a year, they slowly start getting into the hobby and accumulating the necessary equipment. A semester passes uneventfully, but at the outset of the next they choose *Communications Technology* as an option. As a result, they are sure to meet new people (i.e. achieve proximity). Furthermore, many of their new peers will have chosen the same option because they too like photography (i.e. similarity). Finally, because the student has quietly started getting good at photography, they'll already be good at what they do (i.e. they will have achieved efficacy and that's attractive!). If they make a point of being outgoing and social, they have a good chance of being liked by their new peers. With all three predictors of friendship in place, they are likely to make new friends and fall into another social niche. If they are lucky enough to be very attractive, they'll even become popular within their new context.

The reason why I emphasized that the student choose a goal which is long term in nature is because it ensures that their transformation goes unnoticed by potential tormentors who would happily sabotage it. Furthermore, because of problems with time and timing (see Chapter 10), giving them self an ample time line is often a practical necessity. Choosing a goal that is non-social in nature ensures that they won't beg to be included in activities when things don't go their way. That is, when they don't get the invite, they'll be too distracted to care.

The six part strategy that suggested above *will not* make student friends with a *specific* group of people like the seven part strategy I suggested in Chapter 10. That being said, it's a way better choice! Following the advice in this chapter avoids the "Wannabe's Paradox" and potentially all of the other seven challenges I described. If the student wants to shift their place in the social landscape, they should *not* do what I suggested in Chapter 10. The advice in this chapter, without doubt, is a much happier alternative. In my experience, the people who are first to "find" (and accept) themselves are also the first to succeed socially because it is the easiest and safest way to avoid all of the challenges I described.

...NOT SEEK POPULARITY AS IF IT WAS AN ALL OR NOTHING PHENOMENON.

Popularity is often portrayed in the popular media as all or nothing. Although this juxtaposition serves to emphasize the distinction between popular and unpopular characters, it is far from the truth. The experience of popularity is not only for "popular" students, nor is it exclusive to grade school.

The label "popular" itself means little. Hanging out with the popular clique might be enough to win a student the title of "popular," but it won't guarantee them input of energy. If you think about the revised definitions of "popularity" and "popular" that I gave at the beginning of this chapter, the possibility of experiencing "popularity" without actually being labeled "popular" is implied. Popularity is the receipt of disproportionate amounts of input of energy whereas "popular" is a perception by others—nothing more than a title. The implication, therefore, is that anyone can experience "popularity" without formal recognition because the experience comes *before* recognition by others.

In the context of grade school, the label "popular" is used because the social landscape is relatively stable over time. After high school graduation, the majority of social situations change so quickly that the label "popular" becomes meaningless. This is not because people stop experiencing popularity after grade school. Instead it's because the social landscape of adult life generally changes so fast that the public cannot determine who is worthy of the label.

Even though I was never destined to be "that guy" in grade school, this doesn't mean that I will never experience popularity (i.e. disproportionate amounts of input of energy). An example from my university career illustrates the point. I love the natural sciences, so I opted to complete an independent study in biochemistry as one of my degree electives. As part of the final project, I had to present my research at a one day symposium. From early morning to mid-afternoon, student after student stood up and gave a dry and boring presentation. My presentation was (by comparison) a riot: it was direct, funny, and scientifically accurate. It was a beautiful demonstration of efficacy and didn't go unnoticed by the audience. At the break, both students and teachers gravitated towards me. They wanted to talk with me, ask me who I was, and congratulate me on the presentation. For that brief, shining moment, I was experiencing a taste of popularity. So many people were talking to me at once that I had to put some on hold while responding to others. Everyone was so incredibly open and friendly that I felt as if I could do and/or say nothing wrong. After the break, the symposium wrapped up, the crowd dispersed, and my fleeting taste of popularity vanished long before I could ever be deemed "popular."

Perhaps a student, like me, is fated never to be "that guy." If they are, they shouldn't be too disappointed. Think about my guitar playing friend from Chapter 3 who, despite being less popular than most, managed to woo the Swedish exchange student with one demonstration of pure talent.

Consolation for a dissatisfied student may also come from redefining the group of interest. Some, on reflection, may realize that whenever they associate with a particular subset of students (for example, a religious minority) they experience "popularity" but would never be considered "popular" in the context of the entire school. So long as the student knows what to look for, they'll be able to identify when input of energy is being disproportionately directed their way and appreciate it for what it is. Remember: "popularity" isn't just for the "popular" students and this is the number one insight I hope readers take away from this book.

...KNOW MYSELF AND KNOW THE GROUP.

Popularity depends on being attractive and being attractive depends on holding the keys to other people's wants and desires. Therefore, without knowledge of them self and the group, a student cannot hope to predict their potential for popularity. If they want to take control of their social destiny, they can start by considering their strengths and weaknesses and the wants and desires of their peers. If they conclude that their strengths can satisfy the wants of the people around them, they can expect to be highly attractive. If they are forced to conclude, in contrast, that their weaknesses will make them unattractive, they should not expect any miracles.

Early in my undergraduate degree, I attended a party populated by beer drinking hockey players; there I met a guy named Brent who was highly respected among our mutual friends. His name I knew but not his face so when I discovered that I was standing across from him, I held out my hand and introduced myself. He shook my hand but his response was quick and abrupt, "Yeah, I know you. We were in the same biology lab." Taken aback by his tone of voice, I apologized and said, "I'm sorry I must not have noticed you." To which he curtly replied, "Yeah, no doubt. You guys were all dicks and just ignored me."

This story aptly demonstrates how important it is for a student to match their strengths to the social context they're

in. If Brent had known me from the local hockey arena instead of the biology lab, I can assure you that it would have
been *him* ignoring *me*. Students in a biology lab are looking
to ace exams and assignments and, because my strengths are
more academic than athletic, I am more attractive in the context of a laboratory than a rink. Students playing intramural
hockey, on the other hand, are looking to win and because
I'm a dead weight when it comes to hockey, I am less attractive under such circumstances. For me, it's more sensible to
seek the experience of popularity in places such as the undergraduate biology lab instead of the local hockey arena. For
Brent, the exact opposite is true.

One of the suggestions that Meg Cabot gives in *How to Be
Popular* is to cultivate extracurricular interests of all sorts.

> *It doesn't make a bit of difference whether your hobby is sewing,
> gardening, cooking, stamp collecting, or horseback riding. An
> interest makes YOU interesting to others."*[95]

Although I wholeheartedly agree with Cabot that every
one of us should cultivate talents of all sorts, I disagree that
the choice of hobby makes no difference. Matching talents to
the social context is critical for a student looking to experience popularity.

...NOT CONFUSE BEING LIKED WITH POPULARITY OR VICE VERSA.

One of the biggest sources of confusion when it comes to
understanding grade school social dynamics is the distinction
between *liking* and *attraction*. In website after website, movie
after movie, and book after book, authors and screen writers
confuse the effects of being liked by peers with those of being attractive. Remember that how a student relates to others

---

95 Cabot, 2006, p. 184

is what leads to them to being liked or disliked. How others relate to them is what leads to popularity (see Chapter 6).

If a student is popular, they shouldn't believe that people automatically like them because it makes them seem arrogant and out of touch. As demonstrated by Gretchen Wieners' fall from the platform in *Mean Girls*, being popular is not the same as being liked. If it was, her peers would have caught her (see the end of Chapter 7). Without using the modified definitions of "popular" and "popularity" suggested in this chapter, this scene is impossible to explain. If Gretchen is popular, why does no one like her? If no one likes her, why is she so popular? The answer is in the distinction between liking and attraction and the behavioural consequences of both.

...NOT TRY TO ACHIEVE POPULARITY BY BEING NICE TO EVERYONE.

A common mistake is students attempting to achieve popularity by being nice to everyone. Just as popularity doesn't guarantee liking (as exemplified by Gretchen Wieners) liking does not guarantee popularity. In fact, if a student tries too hard to be nice to everyone, the strategy is likely to backfire because desperation makes them unattractive. In practical language, they shouldn't make a show of holding the door, buying coffee, helping carry lightweight objects, apologizing for the smallest things, and so forth in an effort to win friends.

...NOT USE AGGRESSION IN AN ATTEMPT TO GAIN POPULARITY.

The idea that popular students earn their status through acts of calculated strategy is a myth. Popularity is not the result of social manipulation or acts of aggression. Once a student has achieved an elevated place in the Hierarchy of Attraction, they need do little more than wait for input of energy (see Chapter 6).

The reason this myth exists is because Queen Bees and Kingpins are both popular and aggressive and even they might think that their popularity is the result of aggression. Fictional books and movies often perpetuate this myth by fabricating "rise to the top stories" and *Mean Girls* is an excellent example. The main character Cady and her two outcast friends literally devise a plan to "overthrow" the Queen Bee, Regina George. The result is a series of well-planned acts of aggression aimed at Regina that include:

- duplicity on the part of Cady by pretending to be her friend and then gossiping incessantly about all the "dumb stuff" she does;
- petty pranks like giving her foot cream instead of face cream;
- lies so that she eats nothing but protein bars and gains weight;
- maliciously turning her two best friends against her; and
- stealing her boyfriend.

According to the movie, the end result of all these targeted acts of aggression is that Cady becomes the new Queen Bee—the most popular girl in the school. Regina, on the other hand, is banished from the head table in the cafeteria and made a laughing stock. Implied by the script is that aggression leads to popularity.

When considering grade school social dynamics, think of *popularity* and *liking* as largely independent social constructs. Aggression does not cause popularity nor prevent it. The notion that exclusivity is required in the pursuit of popularity is mistaken and the Hollywood Protagonists amongst us prove this every day.

Ultimately, aggression will always lead to dislike but popular students get away with it because input of energy compels their peers to forgive them (see Chapter 10, question 2). For unpopular students, however, the idea that popularity can be usurped from others is a dangerous misconception and *un*attractive students who act aggressively in an attempt to do so will find that it backfires by giving popular students an excuse to retaliate.

...KNOW WHEN NOT TO FEAR THREATS OF RELATIONAL AGGRESSION.

In the movie *Heathers*, the Queen Been Heather invites Veronica to an exclusive party. One too many drinks later, Veronica starts to feel sick and pleads with Heather to take her home. Instead, Heather berates Veronica for rejecting one of the college boy's sexual advances and refuses to leave. Unable to hold her sickness and livid at how she's being treated, Veronica vomits all over the floor and then storms out of the house. Heather confronts her outside and shouts angrily, "You stupid fuck!"

"You Goddamn bitch," Veronica retorts.

"You were nothing before you met me. You were playing Barbies with Betty Finn. You were a bluebird, a brownie, a Girl Scout cookie. I got you into a Remington party. And what's my thanks? It's on the hallway carpet. I got paid in puke!"

"Yeah, well lick it up baby, lick it up."

"Monday morning you're history [Veronica]. I'll tell everyone about tonight. Transfer to Washington, transfer to Jefferson, no one at Westerberg is going to let you play their reindeer games."

If this situation played out in real life, what power does Heather really have over Veronica? Can she really cause the type of social humiliation and isolation she threatens? The reality is that Heather can't do much. Veronica is attractive in her own right because she's intelligent, sociable, physically attractive, and wealthy. She embodies all of the qualities that place her high in the Hierarchy of Attraction and, as a result, benefits from input of energy in the same way Heather does. In this situation, the Heather's power is limited because she's faced with an equally attractive rival. No matter what slanderous and vicious rumours she spreads, input of energy will compel other students to overlook any social blunder Veronica might make. Even without Heather, Veronica would continue to receive party invitations and other positive attention from her peers.

Because they have so much social influence, popular students begin to think that they control the school's social scene. The truth, however, is that input of energy is a fickle thing. As soon as a more attractive student comes along, allegiances can shift. By understanding the cause of popularity, a student will be able to call "bullshit" on threats such as Heather's.

...BE CREATIVE IN MY APPLICATION OF THE THEORY.

I miss grade school. I really do. Even if I was never destined to be "that guy," I loved the intrigue, the politics, and the fascinating demonstrations of social behaviour. Sometimes, I flip nostalgically through my notebooks and reminisce about nights spent perplexed by the phenomenon that is popularity.

I'll never get to re-live grade school, but human nature remains the same after graduation, which means that understanding the psychological "rules of the game" still gives me a certain advantage. I make use of the concepts discussed in this book on a daily basis to explain the social world around me and to guide my own behaviour. After all, even if the phenomenon of popularity rarely emerges out of the grade school context, the behaviours it is based on surface time and again in a myriad of different situations.

As a "career" student thus far, I feel confident giving specific advice about what students can do. Having never been a parent or school administrator, I am not so confident giving specific advice about what can be done in these capacities. Any advice I could give would be purely theoretical and quite possibly naively unrealistic. Regardless, I will try to give one example: when I was in elementary, the French immersion cohort was split into two classes. I do not know what criteria went into deciding who was in what class but my memory is that it was more or less random year after year.

Now, imagine if all my peers known to struggle socially had been perpetually placed in the same class. My teachers would have been, in effect, facilitating friendship cycles between them by interfering at the level of proximity. Under the guise of random class selection, these students would have been given an invisible leg up. The idea being that strength in numbers would shield them from the bullying when they are alone without a clique. An analogous situation where bullies are isolated from their enablers is easily imagined. Such simple modifications could have made a big difference to some of my peers growing up. Perhaps this suggestion is simplistic, unrealistic, or simply unhelpful—I wouldn't know as I have never been a parent or an educator.

Regardless of the quality of the suggestion, grade school social dynamics create a system that can be studied and manipulated. Now that you are aware of what forces guide the emergence of popularity, I hope that you will be able to make creative use of what you know. I cannot stress enough the fact that the experience of popularity is not just for the "popular" students. Through the clever application of knowledge and effort, any student, or adult, can find their unique way of experiencing it.

THE ORIGINAL ESSAY

This book is partially based on an essay I wrote shortly after graduating from high school. Like most students in grades 9 through 12, I was mesmerized by popularity and how it was achieved. For those four years, I secretly studied my friends and peers intent on uncovering its secrets. Of all my peers, the most influential was a girl who was both well liked and popular, the original Hollywood Protagonist to whom this book is dedicated.

THE HIERARCHY OF ATTRACTION, INPUT OF ENERGY, RESPECT, AND FRIENDSHIP

What makes someone popular? What is it about some people that consistently draws us to them, makes us confide in them, and serve them? What makes these rare, but amazing people? Imagine the possibilities if you had this information and could consciously apply it to your life. In any social situation you would have the ability to attract others, and to keep them attracted. You could become a central, important, well-informed, sought-after figure—but how?

Defined simply, what is popularity other than having a large percentage of people attracted to you? Attraction is something we all feel, contribute to, and participate in. Some people are more attractive than others, and this is where popularity begins: being attractive.

THE HIERARCHY OF ATTRACTION

Commonly used, the word attraction connotes sex appeal. However attraction, by definition, is any desire to be around someone for any reason including, but not limited to, physical appearance. Attraction can be the result of personality, sexuality, spirituality, wealth, intelligence, appearance, humour, talent, etc. Anything that makes us want to be near someone constitutes attraction.

All people can be placed in a "Hierarchy of Attraction". Those who are at the top are the most attractive, and those towards the bottom, least attractive. Hierarchies will always exist because true equality is a utopian fantasy. Relativity proves this. If you have ever liked someone, that action proves that there is someone you dislike. Likewise if there were no ugly people there would be no beautiful people, if there were no talented people there could be no untalented people and so on. Hence, the fact that we are attracted to some and unattracted to others proves that a Hierarchy exists.

Because attraction is natural, everyone has their own personal hierarchies in which they classify those they meet and because all hierarchies are the product of opinion, no two people will share the exact same Hierarchy. Still, popularity is dependent on being attractive to a large percentage of persons; and thus, to be popular you must occupy a high rung in the 'general Hierarchy.' The general Hierarchy works like such: there are infinite degrees of attractiveness and in reality no set levels or rungs. A small percentage of people are near the top, the average is near the middle, and a small percentage is near the bottom. People are attracted to those above them, and therefore attraction flows up. Those at the top are attractive to a high percentage of people and those at the bottom are attractive to a low percentage. Here is an example: a supermodel would not marry a fat slob, whereas fat slobs, white collared workers, athletes, and millionaire reality television personalities, would all love to marry a supermodel.

It should be noted that a person's position in the general Hierarchy, or any individual hierarchies, isn't stagnant because attraction is not based on something unchangeable like body type. Through effort or lethargy you can either ascend or descend any Hierarchy. For example, if you learn to play guitar you could ascend someone's Hierarchy where as if you possessed no musical talent you would descend. However, learning to play guitar is by no means the only way to climb a Hierarchy. There are numerous ways in which you can ascend. For example, being the quarter back of the football team, the lead in a play, dressing nicely, walking confidently, driving a nice car, learning to sing or act, being wealthy, kind, strong, funny… these are a few examples of what makes us more attractive—and only a few.

Unfortunately, trying to climb people's hierarchies, for the most part, isn't easy and takes consistent effort; however, it is a natural conscious and subconscious occurrence. Why else would you do your hair, or put on cologne before a date? This brings the discussion to:

INPUT OF ENERGY

The concept of input of energy is very simple and can be summed up in a single rule: if you are attracted to someone, you input energy into that relationship. Input of energy is a conscious and subconscious occurrence. It is anything from thinking to fantasizing about someone, making an effort to be near them to laughing at unfunny jokes they tell. The concept of input of energy isn't a metaphor or a symbol. It only has one meaning: whatever you do in a relationship that takes energy is 'input of energy'.

Input of energy is a linear concept. The amount of energy you input into a relationship is directly proportional to how attracted you are to someone. Consider Valentines Day, those who are unattractive receive nothing, whereas those who are very attractive have people actively searching them out at lunch, knowingly embarrassing themselves in front of friends; just to deliver that box of chocolates, that lame trinket, or perhaps a Teddy Bear in the cafeteria.

Evidence of input of energy can be found everywhere because it is a natural occurrence. For example: Romeo climbs the balcony to be with Juliet. The man gives his jacket to his date so that she is not cold. Your girlfriend gives you a massage because you have had a bad day. In every case, one of the individuals is consciously inputting energy into the relationship due to an attraction. However, compared to its conscious form, subconscious input of energy is subtler and therefore the best examples of it can be found in our own lives. When you have the choice of sitting alone or beside a friend who is across the room, what do you normally choose? Barring unusual circumstances, you choose your friend because you are attracted to them—you want to be near them.

It should be noted however, that attraction is not the only reason people input energy into a relationship. Individuals may input energy in anticipation of receiving something in return, due to various circumstances, are being forced to input energy, or are genuinely kind people. Because of this, input of energy is not a definitive test, only a potential indicator, of attraction. However, understanding the concept of input of energy is fundamental to understanding popularity.

THE CRUCIAL ELEMENT: RESPECT

When people input energy into a relationship, the 'attractor' can respond to the 'attracted' in different ways. If there is mutual attraction the input of energy will be responded to with enthusiasm, happiness, excitement, and other favourable signs. However, if the attraction isn't mutual, then the outcome will be different and it is here that popular people differentiate themselves. Generic people tend to respond to unwanted input of energy with disdain or callousness. If you have ever been rejected by someone you have approached then you will understand what this denial is like. Popular people don't do this; they respond to unwanted input of energy with respect. This does not mean that they have an attraction to the attracted, or that they will be overly friendly, it simply means that they won't give clear and glaring signs that the input of energy is unwanted. This leaves the attracted with a positive feeling making the attractor even more alluring. Consider the next two scenarios:

Gordon is an average boy who, much to his dismay, is only 145 pounds and not especially good-looking. Although well motivated, Gordon enjoys studying and writing essays and thus, isn't very high in the Hierarchy of Attraction. In contrast, Daisy is a beautiful young brunette who is athletic, intelligent, and has leads in school plays—Daisy is high in the Hierarchy of Attraction. As we would expect, Gordon is attracted to Daisy but unfortunately for him, this attraction is not mutual. Still, due to his attraction, Gordon inputs energy into his relationship with Daisy by striking up a conversation with her in the next time they make eye contact. Unfortunately for Gordon though, Daisy is a bitch and his friendly, "Hi!" is met with the cold shoulder. Consequently, Gordon will leave this encounter feeling insecure and disappointed due to Daisy's reaction. Gordon won't re-approach Daisy because he knows the outcome will be unpleasant. In fact, he will avoid Daisy knowing the misery of feeling unwanted. Unless Gordon's attraction to Daisy is extreme, he will not be able to work up the courage (large input of energy) to try again. Either way, Gordon's attraction to Daisy will have decreased.

Alternately, what if Daisy wasn't a bitch? What if Gordon's friendly "Hi!" is met with another friendly "Hi!" What if Daisy humoured Gordon by kindly answering his questions and responding to his conversation until it naturally came to an end? Would Gordon not leave the encounter feeling good knowing that his feelings were respected? More importantly what if Daisy consistently respected Gordon, would he not begin to associate the feeling of security with being near Daisy? When you respect someone it makes them feel good because they feel secure. A feeling which comes with knowing that every aspect of you is being respected: your appearance, feelings, privacy, belief, etc. The result of this outcome will be that Gordon's self-esteem and sense of acceptance will increase, and he will naturally return to Daisy much in the same way that he would return to a gold mine were he to find one.

Now imagine if Daisy were to respond unconditionally and consistently to all people, including those she found unattractive, with unconditional respect. Eventually a high percentage of people would begin to associate the feeling of security with being near Daisy and would develop a prolonged attraction to her. Daisy could then be termed 'popular.'

At this point it is necessary to broaden the definition of respect. As used in this essay, respect is a title given to a union of several qualities such as kindness, consideration and empathy. I have chosen the word respect simply because so many other attributes can be defined in terms of it. E.g., kindness is respect for someone's feelings; consideration is respect for someone's belongings; etc. And so, showing respect covers more than a single attribute and can be very loosely defined as—in an un-patronizing way and without kissing ass—doing and saying what is necessary to increase a person's sense of well being. Unfortunately there is no rule which can be used to define what would constitute showing respect in every situation: the number of relationships, as well as the vast number of variables that define each individual relationship, is simply too large.

A theory of popularity can now be formulated and stated as a rule: those who are high in the general Hierarchy, and who respond to input of energy with varying degrees of respect become popular. It should be noted that nobody is either popular or unpopular. Popularity is not an absolute and is instead measured in degrees. The higher you are in the Hierarchy and the more unconditional respect you show the more popular you will become. At a certain point however, some people transcend popularity and become something else. Those who consistently demonstrate a sincere respect for everyone are those who create an everlasting sovereignty. These are the people whose time we actively bid for because we know the wonderful feeling of being around them. Because they have the ability to make everyone feel good and accepted, these are truly amazing people.

FRIENDSHIP

Unfortunately, amazing people are extremely rare. Learning to play guitar and doing copious amounts of sit-ups is easy. Showing unconditional respect is the difficulty. Because I am not one of these people I can only speculate on what enables amazing people to be who they are. Whether the "unconditional respect" character strength is due to nature or nurture I don't know. What I assume is that these people are so confident and secure with who they are, that they are not concerned about who they associate with. They do not require the ego trip that comes with putting others down, and they are kind for what seems to be no other reason than that. We are all attracted to these people because, although our attraction may not be mutual, they let us believe that it is. An amazing person might loath your personality, your appearance and demeanour, they may hate the sight of you, but they will never let you know this. Amazing people seem to be friends with everyone, and to you they are your friend because to you they show respect.

This realization implies a very important conclusion. If we are all friends with amazing people due to a mutual, or a perceived mutual attraction, then what is friendship other than a mutual, or a perceived mutual attraction? If attraction is based on respect, isn't friendship? Consider, how many jerks do you actively seek out? How many assholes do you voluntarily return to be around? Not everyone has the capacity to be an amazing person or even to be considered popular. However, everyone has the capacity to be mutually attracted and attractive to some—though be it a small number—and in other words: to make and keep friends. Hence, the secret of popularity is good, but the secret of friendship is better. So if there was one piece of advice I could give someone, one sentence that summed up the most important conclusion of this essay, or communicated the best theory that I have ever had, it would be that "friendship is based on respect." This is the best lesson I have ever learned.

FURTHER READING

B efore developing into its current form, *Popularity Explained* was an independent study that I completed as part of my undergraduate degree in psychology. Below is the original list of published references that I used. Although I haven't directly cited all of these sources in the book, the following scholars warrant due credit and recognition. Their dedication to research makes books like this possible.

Abel, M. H., & Watters, H. (2005). Attributions of guilt and punishment as functions of physical attractiveness and smiling. *Journal of Social Psychology, 145,* 687-702.

Adler, P. A., & Adler, P. (1995). Dynamics of inclusion and exclusion in preadolescent. *Social Psychology Quarterly 58(3),* 145-162.

Adler, P. A., Kless, S. J. & Adler, P. (1992). Socialization to Gender Roles: Popularity among Elementary School Boys and Girls. *Sociology of Education, 65,* 169-187.

Banerjee, R. (2002). Audience effects on self-presentation in childhood. *Social Development, 11(4),* 487-507.

Barr, A., Bryan, A. & Kenrick, D. (2002). Sexual peak: Socially shared cognitions about desire frequency, satisfaction in men and women. *Personal Relationships, 9,* 287-299.

Bennett, M., & Yeeles, C. (1990). Children's understanding of the self-presentational strategies of ingratiation and self-promotion. *European Journal of Social Psychology, 20,* 455–461.

Berridge, K. C. & Robinson, T. E. (1998). What is the role of dopamine in reward: hedonic impact, reward learning, or incentive salience? *Brain research Reviews, 28(3),* 309-369.

Berridge, K. C., Robinson, T. E. & Aldridge, J. W. (2009). Dissecting components of reward: 'liking', 'wanting', and learning. *Current Opinion in Pharmacology, 9(1),* 65-73.

Bierhoff, H. W. (1989) *Person perception and attribution.* New York, NY: Springer-Verlag.

Boyatzis, C. J., Baloff, P. & Durieux, C. (1998). Effects of perceived attractiveness and academic success on early adolescent peer popularity. *The Journal or Genetic Psychology, 159(3),* 337-344.

Brendgen, M. & Little, T. D. (2000). Rejected children and their friends: A shared evaluation of friendship quality? *Merrill-Palmer Quarterly,* 46 (1), 45-70.

Bukowski, W. M. & Pizzamiglio, M. T., Newcomb, A. F. & Hoza, B. (1996). Popularity as an affordance for friendship: The link between group and dyadic experience. *Social Development, 5 (2),*189-202.

Byrne, D. & Griffit, W. (1973). Interpersonal attraction. *Annual Review of Psychology, 24,* 317-336.

Caplan, C. (2010). Bullying girls in and out of cliques. In S. R. Gunton (Ed.), *Cliques,* (pp. 17-32). Detroit, MI: Greenhaven Press.

Carnegie, D. (1937). *How to win friends and influence people.* New York, NY: Simon and Schuster.

Cillesen, A. H. N., & Mayeux, M. (2004). From censure to reinforcement: Developmental changes in the association between aggression and social status. *Child Development, 75(1)*, 147-163.

Cillessen, A. H. (2011). Toward a theory of popularity. In A. H., Cillessen, & D. Schwartz, L. Mayeux, (Eds.), *Popularity in the Peer System* (pp. 273-299). New York, NY, USA: Guilford Press.

Closson, L. M. (2008). Status and gender differences in early Adolescents' descriptions of popularity. *Social Development 18(2)*, 412-426.

Closson, L. M. (2009). Status and gender differences in early adolescents' descriptions of popularity. *Social Development, 18(2)*, 412-426.

DePaulo, B. M. (1992). Nonverbal behaviour and self-presentation. *Psychological Bulletin, 111(2)*, 203-243.

Dijkstra, J. K., Cillessen, A. H. N., Lindenberg, S. & Veenstra, R. (2010). Basking in reflected glory and its limits: Why adolescents hang out with popular peers. *Journal of Research on Adolescence, 20(4)*, 942-958.

Dodge, K. A., Schlundt, D. C., Schocken, I., Delugach, J. D. (1983). Social competence and children's sociometric status: The role of peer group entry strategies. *Journal of Developmental Psychology, 29(3)*, 309-336.

Dollinger, S. J. (2002). Physical attractiveness, social connectedness, and individuality: An autophotographic study. *Journal of Social Psychology, 142*, 25-32.

Dunn, M. J. & Searle, R. (2010). Effects if manipulated prestige-car ownership on both sex attractiveness ratings. *The British Journal of Psychology, 101*, 69-80.

Erwin, P, G. (1981). The role of attitudinal similarity and perceived acceptance evaluation in interpersonal attraction.
The Journal of Psychology, 109, 133-136.

Fisher, H. (1993). *Anatomy of Love: A natural history or monog-
amy, adultery, and divorce.* New York, NY: W. W. Norton.

Fisher, H., Aron, A., Mashek, D., Li, M. & Brown, L. L. (2002)
Defining the brain systems of lust, romantic attraction,
and attachment. *Archives of Sexual Behaviour, 31(5),* 413-
419.

Flora, C. (2004). The once over: Can you trust first impressions? *Psychology Today.com.* Retrieved from http://
www.psychologytoday.com/articles/200407/the-once-
over?page=2

Garcia, S., Stinson, L., Ickes, W., Bissonnette, V., & Briggs, S.
R. (1991). Shyness and physical attractiveness in mixed-
sex dyads. *Journal of Personality and Social Psychology, 61,*
35-49.

Gross, A. E. & Crofton, C. (1977). What is good is beautiful.
Sociometry, 40(1), 85-90.

Horton, R. S. (2003). Similarity and attractiveness in social
perception: Differentiating between biases for the self
and the beautiful. *Self and Identity,* 2, 137-152.

Hosoda, M., Stone-Romero, E., & Coats, G. (2003). The ef-
fects of physical attractiveness on job-related outcomes:
A meta-analysis of experimental studies. *Personnel
Psychology,* 56, 431-462.

Howe, C. (2010). *Peer Groups and Children's Development.*
Malde, MA: Wiley-Blackwell.

Kleck, R. E., Richardson , S. A. & Ronald, L. (1974). Physical
appearance cues and interpersonal attraction in children. *Child Development,* 45, 305-310).

Kunin, C. C., & Rodin, M. J. (1982). The interactive effects
of counselor gender, physical attractiveness and status

on client self-disclosure. *Journal of Clinical Psychology, 38,* 84-90.

LaFontana, K. M., & Cillessen, A. H. N. (2002). Children's perceptions of popular and unpopular peers: A multimethod assessment. *Developmental Psychology, 38(5),* 635–647.

LaFreniere, P. & Charlesworth, W. R. (1983). Dominance, attention, and affiliation in a preschool group: A nine-month longitudinal study. *Ethology and Sociobilogy, 4(2),* 55–67.

Lemay, E. P., Clark, M. S. & Greenberg, A. (2010). What is beautiful is good because what is beautiful is desired: Physical attractiveness stereotyping as projection of interpersonal goals. *Personality and Social Psychology Bulletin, 36 (3),* 339-353.

Levine, S. P., & Feldman, R. S. (1997). *Self-presentational goals, self-monitoring, and nonverbal behaviour. Basic and Applied Social Psychology, 79(4),* 505-518.

Levinger, G. (1974). A three-level approach to attraction: Toward an understanding of Pair Relatedness. In T. L. Huston (Ed.), *Foundations of interpersonal attraction* (pp. 99-120). New York, NY: Academic Press.

Lindstrom, W. A. & Lease, M. A. (2005). The role of athlete as contributor to peer status in school-age and adolescent females in the United States: From pre-title IX to 2000 and beyond. *Social Psychology of Education, 8,* 223-244.

McCall, G. J. (1974). A symbolic interactionist approach to attraction. In T. L. Huston (Ed.), *Foundations of interpersonal attraction* (pp. 217-231). New York, NY: Academic Press.

McCall, M. (1997). The effects of physical attractiveness on gaining access to alcohol: When social policy meets social decision making. *Addiction, 92,* 597-600.

Mims, P. R., Hartnett, J. J., & Nay, W. R. (1975). Interpersonal attraction and help volunteering as a function of physical attractiveness. *Journal of Psychology: Interdisciplinary and Applied, 89*, 125-131.

Newcomb, A. F. & Bagwell, C. L. (2009). Children's friendship relations: A meta-analytic review. *Psychological Bulletin, 117(2)*, 306-347.

Newcomb, A. F., Bukowski, W. M., & Pattee, L. (1993). Children's peer relations: A meta-analytic review of popular, rejected, Neglected, controversial, and average sociometric status. *Psychological Bulletin, 113*, 99-128.

Parker, J. G., & Asher, S. R. (1993). Friendship and friendship quality in middle childhood: Links with peer group acceptance and feelings of loneliness and social dissatisfaction. *Developmental Psychology, 29*, 611–621.

Parker, J. G., Rubin, K. H., Price, J., & DeRosier, M. (1995). Peer relationships, child development, and adjustment: A developmental psychopathology perspective. In D. Cicchetti & D. J. Cohen (Eds.), *Developmental psychopathology: Vol. 2. Risk, disorder, and adaptation* (pp. 96–161). Oxford: Wiley.

Principe, C. C. & Langlois, J. H. (2010). Faces differing in attractiveness elicit corresponding affective responses. *Cognition and Emotion, 25(1)*, 140-148.

Principe, C. P. & Langlois, J. H. (2011). Faces differing in attractiveness elicit corresponding affective responses. *Cognition and emotion, 25(1)*, 140-148.

Quereshi, M. Y., & Kay, J. P. (1986). Physical attractiveness, age, and sex as determinants of reactions to resumes. *Social Behaviour & Personality, 14*, 103-112.

Rall, M., Greenspan, A., & Neidich, E. (1984). Reactions to eye contact initiated by physically attractive and unattractive men and women. *Social Behavior and Personality, 12,* 103-109.

Ramsey, J.L., & Langlois, J.H. (2002). Effects of the "beauty is good" stereotype of children's information processing. *Journal of Experimental Child Psychology, 81,* 320–340.

Rosen, L. H. & Underwood, M. K. (2010). Facial attractiveness as a moderator of the association between social and physical aggression and popularity in adolescents. *Journal of School Psychology, 48,* 313–333.

Rotem, K. (1995). The effect of physical attractiveness comparison on choice of partners. *Journal of Social Psychology, 135,* 153-165.

Sandstrom, M. J. & Cillessen A. H. N. (2006). Likeable versus popular: Distinct implications for adolescent adjustment. *International Journal of Behavioral Development, 30 (4),* 305–314.

Sangrador, J. L., & Yela, C. (2000). What is beautiful is loved: Physical attractiveness in love relationships in a representative sample. *Social Behavior & Personality, 28,* 207-219.

Shafter, D. R., Kipp, K., Wood, E. & Willoughby, T. (2010). *Developmental Psychology: Childhood and Adolescence (Third Canadian Ed.).* Scarborough, ON: Nelson.

Shaw, J. I. & Skolnick, P. (1973). An investigation of relative preference for consistency motivation. *European Journal of Social Psychology, 3(3),* 271-280.

Sherman, A. M., deVries, B. & Lansford, J. E. (2000). Friendship in childhood and adulthood: Lessons across the life span. *Int. J. Aging and Human Development, 51(1),* 31-51.

Vaillancourt, T. & Hymel, S. (2006). Aggression and social status: The moderating roles of sex and peer-valued characteristics. Aggressive Behaviour, 32, 396-408.

Vannatta, K., Gartstein, M. A., Zeller, M., & Noll, R. B. (2009) Peer acceptance and social behavior during childhood and adolescence: How important are appearance, athleticism, and academic competence? *International Journal of Behavioral Development, 33(4)*, 303-311.

Watling, D. & Banerjee, R. (2007). Children's differentiation between ingratiation and self-promotion. *Social development, 16 (4)*, 758-776.

Wiederman, M. W., & Hurst, S. R. (1997). Physical attractiveness, body image, and women's sexual self-schema. *Psychology of Women Quarterly, 21*, 567-581.

ACKNOWLEDGEMENTS

There is no question that the first acknowledgement must go to my parents. I wrote the first draft of this book between May and August, 2011, while living in their home. Over the course of those four months, not once did they pester me to get a real job. While I wrote, they allowed me to live for free giving me the chance to focus my attention. Without their support, I could never have gotten this book written in such a short time. I also owe a debt of gratitude to them for supporting my entire my post-secondary education. Much of this book's content was inspired by my undergraduate degree in psychology which is entirely thanks to them. A special nod goes out to my mother who has willingly and happily edited all my writing since grade school. She is one of the few people who actually read the independent study that preceded this book.

To the authors Rosalind Wiseman, Rachel Simmons, and Meg Cabot. Rosalind, your excellent book, *Queen Bees and Wannabes*, is truly a classic. Unlike many, you provide a frank and honest assessment of grade school. As I wrote my own book, I felt totally confident quoting you as an expert. I specifically chose to use the term "Queen Bee" as an acknowledgement of your work and insight. Rachel, thank you for writing *Odd Girl Out* and *Odd Girl Speaks Out*. It wasn't possible for me to do similar research and so I was dependent on authors such as yourself to do it for me. I hope that victimized girls who happen across my book will be directed to yours. Meg, although I often disagree with your advice in *How to Be Popular*, thank you for writing. More than once I use an example from your book to make a point in mine. I hope you will forgive me for being a callous academic at times.

To my brothers: Refah, thanks for the YouTube video and for reading the independent study. When I asked you if my ideas were original you said, "No" but that I was "the first to combine them in this particular order"—good enough to keep me motivated and writing. Also, thank you for all the free Photoshop. I hope to pay you back in time. Soraj, thanks for telling me about your friends and the social dramas of your school while we did the dishes. Also for doing the original sound recordings.

On the subject of research, thank you to all of the cited authors. Notably, Antonius Cillessen, Kathryn LaFontana, Peter and Patricia Adler, Helen Fisher, and Kent Berridge. I studied your research extensively during the process of writing.

Input of Energy: a brilliant term. James Fuite, it was immediately after our discussion by the lake that everything came together. I remember very vividly lying in bed for several hours immediately after, wide awake, as each element fell into place for the first time. A few months later, I would write the essay.

Thanks to Dr. S. A. who supervised the independent study that preceded this book. *Psych 3330* will always be my favourite course completed at the University of Lethbridge. Thanks for the discussion and input. I now understand why none of my friends are ugly.

Many thanks go out to Jacqueline Burt. Your belief in me at the beginning of the project and your assistance throughout were much appreciated. When you see commas before quotes and capitalized table headings, I hope you will recognize your influence.

To all the people I have secretly studied over the years, please forgive me.

And finally, a special thanks to the original Hollywood Protagonist. So many awkward moments... sorry about that. My hope is that one day you'll happen across this book and suddenly realize what was motivating my behaviour. If ever you noticed me staring from across room with a look of perplexed amazement, now you know why. Take it as a compliment. Although you probably do not feel as if you did anything special, your example inspired the original essay whereon this book is ultimately based.

BIBLIOGRAPHY

Chapter 1 *Introduction*

1. LaFontana, K. M. & Cillessen, A. H. N. (2009). Developmental changes in the priority of perceived status in childhood and adolescence. *Social Development, 19(1)*, 130-147.

2. Wellman, B. (1926). The school child's choice of companions. *The Journal of Educational Research, 14(2)*, 126-132.

3. Chang, D. (2010). What I did to be popular. In S. R. Gunton (Ed.), *Cliques* (pp. 67-70). Detroit, MI: Greenhaven Press.

4. Adler, P. A. & Adler, P. (1995). *Peer Power: Preadolescent Culture and Identity.* Saint John, NB: Rutgers University Press.

5. Dunnington, M. H. (1957). Behavioural differences in sociometric status groups in a nursery school. *Child Development, 25*, 103-111.

6. Mayeux, L., Houser, J. & Dyche, K. (2011). Social acceptance and popularity: Two distinct forms of peer status. In A. H., Cillessen, D. Schwartz, L. & Mayeux, (Eds.), *Popularity in the Peer System* (pp. 79-102). New York, NY, USA: Guilford Press.

7. Columbia Pictures (2001). Not Another Teen Movie.

Chapter 2 *The Students Among Us*

8. Gronlund, N. E. (1959). *Sociometry in the Classroom.* New York, NY: Harper.

9. Coie, J. D., Dodge, K. A., & Coppotelli, H. (1982). Dimensions and types of social status: A cross-age perspective. *Developmental Psychology, 18,* 557-570.

10. Kosir, K. & Pecjak, S. (2005). Sociometry as a method for investigation peer relationships: What does it really measure? *Educational Research, 47(1),* 127-144.

11. Wiseman, R. (2002). *Queen Bees & Wannabes.* New York, NY: Crown Publishers.

12. Wiseman, R. (2002). *Queen Bees & Wannabes* (p. 25). New York, NY: Crown Publishers.

13. Aikins, J. W. (2011). Prosocial skills, social competence, and popularity. In A. H., Cillessen, D. Schwartz & L. Mayeux, (Eds.), *Popularity in the Peer System* (pp. 140-162). New York, NY: Guilford Press.

14. Wiseman, R. (2002). *Queen Bees & Wannabes* (p. 28). New York, NY: Crown Publishers.

15. Cabot, M. (2006). *How to Be Popular* (p. 167). New York, NY: HarperTempest

16. Cabot, M. (2006). *How to Be Popular* (p. 104). New York, NY: HarperTempest

17. Wiseman, R. (2002). *Queen Bees & Wannabes* (p. 23). New York, NY: Crown Publishers.

18. Adler, P. A. & Adler, P. (1996). Preadolescent clique stratification and the hierarchy of identity. *Sociological Inquiry, 66(2),* 111-142.

19. Steve, M. (2010). I was bullied because I was different. In S. R. Gunton (Ed.), *Cliques* (pp. 53-55). Detroit, MI: Greenhaven Press.

20. Chang, D. (2010). What I did to be popular. In S. R. Gunton (Ed.), *Cliques* (pp. 67-70). Detroit, MI: Greenhaven Press.

Chapter 3 *The Hierarchy of Attraction*

21. Wiseman, R. (2002). *Queen Bees & Wannabes* (p. 180). New York, NY: Crown Publishers.

22. Berscheid, E. & Walster, E. H. (1969). *Interpersonal Attraction.* Reading, MA: Addison-Wesley.

23. Cialdini, R. B. & Richardson, K. D. (1980). Two indirect tactics of impression management: Basking and blasting. *Journal of Personality and Social Psychology, 39,* 406–416.

24. Tracy, J. L. & Beall, A. T. (in press). Happy guys finish last: The impact of emotion expressions on sexual attraction. © 2011 American Psychological Association. DOI: 10.1037/a0022902

Chapter 4 *Input of Energy*

25. Fisher, H. (2000). Lust, attraction, attachment: Biology and evolution of the three primary emotion systems for mating, reproduction and parenting. *Journal of Sex Education and Therapy, 25(1),* 96-105.

26. Kolb, B. & Wishaw, I. Q. (2005). *An Introduction to Brain and Behaviour.* New York, NY: Worth Publishers.

27. Cloutier, J., Heatherton, T. F., Whalen, P. J. & Kelley, W. M. (2008). Are attractive people rewarding? Sex differences in the neural substrates of facial attractiveness. *Journal of Cognitive Neuroscience, 20(6),* 941-91.

28. Moore, M. M. (2010). Human nonverbal courtship behaviour—A brief historical review. *Journal of Sex Research, 47(2-3),* 171-180.

29. Quilliam, S. (2004). *Body language.* Buffalo, NY: Firefly Books.

30. Garcia, S., Stinson, L., Ickes, W., Bissonnette, V. & Briggs, S. R. (1991). Shyness and physical attractive-

ness in mixed-sex dyads. *Journal of Personality and Social Psychology, 61*, 35-49.

31. Brundage, L. E., Derlega, V. J. & Cash, T. F. (1977). The effects of physical attractiveness and need for approval on self-disclosure. *Personality and Social Psychology Bulletin, 3*, 63-66.

32. Andersen, S. M. & Bem, S. L. (1981). Sex typing and androgyny in dyadic interaction: Individual differences in responsiveness to physical attractiveness. *Journal of Personality and Social Psychology, 41*, 74-86.

33. Ahearne, M., Gruen, T. W. & Jarvis, C. B. (1999). If looks could sell: Moderation and mediation of the attractiveness effect on salesperson performance. *International Journal of Research in Marketing, 16(4)*, 269-284.

34. Ray, B. & Rumsey, N. (1988). *The Social Psychology of Facial Appearance.* New York, NY: Springer-Verlag.

35. Wiseman, R. (2002). *Queen Bees & Wannabes* (p. 39). New York, NY: Crown Publishers.

36. Fisher, H. (2000). Lust, attraction, attachment: Biology and evolution of the three primary emotion systems for mating, reproduction and parenting. *Journal of Sex Education and Therapy, 25(1)*, 96-105.

37. Wiseman, R. (2002). *Queen Bees Wannabes* (p. 205). New York, NY: Crown Publishers.

38. Cabot, M. (2006). *How to Be Popular* (p. 164). New York, NY: HarperTempest

39. Wilson, D. W. (1978). Helping behaviour and physical attractiveness. *Journal of Social Psychology, 104*, 313-314.

40. Wilson, T. D. (2002). *Strangers to Ourselves: Discovering the Adaptive Unconscious* (p. 6). Cambridge, MA: The Belknap Press of Harvard University Press.

41. Gladwell, M. (2005). *Blink* (p. 74). New York, NY: Little, Brown and Company

42. Wilson, T. D. (2002). *Strangers to Ourselves: Discovering the Adaptive Unconscious* (p. 34). Cambridge, MA: The Belknap Press of Harvard University Press.

43. Cabot, M. (2006). *How to Be Popular* (p. 200). New York, NY: HarperTempest

Chapter 5 *Attraction Liking and Attachment*

44. Hanson, D. (2010). Liking it vs. wanting it: The joylessness of drug addiction. *The Addiction Inbox.* Retrieved online July, 2011 @ http://addiction-dirkh.blogspot.com/2010/04/liking-it-vs-wanting-it.html

45. Berridge, K. C. (2002). Irrational pursuit: Hyper-Incentives from a visceral brain. In I. Brocas & J. D. Carrillo, (Eds.). *The Psychology of Economic Decisions Volume 1.* Oxford, NY: Oxford University Press.

46. Berridge, K. C. (n.d.). Neuroscience of Liking & Wanting. *Affective Neuroscience & Biophsychology Lab.* Retrieved online July, 2011 @ http://www.lsa.umich.edu/psych/research&labs/berridge/research/affectiveneuroscience.html

47. Zajonc, R. B. (2001). Mere exposure: A gateway to the subliminal. *Current Directions in Psychological Science, 10(6)*, 224-228.

48. Zeki, S. (2007). The neurobiology of love. *FEBS Letters, 581*, 2575-2579.

49. Young, L. J. & Wang, Z. (2004). The neurobiology of pair bonding. *Nature Neuroscience, 7(10)*, 1048-1056.

50. Insel, T. R. & Young, L. J. (2001). The neurobiology of attachment. *Nature Neuroscience, 2*, 129-138.

51. Fisher, H. (2000). Lust, attraction, attachment: Biology and evolution of the three primary emotion systems for mating, reproduction and parenting. *Journal of Sex Education and Therapy, 25(1)*, 96-105.

52. Chang, D. (2010). What I did to be popular. In S. R. Gunton (Ed.), *Cliques* (p. 89). Detroit, MI: Greenhaven Press.

53. Simmons, R. (2002). *Odd Girl Out* (p. 89). New York, NY: Harcourt, Inc.

54. Anonymous (2008). Is it possible to love someone without liking them? *TrèsSugar*. Retrieved online June, 2011 @ http://www.tressugar.com/DearSugar-Needs-Your-Help-Possible-Love-Someone-Without-Liking-Him-1078577

55. Barnett, O. W. (2001). Why battered women don't leave. *Trauma Violence Abuse January, 2(1)*, 3-35.

56. Simmons, R. (2002). *Odd Girl Out* (p. 165-166). New York, NY: Harcourt, Inc.

57. Lewandowski, G. W., Aron, A. & Gee, J. (2007). Personality goes a long way: The malleability of opposite-sex physical attractiveness. *Personal Relationships, 14*, 571–585.

Chapter 6 *The Emergence of Popularity*

58. Allport, G. W. & Odbert, H. S. (1936). Traitnames: A psycho-lexical study. *Psychological Monographs, 47*, 1-171.

59. Blanco, J. (2010). Finding My Own Crowd. In S. R. Gunton (Ed). *Cliques* (pp. 97-105). Detroit, MI: Greenhaven Press.

60. Wiseman, R. (2002). *Queen Bees & Wannabes* (p. 201). New York, NY: Crown Publishers.

61. Wiseman, R. (2002). *Queen Bees & Wannabes* (p. 39 & 178). New York, NY: Crown Publishers.

Chapter 7 *Liking and Disliking*

62. Digman, J. M. (1990). Personality structure: Emergence of the five-factor model. *Annual Review of Psychology, 41*, 417–440.

Chapter 8 *The Situation*

63. Maslow, A. H. (1987). *Motivation and Personality.* New York, NY: Harper and Row.
64. Hay, I. & Ashman, A. F. (2003). The development of adolescents' emotional stability and general self-concept: The interplay of parents, peers, and gender. *International Journal of Disability, Development, and Education, 50*, 77–91.
65. LaFontana, K. M. & Cillessen, A. H. N. (2009). Developmental changes in the priority of perceived status in childhood and adolescence. *Social Development, 19(1)*, 130-147.
66. Wiseman, R. (2002). *Queen Bees & Wannabes.* (p. 186). New York, NY: Crown Publishers.
67. Baskin, J., Newman, L., Pollitt-Cohen, S. & Toombs, C. (2006). *The Notebook Girls.* New York, NY: Warner Books.
68. Call, V., Sprecher, S. & Schwartz, P. (1995). Frequency and incidence of sex in marriage. *Journal of Marriage and Family, 57(3)*, 639-652.
69. Barr, A., Bryan, A. & Kenrick, D. (2002). Sexual peak: Socially shared cognition about desire frequency and satisfaction in men and women. *Personal Relationships, 9*, 287-299.

70. W. J. (2009). It's high school—with scalpels. *JeffreyMD*. Retrieved online April, 2011 @ http://www.jeffreymd.com/?s=popular

71. Anonymous (2010). Social life in medical school. *Student Doctor Network Forums*. Retrieved online April, 2011 @ http: // forums.studentdoctor.net / archive / index.php / t-741177.html

Chapter 9 *Friendship and the Genesis of Cliques*

72. Anonymous (2004a). Friend trouble. In R. Simmons (Ed.), *Odd Girl Speaks Out* (pp. 115-118). San Diego, CA: Harcourt, Inc.

73. Wiseman, R. (2002). *Queen Bees & Wannabes* (p. 39). New York, NY: Crown Publishers.

Chapter 10 *Breaking In and Painful Self Discovery*

74. Wikihow (2013). How to Be Popular. Retrieved online January, 2013

75. Gladwell, M. (2008). *Outliers*. New York, NY: Little, Brown and Company

Chapter 11 *Some Questions Answered*

76. Simmons, R. (2002). *Odd Girl Out* (p. 94 & 98). New York, NY: Harcourt, Inc.

77. Hunter, A. (2010). We had a popularity plan. In S. R. Gunton (Ed). *Cliques* (pp. 84-96). Detroit, MI: Greenhaven Press.

78. Cabot, M. (2006). *How to Be Popular* (p. 137). New York, NY: HarperTempest

79. Cabot, M. (2006). *How to Be Popular* (p. 63). New York, NY: HarperTempest

80. Wiseman, R. (2002). *Queen Bees & Wannabes*. New York, NY: Crown Publishers.

81. Anonymous (2004). I just stood by and let it happen. In R. Simmons (Ed.), *Odd Girl Speaks Out* (pp. 125-127). San Diego, CA: Harcourt, Inc.

82. Wiseman, R. (2002). *Queen Bees & Wannabes* (p. 67). New York, NY: Crown Publishers.

83. Cabot, M. (2006). *How to Be Popular* (p. 187). New York, NY: HarperTempest

84. Wiseman, R. (2002). *Queen Bees & Wannabes* (p. 112 & 122). New York, NY: Crown Publishers.

85. Wilson, T. D. (2002). *Strangers to Ourselves: Discovering the Adaptive Unconscious* (p. 71). Cambridge, MA: The Belknap Press of Harvard University Press.

86. Wiseman, R. (2002). *Queen Bees & Wannabes* (p. 201). New York, NY: Crown Publishers.

87. Ramsey, J. L., Langlois, J. H., Hoss, R. A., Rubenstein, A. J. & Griffin, A. M. (2004). Origins of a stereotype: categorization of facial attractiveness by 6-month-old infants. *Developmental Science, 7(2)*, 201-211.

88. Wiseman, R. (2002). *Queen Bees & Wannabes* (p. 81). New York, NY: Crown Publishers.

89. Chang, D. (2010). What I did to be popular. In S. R. Gunton (Ed.), *Cliques* (pp. 67-70). Detroit, MI: Greenhaven Press.

90. Meston, C. M. & Frohlick, P. F. (2000). The neurobiology of sexual function. *Archive of General Psychiatry, 57*, 1012-1030.

91. Guastella, A. J., Mitchell, P. B. & Mathews, F. (2008). Oxytocin enhances the encoding of positive social memories in humans. *Biological Psychiatry, 64*, 256-258.

92. Zeki, S. (2007). The neurobiology of love. *FEBS Letters,* *581,* 2575-2579.

Chapter 12 *Practical Advice and Conclusions*

93. Wikihow (2013). How to Be Popular. Retrieved online January, 2013

94. MSNBC (2012). Bradley Cooper, Willie chat in French; women swoon. Retrieved online, December, 2012

95. Cabot, M. (2006). *How to Be Popular* (p. 184). New York, NY: HarperTempest

To order more copies of this book, find books by other
Canadian authors, or make inquiries about publishing your own
book, contact PageMaster at:

PageMaster Publication Services Inc.
11340-120 Street, Edmonton, AB T5G 0W5
books@pagemaster.ca
780-425-9303

catalogue and e-commerce store
www.ShopPageMaster.ca

A. L. Freedman has a double degree in psychology and general management from the University of Lethbridge. On graduating, he was awarded a gold medal for his academic achievements. Currently he studies medicine at the University of Alberta and is pursuing a specialty in rural family medicine.

In his free time, Alex enjoys piano, writing, swimming, and travelling. He has worked in Tanzania, Mexico, and the North West Territories and has visited the USA, China, Rwanda, France, Uganda, and Nicaragua. In his own words, "People fascinate me. I feel privileged to have met so many in so many different countries."

Psychology has been, and will always be, one of his primary interests.

Contact: popularityexplained@gmail.com